Ready-to-Use

WRITING PROFICIENCY LESSONS & ACTIVITIES

10th Grade Level

Carol H. Behrman

JOSSEY-BASS
A Wiley Imprint
www.josseybass.com

WITHDRAWN

Published by Jossey-Bass
A Wiley Imprint
989 Market Street, San Francisco, CA 94103-1741   www.josseybass.com

The materials that appear in this book (except those for which reprint permission must be obtained from the primary sources) may be freely reproduced for educational/training activities. There is no requirement to obtain special permission for such uses. We do, however, ask that the following statement appear on all reproductions:

This free permission is limited to the reproduction of material for educational/training events. Systematic or large-scale reproduction or distribution (more than one hundred copies per year)—or inclusion of items in publications for sale—may be done only with prior written permission. Also, reproduction on computer disk or by any other electronic means requires prior written permission. Requests for permission should be addressed to the Permissions Department, John Wiley & Sons, Inc., 111 River Street, Hoboken, NJ 07030, (201) 748-6011, fax (201) 748-6008, e-mail: permcoordinator@wiley.com.

Jossey-Bass books and products are available through most bookstores. To contact Jossey-Bass directly, call our Customer Care Department within the U.S. at (800) 956-7739, outside the U.S. at (317) 572-3993 or fax (317) 572-4002.

Jossey-Bass also publishes its books in a variety of electronic formats. Some content that appears in print may not be available in electronic books.

Library of Congress Cataloging-in-Publication Data
Behrman, Carol H.
    Ready-to-use writing proficiency lessons & activities, 10th grade
level / Carol H. Behrman.— 1st ed.
        p. cm.
    ISBN 0-7879-6600-2 (pbk.)
    1. English language—Composition and exercises—Study and teaching
(Secondary)—Activity programs—United States. 2. Tenth grade
(Education)—United States. I. Title.
    LB1631.B379 2004
    808'.042'0712—dc22

                                        2003017862

Printed in the United States of America
FIRST EDITION
PB Printing   10 9 8 7 6 5 4 3 2 1

DEDICATION

To Edward, my partner in this and everything

ABOUT THE AUTHOR

Carol H. Behrman was born in Brooklyn, New York, graduated from City College of New York, and attended Columbia University's Teachers College, where she majored in education. For many years, Mrs. Behrman taught at high schools in New York City and at the Middle School in Glen Ridge, New Jersey, where she created a program that combined language arts with word-processing instruction. She has written twenty-four books, fiction and nonfiction for children and young adults, and five writing activity textbooks, and has conducted numerous workshops on the writing process for students, teachers, and aspiring writers. She has served as writer-in-residence at Chautauqua Institution and has been an adjunct lecturer at Seton Hall and New York University's Writing Center.

Mrs. Behrman is also the author of *Writing Proficiency Lessons and Activities, 8th Grade Level* (2003), *Writing Proficiency Lessons and Activities, 4th Grade Level* (2002), *Writing Skills Problem Solver* (2000), *Writing Activities for Every Month of the School Year* (1997), *Write! Write! Write!* (1995), all from Jossey-Bass, and *Hooked on Writing!* (1990) from The Center for Applied Research in Education. She currently resides in Sarasota, Florida.

ABOUT THIS WRITING TESTPREP TEACHING RESOURCE

Ready-to-Use Writing Proficiency Lessons and Activities gives classroom teachers and language arts specialists a powerful and effective tool for addressing writing standards and competencies at the tenth-grade level. This resource offers a variety of easy-to-use, reproducible activity sheets that provide review and application of basic language skills, as well as extensive practice in producing the types of writing called for in standardized tests. The activities are grouped into the following nine sections:

- **Section 1:** "Choosing the Right Word" provides twenty-four activities to help students select the most appropriate word and use it correctly when they write. Words that are often confused, spelling demons, homophones, adjectives, sensory words, similes, and metaphors are included in these pages.

- **Section 2:** In "Making Mechanics and Usage Work for You," twenty-eight activities provide a review of writing mechanics including capitalization, punctuation, pronoun usage, and plurals.

- **Section 3:** The twenty activities in "Writing Sentences" review basic strategies (and more) for writing interesting and effective sentences. Sentence-writing is the groundwork of all written communication; projects in this section include such topics as subjects and predicates, subject-verb agreement, types of sentences, and avoiding fragments and run-ons.

- **Section 4:** In "Writing Paragraphs," twenty-nine activities review the essentials of a well-constructed paragraph. Included are strategies for creating effective topic sentences, developing topics efficiently, and producing strong concluding sentences, using the steps of the writing process.

- **Section 5:** The twenty-six activities in "Essay-Writing Techniques" provide extensive practice in using the writing process to produce effective essays. Included are prewriting activities such as brainstorming, clustering, and outlining; using creative, stimulating introductions; developing the topic in an interesting, relevant way; writing strong concluding paragraphs; and avoiding common pitfalls such as straying from the topic, using irrelevant details, and so on.

- **Section 6:** In "Writing Informative/Expository Essays," seven 3-part projects (prewriting activities, writing a first draft, and revising and writing a final copy) guide students through the steps necessary to effectively produce information on a variety of interesting topics.

- **Section 7:** In "Writing Persuasive Essays," seven 3-part writing projects (prewriting activities, writing a first draft, and revising and writing a final copy) give students guided practice in producing persuasive essays that are cogent and convincing.

- **Section 8:** "Narrative Writing" offers seven 3-part projects. Students will work from a variety of stimulating prompts to produce both realistic and imaginative narrative essays.
- **Section 9:** "Writing Letters" provides students with six 3-part activities that review the purposes and components of letters that inform, narrate, or persuade.

Teacher Preparation and Lessons

Teacher lesson plans and detailed instruction precede each section of activities. Answer keys are provided where appropriate. The activities in Sections 1 through 3 can be used—either as part of a larger language arts program or specifically for test preparation—to introduce, review, and reinforce basic language skills with individual students, small groups, or the entire class. Students should be encouraged to apply these skills as they complete the writing activities in Sections 4 through 9. You may wish to select skill pages and assign them before students begin a specific writing assignment or a practice test.

Review Tests, Practice Tests, and Standardized Assessment

The review tests at the end of Sections 1 through 3 can be used as pretests or posttests to assess basic language skills. They can indicate to the teacher which activities should be emphasized and used in complete class instruction, small group work, or individual remediation.

The Practice Tests at the end of Sections 4 through 9 take students through the writing process for producing a passage based on a prompt. Distribute a Practice Test and an Answer Sheet to each student. Point out the importance of reading and following directions carefully, especially when taking standardized tests. Make sure students understand the formats of the practice test items. A checklist at the beginning of each test reminds students which skills and techniques are required for each type of writing. Many of these competencies are also listed on the scoring guide accompanying each test. These scoring guides are included to assist you in assessing students' writing on the test. Students may find it helpful to use these guides to assess their own writing as well as the sample student-writing passages provided with the tests. Make sure that when students assign a score to a sample writing passage, they are able to support their decision with evidence. Scores for the sample writing passages and a rationale for each are provided at the end of the Teacher Preparation pages for each section. Class analysis and discussion of this scoring may help clarify student goals in their own writing.

Information on standardized writing tests and scoring rubrics for various states appear at the beginning of Sections 5 through 9. The scoring guides accompanying the writing practice tests were adapted from the NAEP (National Assessment of Education Progress) rubrics. You may wish to compare these guidelines with those for your individual state when scoring students' writing samples.

Writing Proficiency Lessons and Activities books are also available from Jossey-Bass at the fourth-grade level and the eighth-grade level. The lessons, activities, and sample test items in all three grade-level volumes are invaluable tools for helping students to master basic language and writing skills in preparation for taking standardized tests. Even more important, they will help students develop a sound foundation for becoming proficient writers.

CONTENTS

SECTION 2
MAKING MECHANICS AND USAGE WORK FOR YOU   35

SECTION 3
WRITING SENTENCES   77

REVIEW TEST: WRITING SENTENCES   **105**

SECTION 4
WRITING PARAGRAPHS   **109**

PRACTICE TEST: WRITING PARAGRAPHS   145

SECTION 5
ESSAY-WRITING TECHNIQUES   151

SECTION 6
WRITING INFORMATIVE/EXPOSITORY ESSAYS   189

SECTION 7
WRITING PERSUASIVE ESSAYS   219

SECTION 8
NARRATIVE WRITING   249

SECTION 9
WRITING LETTERS   279

Appendix
PREPARING YOUR STUDENTS
FOR STANDARDIZED PROFICIENCY TESTS   **309**

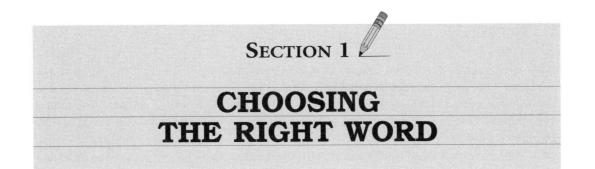

SECTION 1

CHOOSING THE RIGHT WORD

Teacher Preparation and Lessons

The exercises in this section are designed to enlarge the students' vocabulary so that they can write with more accuracy and precision. Activities 1–1 through 1–6 concentrate on words often confused. Activities 1–7 through 1–12 focus on prefixes, suffixes, and synonyms. Activities 1–13 through 1–17 help students improve their use of literal and figurative language. Activities 1–18 through 1–24 focus on using parts of speech correctly. You may wish to use the REVIEW TEST at the end of the section as a pretest and/or a posttest. Answer keys for this section can be found on pages 4 to 7.

ACTIVITIES 1–1 through 1–6 offer a selection of **words often confused.** Introduce this segment by writing the following sentences on the board:

> *The state attorney persecuted the defendant.*
> *The state attorney prosecuted the defendant.*

Elicit the meaning of *prosecute* and *persecute* from the students. Discuss how the use of the wrong word gives a completely different interpretation to the sentence. Write the following pairs of words on the board: *descendant/ancestor, personal/personnel, conscious/conscience.* Discuss the meanings of these words and why they are sometimes confused. Distribute **Activity 1–1 Words Often Confused (Part One).** Direct students to read the explanation and examples at the top of the page, and then complete the activity. For **Activities 1–2 to 1–5 Words Often Confused (Part Two, Part Three, Part Four, and Part Five),** follow these steps: (1) Distribute the activity sheet. (2) Read and discuss the explanations and examples of words often confused on each page. Have students complete the activity, and then share and correct the answers. Distribute **Activity 1–6 Words Often Confused (Review).** The results of this review can help the teacher determine whether more work is needed either individually or in class on these words often confused.

ACTIVITY 1–7 adds some less well-known **prefixes** to the students' developing vocabulary. Write the word *super* on the board. Ask the students to supply words that begin with *super.* Write these words on the board (for example, *Superman, superhero, superstar, superior,* and so on). Inform the students that *super* is derived from Latin and that both Latin and Greek have given us many prefixes that are now part of the English language. Distribute **Activity 1–7 Prefixes.** Read and discuss the Greek and Latin prefixes that are presented. Ask the students to add other examples. Have students complete the sentences at the bottom of the page and share them aloud with the class.

ACTIVITIES 1–8 through 1–11 present information and exercises about the use of **suffixes.** Write the following word pairs on the board: *terror/terrorize, memory/memorize, popular/popularize.* Elicit from the students that each pair contains a root word and the same root word with a suffix added. Elicit that the suffix *ize* means *cause to become.* Discuss how suffixes can be used to change the form or meanings of words. Write the following words on the

1

board: *careful, careless, carefree.* Discuss how different suffixes give different meanings to the root word. Distribute **Activity 1–8 Suffixes (Part One)**. Read and discuss the examples and their meanings. Read and discuss the directions for the completion of the activity. When it has been finished, have the class read several examples aloud. Write the following words on the board: *love, lovely, loving.* Elicit from the class the fact that the final *e* is kept when adding a suffix beginning with a consonant, but it is dropped when adding a suffix that begins with a vowel. Write the following pairs of words on the board: *easy/easily, angry/angrily.* Point out that when a root word ends with a *y*, it is changed to an *i* before a suffix. Encourage the students to contribute additional examples. Distribute **Activity 1–9 Suffixes (Part Two)**. Read aloud the four rules and examples presented in this activity. Have the students complete the activity. Distribute **Activity 1–10 Suffixes (Part Three)**. Read and discuss the lists of words using *er, or, ar, able,* and *ible.* Stress the importance of memorizing these words. Ask the students to add words to these lists. When the activity has been completed, read several sentences aloud for each suffix. Distribute **Activity 1–11 Prefixes and Suffixes (Review)**. Read and discuss the directions. When the activity has been completed, have the class read several examples aloud for each prefix and suffix.

ACTIVITY 1–12 involves the use of **synonyms.** Write the following short paragraph on the board.

> *John stopped when he heard a noise. The noise stopped. John started walking. Then the noise came again. John stopped.*

Elicit the three-time repetition of the word *stopped.* Ask students to supply **synonyms** that could be used to replace some of these repetitions and list them (*halted, disappeared, ended, ceased,* and so forth). Discuss how synonyms can be used successfully to avoid repetition. Distribute **Activity 1–12 Synonyms**. Read the directions out loud. When the activity has been completed, have the students read several examples of each sentence aloud.

ACTIVITIES 1–13 through 1–15 review the use of **similes** and **metaphors.** Say to the students, "*I am so tired. In fact, I am as tired as . . .*" Invite students to complete the sentence. Point out that they have already been using **similes**. Distribute **Activity 1–13 Similes**. Read aloud the explanation at the top of the page. Emphasize the desirability of using original rather than trite similes. When students have completed the assignment, have them read several examples of each simile aloud. Distribute **Activity 1–14 Metaphors**. Read and discuss the description of **metaphors** and how they differ from similes. Point out in particular that a metaphor does not use the words *as* or *like.* Have students complete Part A, then discuss the results. Ask the students to complete Part B, encouraging them to use original, not trite, metaphors. Read a selection of the results out loud. **Activity 1–15 Similes and Metaphors (Review)** can be used to evaluate the students' understanding of these figures of speech. Use the results to determine if more practice is needed on a class or individual basis.

ACTIVITIES 1–16 and 1–17 cover the use of **sensory language.** Distribute **Activity 1–16 Sensory Language (Part One)**. Read and discuss the explanation and examples. Read the directions. When the activity has been completed, have the class read several examples for each sense aloud. Distribute **Activity 1–17 Sensory Language (Part Two)**. Read the directions. Have students share the results either in small groups or with the whole class.

ACTIVITIES 1–18 through 1–21 relate to the correct and effective use of **verbs.** Write the following words on the board: *see, go, say.* Point out that these verbs are action words, but the action is rather weak. Elicit stronger verbs that are more exciting for *see,* such as *stare, glare,* and *squint.* Do the same for *go* (for example, *rush, creep, stumble*) and *say* (for example, *scream, hiss, grumble*). Distribute **Activity 1–18 Strong, Active Verbs** and read the directions out loud. When the students have completed rewriting the paragraph, divide the class into small groups for reading and discussion. Distribute **Activity 1–19 Transitive and Intransitive Verbs.** Read and discuss the definitions and examples. Ask the students to offer additional examples. Read and discuss the directions for the assignment. The teacher can analyze the results to determine whether additional instruction and/or practice is needed either on a class or individual basis. Distribute **Activity 1–20 Linking Verbs.** Read and talk about the explanation and examples, pointing out that a **linking verb** is one type of **intransitive** verb. Have the students complete the assignment. Share the results in small groups or as a classroom activity. Distribute **Activity 1–21 Irregular Verbs.** Read and analyze the explanation and examples. Have the class complete the assignment and use the results to determine if more time on this subject is needed on either a class or individual basis.

ACTIVITIES **1–22 and 1–23** review **adjectives.** Write these sentences on the board:

> *The girl was alone in the room.*
> *The pale, frightened girl was alone in the strange, dark room.*

Discuss how the **adjectives** in the second sentence paint a stronger, more vivid picture. Distribute **Activity 1–22 Adjectives (Part One).** Read the explanation and directions aloud. When students have completed the assignment, share the results by reading the sentences aloud in small groups or to the class. Follow the same procedure for **Activity 1–23 Adjectives (Part Two).**

ACTIVITY **1–24** points out some common **illiteracies.** Distribute **Activity 1-24 Illiteracies.** Read and discuss the explanation and examples. When students have completed the assignment, use the results to determine whether more practice is needed in this area.

ANSWER KEY

1–1. WORDS OFTEN CONFUSED (PART ONE)

1. conscience
2. personnel
3. conscious
4. descendant

5. ancestors
6. prosecute
7. persecute
8. personal

1–2. WORDS OFTEN CONFUSED (PART TWO)

1. among
2. between
3. breathe
4. breath

5. accept
6. except
7. besides
8. beside

1–3. WORDS OFTEN CONFUSED (PART THREE)

1. infer
2. implies
3. morale
4. moral

5. formally
6. formerly
7. export
8. import

1–4. WORDS OFTEN CONFUSED (PART FOUR)
Sentences will vary.

1–5. WORDS OFTEN CONFUSED (PART FIVE)

1. laid
2. lays, laid
3. lay

4. lays
5. lie
6. laid

7. lie
8. lies
9. laid

1–6. WORDS OFTEN CONFUSED (REVIEW)

1. b
2. c
3. a
4. a

5. b
6. a
7. c
8. b

1–7. PREFIXES
Sentences will vary.

1–8. SUFFIXES (PART ONE)
Sentences will vary.

1–9. SUFFIXES (PART TWO)

1. changeable
2. spitting
3. noticeable

4. motorist, driving
5. happiness
6. careless, statements

7. lovely, caring
8. arrangement
9. noticeable

1–10. SUFFIXES (PART THREE)
Sentences will vary.

1–11. PREFIXES AND SUFFIXES (REVIEW)
Part A.
Answers will vary.

Part B.
Answers will vary.

1–12. SYNONYMS
Answers will vary.

1–13. SIMILES
Answers will vary.

1–14. METAPHORS
Part A.
Metaphors to be underlined are the following: jewels glinting under the sun, diamonds and pearls ride the white-crested waves, blinded

Part B.
Sentences will vary.

1–15. SIMILES AND METAPHORS (REVIEW)
Answers will vary.

1–16. SENSORY LANGUAGE (PART ONE)
Lists will vary. Here are some possible additions:

1. *Touch:* smooth, crinkly, hard, sharp
2. *Taste:* sweet, hot, cold, spicy
3. *Sight:* blue, dim, dark, light, round, glittering
4. *Sound:* loud, hiss, croak, roar, bark
5. *Smell:* nasty, sweet, sour, rotten

1–17. SENSORY LANGUAGE (PART TWO)
Part A.
Sentences will vary.

Part B.
Answers will vary. Some possibilities are as follows:

1. *Worm:* slimy, soft, wriggly
2. *Ocean:* blue, stormy, calm, vast, white-crested
3. *SUV:* cool, roomy, sleek, mighty
4. *Rap artist:* cool, popular, star
5. *Sci-fi film:* eerie, futuristic, scary, imaginative
6. *Pizza:* cheesy, tasty, crusty
7. *Football stadium:* roaring, huge, noisy, crowded
8. *Dog:* loving, furry, loyal

1–18. STRONG, ACTIVE VERBS
The verbs (and pronoun/verb contractions) to be circled are: saw, went, took, went, got, went, was, got, said, what's, asked, moved, I'm, said, looked, are, said, was going, pushed, went, is, said, You're.
Rewritten paragraphs will vary.

1–19. TRANSITIVE AND INTRANSITIVE VERBS

1. pitied (T)
2. laid (T)
3. are complaining (I)
4. looks (I)
5. were (I)

6. tasted (T)
7. tasted (I)
8. purrs (I)
9. scratched (T)
10. threw (T)

1–20. LINKING VERBS

Sentences will vary.

1–21. IRREGULAR VERBS

1. rang
2. drove
3. sang
4. taken
5. blew

6. brought
7. forgot
8. sworn
9. sped
10. chosen

1–22. ADJECTIVES (PART ONE)

Sentences will vary.

1–23. ADJECTIVES (PART TWO)

Sentences will vary.

1–24. ILLITERACIES

1. (circled) goes; My dad often says, "Watch out for cars when you are on your bike."
2. (circled) this here; This tennis racket is broken.
3. (circled) ain't; Luci isn't so smart as she thinks she is.
4. (circled) drownded; I almost drowned when that idiot pushed me into the pool.
5. (circled) nowheres; My mom told me I was going nowhere until I cleaned up my room.

ANSWERS TO REVIEW TEST (PART ONE)

The following errors should be circled: breathe, peculier, moral, happyer, docters, implied, probible, arrangments, neighber, drived, sensably, accept, sung

The correct paragraph should be written as follows:

My dad went to the hospital last week. He was having shortness of breath and peculiar pains in his chest. We were all worried, but Dad's morale was great. The family felt happier after the tests were completed and we spoke to the doctors. We inferred from their reports that nothing was seriously wrong with Dad and that it was probable he had been doing too much exercise. We made arrangements with a neighbor who drove Dad home. He was told to rest and eat sensibly. Everyone except my sister, Rose, was there to greet him when he arrived. Mom even sang a song to him.

ANSWERS TO REVIEW TEST (PART TWO)

Part A

Possible answers are:

 1. postgraduate, undergraduate, graduating
 2. operator, operated, operating
 3. changeable, changing, changed
 4. forgettable, forgetting, forgetful
 5. mismanage, manager, managed, managing
 6. superstar, starry, starless
 7. unpopular, popularize, popularity
 8. disbelieve, believable, believing
 9. servant, serving, served
10. caring, cared, careless

Part B

1. b
2. c
3. c
4. b
5. c

1–1. WORDS OFTEN CONFUSED (PART ONE)

The following words are often confused. Be sure you use them correctly.

> *Ancestor* refers to a family member who lived before, in the past. (*I met a girl named Tricia Adams who claims that John Adams was her ancestor.*)
> *Descendant* refers to the subject's children, their children, and on into the future. (*I hope that my descendants will live in a peaceful world.*)
>
> *Personal* refers to things or qualities that belong to a particular person. (*Mr. Smith's personal papers are kept in a locked box.*)
> *Personnel* refers to people who are employed in a particular place. (*The personnel at Blake's Department Store are always helpful.*)
>
> *Persecute* means to harass or annoy cruelly and constantly. (*Hitler persecuted the Jews in Nazi Germany.*)
> *Prosecute* means to try a defendant in a courtroom. (*The district attorney prosecutes cases in court.*)
>
> *Conscious* means to be awake or aware. (*The man was badly injured but still conscious.*)
> *Conscience* refers to an inner feeling of right and wrong. (*Your conscience often tells you when you have done something wrong.*)

DIRECTIONS: Circle the correct word to be inserted in each sentence.

1. People who commit terrible crimes seem to have no _____.
   (**conscious, conscience**)

2. Mr. Abado is in charge of hiring _____ for his company.
   (**personal, personnel**)

3. The accident victim was _____ when he arrived at the hospital.
   (**conscious, conscience**)

4. My friend Winston is a _____ of early settlers. (**ancestor, descendant**)

5. His _____ came over on the Mayflower. (**ancestors, descendants**)

6. Is there enough evidence to _____ this defendant? (**persecute, prosecute**)

7. It is wrong to _____ others for their religious beliefs.
   (**persecute, prosecute**)

8. I won't answer your question because it is too _____ (**personal, personnel**)

1–2. WORDS OFTEN CONFUSED (PART TWO)

The following words are often confused. Be sure you use them correctly.

Accept means to take something that is offered. *(Marla was happy to accept her award on graduation day.)*

Except means "but" or "not including." *(Everyone was there except Lance.)*

Breath is a noun. It means "the air you draw into and out of your lungs." *(Eric took a deep breath when he walked out into the fresh air.)*

Breathe is a verb. It means "the act of drawing air into your lungs." *(Go outside and breathe deeply.)*

Among is used with more than two things. *(The rock star walked among his fans at the concert.)*

Between is used with two things. *(The final championship game is between Matthew and Jonathan.)*

Beside means "by the side of" or "next to." *(I don't like to sit beside my brother at the movies because he is a pest.)*

Besides means "also" or "in addition to." *(Who else is going to be there besides you and your cousin?)*

DIRECTIONS: Fill in the blanks below.

1. There is not one good tennis player _____ the girls in my class. **(between, among)**

2. This argument is just _____ you and me. **(between, among)**

3. This room is so stuffy that I cannot _____. **(breath, breathe)**

4. I can hardly take a _____ in this stuffy room. **(breath, breathe)**

5. Every actor would love to _____ an Academy® Award. **(accept, except)**

6. Everyone in the family _____ Jeff loves pizza. **(accept, except)**

7. How many people _____ Sara can roast a turkey? **(beside, besides)**

8. I wish I lived in a house _____ the sea. **(beside, besides)**

1–3. WORDS OFTEN CONFUSED (PART THREE)

The following words are often confused. Be sure you use them correctly.

Import means to bring in. *(The United States imports oil from the Middle East.)*
Export means to send out. *(Mr. Romero's company exports goods from the United States to Mexico.)*

Formally means in a formal or regulated manner. *(You are expected to dress formally for the Grand Ball.)*
Formerly means at a previous time. *(The school I formerly attended is in Ohio.)*

Imply means to indicate something. *(The defendant implied his guilt in his statement to the police.)*
Infer means to draw information from. *(The police inferred from his statement that he was guilty.)*

Moral means related to right and wrong. *(A crime against another person is not a moral act.)*
Moral can also refer to a meaning or lesson gained from a story. *(Each of Aesop's "Fables" has a moral.)*
Morale refers to the condition of individual or group happiness or satisfaction. *(Morale is high among the people who work in that store.)*

DIRECTIONS: Fill in the blanks below.

1. What message do you _____ from the mayor's speech? **(imply, infer)**

2. His speech _____ there is no money in the budget for new programs. **(implies, infers)**

3. The _____ of the public is low when there is a depression. **(moral, morale)**

4. Some students think it is _____ to cheat on a test. **(moral, morale)**

5. Our principal likes to be spoken to _____ as Dr. Brown. **(formerly, formally)**

6. She was _____ principal at a high school in New Jersey. **(formerly, formally)**

7. The United States should _____ its democratic ideals to other countries. **(import, export)**

8. A country does not have to _____ what it can produce itself. **(import, export)**

Name _____ Date _____

1–4. WORDS OFTEN CONFUSED (PART FOUR)

The following words are often confused. Be sure you use them correctly.

Emigrate means to leave a country. *(Joe Morales emigrated from Mexico.)*
Immigrate means to come into a country. *(Joe Morales immigrated to the United States.)*

Compliment means praise. *(Rose liked the compliment about her dress.)*
Complement refers to completing or perfecting something else. *(The dessert was a perfect complement to the meal.)*

Forward means ahead. *(The line moved forward slowly.)*
Foreword means an introduction. *(Did you read the foreword to this book?)*

Incredible means unbelievable or astonishing. *(The story about aliens is incredible.)*
Incredulous means unbelieving or skeptical. (I was incredulous about that story.)
Note: A thing or event is *incredible*. A person is *incredulous*.

Envelop is to cover completely or surround. *(The fog will soon envelop the town.)*
Envelope is a container for a letter. *(Put the stamp on the envelope.)*

DIRECTIONS: Use each of the following words in a sentence. Study the definitions and examples above until you understand the meaning and correct usage of each word.

1. incredible _____

2. incredulous _____

3. emigrate _____

4. immigrate _____

5. compliment _____

6. complement _____

7. envelop _____

8. envelope _____

9. forward _____

10. foreword _____

1–5. WORDS OFTEN CONFUSED (PART FIVE)

The words *lie* and *lay* are often used incorrectly. It is easy to use them in the right way if you follow these simple rules:

> 1. The verb "to lie" means to rest or recline. The subject usually takes a position or is in a position. *Lie* never takes an *object* (a word following the verb that answers the question "what" or "whom").
>
> *Lie* is the present tense of the verb "to lie."
> *Lay* is the past tense of the verb "to lie."
>
> Examples: Jody likes to lie on the beach on summer afternoons. *(present tense; does not have an object)*
>
> Last night, I lay awake for two hours. *(past tense; does not have an object)*
>
> 2. The verb "to lay" means to place or put something down. It always takes an *object* (a word following the verb that answers the question "what" or "whom").
>
> *Lay* is the present tense of the verb "to lay."
> *Laid* is the past tense of the verb "to lay."
>
> Examples: Sheri lays her book upon the table. *(present tense; has an object, "book")*
>
> Yesterday, I laid my keys on the table and forgot where I put them. *(past tense; has an object, "keys")*

DIRECTIONS: Fill in each blank with the correct form of the verb "to lie" or "to lay."

1. Last week, the workmen _____ the new carpet in our living room.

2. He _____ his report on the same desk every day.

3. Josh _____ in the sun too long on Sunday and got a severe burn.

4. I can see Mr. Rosen as he _____ his airline ticket on the counter.

5. The seats adjust so the passenger can _____ back.

6. An hour before dinner last night, Josie _____ the silverware on the table.

7. Mrs. Barney told the kindergarten children to _____ down.

8. Now that it is summer, our dog _____ under the shady tree on hot afternoons.

9. Last Christmas, my father _____ colorful packages under the tree.

1–6. WORDS OFTEN CONFUSED (REVIEW)

DIRECTIONS: Place a checkmark next to the correct sentence in each of the sets below.

1. ❏ a. After the test, I lay down my pen without being conscience I was doing it.
   ❏ b. After the test, I laid down my pen without being conscious I was doing it.
   ❏ c. After the test, I laid down my pen without being conscience I was doing it.

2. ❏ a. Are you inferring that I should lay down for a nap this afternoon?
   ❏ b. Are you implying that I should lay down for a nap this afternoon?
   ❏ c. Are you implying that I should lie down for a nap this afternoon?

3. ❏ a. My Boston ancestors imported lace from Belgium in the nineteenth century.
   ❏ b. My Boston descendants imported lace from Belgium in the nineteenth century.
   ❏ c. My Boston ancestors exported lace from Belgium in the nineteenth century.

4. ❏ a. It is not moral to persecute a person because of his race.
   ❏ b. It is not morale to persecute a person because of his race.
   ❏ c. It is not morale to prosecute a person because of his race.

5. ❏ a. You will be able to breath more easily if you lay on the couch.
   ❏ b. You will be able to breathe more easily if you lie on the couch.
   ❏ c. You will be able to breathe more easily if you lay on the couch.

6. ❏ a. Everyone except Tim is lying down for a nap.
   ❏ b. Everyone accept Tim is laying down for a nap.
   ❏ c. Everyone except Tim is laying down for a nap.

7. ❏ a. Who is going to dress formally for the dance beside Rose?
   ❏ b. Who is going to dress formerly for the dance beside Rose?
   ❏ c. Who is going to dress formally for the dance besides Rose?

8. ❏ a. This is a personnel matter among Matt and me.
   ❏ b. This is a personal matter between Matt and me.
   ❏ c. This is a personal matter among Matt and me.

Name _____ Date _____

1–7. PREFIXES

You are already familiar with many prefixes (syllables added to the beginning of a word to change or modify the meaning) such as *pre, in, dis, mis,* and *non.* But did you know that most English prefixes have their origin in Greek or Latin?

Here are some common Greek prefixes:

Prefix	Meaning	Examples
a	without	anemia, amoral, atypical
mono	one, single, alone	monarchy, monotone, monosyllabic
mis	hate or badly	mischief, misguided, misconduct, misanthrope
poly	many	polygamy, Polynesian
auto	self	autograph, autobiography

Here are some common Latin prefixes:

Prefix	Meaning	Examples
ab	away	abduct, abnormal, abscond
ante	before	antechamber, antecedent
post	after	postpone, postgraduate
semi	half	semiconscious, semiskilled, semicolon
super	above, greater	superhero, superstructure, superstar

DIRECTIONS: For *each* of the prefixes below, write two sentences containing words with that prefix.

1. a- _____

_____

2. mono- _____

_____

3. mis- _____

_____

4. super- _____

_____

5. post- _____

_____

Name _____   Date _____

1–8. SUFFIXES (PART ONE)

Suffixes are syllables added at the end of words to change their meanings or form new words. Here is a partial list of common suffixes and examples of their use:

Suffix	Meaning	Examples
ant	one who is	descendant, servant, inhabitant
er	one who does	buyer, seller, writer, farmer
ist	one who believes in or does	atheist, typist, deist
or	one who does	operator, legislator, professor
ful	full of	beautiful, peaceful, tasteful
ic	like	fantastic, manic, demonic
ish	like	foolish, stylish
ize	cause to become	popularize, stylize, standardize
less	without	careless, hopeless, homeless
ly	in the manner	foolishly, carelessly, quietly
sion, tion, ation	process of, state of being	depression, immersion, rejection, elation, operation, desperation
ward	in the direction of	toward, homeward, forward
hood	condition of	childhood, adulthood
ness	condition of	goodness, happiness, foolishness

DIRECTIONS: Write ten sentences. Each sentence should contain at least one word with a suffix.

1. _____

2. _____

3. _____

4. _____

5. _____

6. _____

7. _____

8. _____

9. _____

10. _____

1–9. Suffixes (Part Two)

Here are some rules to follow when adding suffixes.

---

1. **Do not** drop the final *e* of the base word when adding a suffix that begins with a consonant. **Examples:** *care + less = careless, state + ment = statement, love + ly = lovely.*

2. **Drop** the final *e* in a word before adding a suffix that begins with a vowel. **Examples:** *care + ing = caring, state + ed = stated, love + able = lovable.* **Exception:** Do not drop the final *e* in some words that end with *ce* or *ge*, such as *peaceful, changeable, noticeable.*

3. When the root word ends in *y*, change the *y* to an *i* before a suffix. **Examples:** *easy + ly = easily, ready + ness = readiness, duty + ful = dutiful.*

4. When you add a suffix that begins with a vowel to a word that ends with a consonant preceded by a vowel, double the final consonant. **Examples:** *forget + able = forgettable, slip + ing = slipping, spit + ing = spitting.* **Exception:** Do not double the final consonant in words of more than one syllable if the accent does not fall on the last syllable. **Examples:** *labor + ing = laboring, motor + ist = motorist, differ + ence = difference.*

DIRECTIONS: Circle the correct spelling in parentheses for each sentence.

1. My Uncle Jason has very _____ (**changeable, changable**) moods.

2. _____ (**Spiting, Spitting**) on the ground is a disgusting habit.

3. The scar on Maria's forehead is not _____ (**noticable, noticeable**) because it is covered by her bangs.

4. The _____ (**motorrist, motorist**) in the blue Camaro is _____ (**driving, driveing**) too fast.

5. My _____ (**happiness, happyness**) was complete when I got an A in science.

6. It is _____ (**careless, carless**) to make _____ (**statments, statements**) without thinking.

7. Mrs. Arcaro is a _____ (**lovly, lovely**) and _____ (**caring, careing**) teacher.

8. The _____ (**arrangment, arrangement**) of the furniture is perfect for that room.

9. Is the spot on this jacket _____ (**noticable, noticeable**)?

Name _____ Date _____

1–10. SUFFIXES (PART THREE)

Do you know whether to use *er, or,* or *ar* at the end of a word? There are no rules to follow for these suffixes. It is necessary to memorize them. The same is true for *able* and *ible.* Here are some common words containing these suffixes that you can memorize.

Words Using *er, or,* and *ar*	Words Using *able* or *ible*
announcer, baker, barber, believer, cheater, commissioner, computer, lawyer, manager, messenger, passenger, quieter	acceptable, attainable, believable, charitable, comfortable, honorable, irritable, lovable, noticeable, peaceable, probable, regrettable, unspeakable, usable, valuable
ancestor, author, behavior, counselor, creator, doctor, elevator, major, minor, neighbor, pastor, professor, supervisor	admissible, digestible, edible, eligible, flexible, forcible, horrible, invisible, irresistible, legible, responsible, sensible, visible
burglar, calendar, circular, collar, grammar, liar, particular, peculiar, regular, similar, stellar, sugar, unpopular, vinegar, vulgar	

DIRECTIONS: Write a sentence that contains at least one word with the suffix indicated at the beginning.

1. -ar _____

2. -ar _____

3. -er _____

4. -er _____

5. -or _____

6. -or _____

7. -able _____

8. -able _____

9. -ible _____

10. -ible _____

1–11. PREFIXES AND SUFFIXES (REVIEW)

A. DIRECTIONS: Change each of the words below by adding a prefix. Then write a sentence containing the new word.

Base Word	New Word with Prefix	Sentence
1. like	_____	_____
2. conscious	_____	_____
3. gram	_____	_____
4. moral	_____	_____
5. test	_____	_____
6. graduate	_____	_____
7. light	_____	_____

B. DIRECTIONS: Change each of the words below by adding a suffix. Then write a sentence containing the new word.

Base Word	New Word with Suffix	Sentence
1. care	_____	_____
2. forget	_____	_____
3. peace	_____	_____
4. regret	_____	_____
5. force	_____	_____
6. ready	_____	_____
7. accept	_____	_____

Name _____   **Date** _____

1–12. SYNONYMS

It is boring to repeat the same word over and over again. That is where **synonyms** (words with the same meaning) come in handy.

Here is an example of writing that is repetitious: "John *stopped* when he heard a noise. The noise *stopped*. John started walking. Then the noise came again. John *stopped*."

Wouldn't this be better? "John *stopped* when he heard a noise. The noise *disappeared*. John started walking. Then the noise occurred again. John *came to a halt*."

DIRECTIONS: Write as many synonyms as you can for each of the words below.

1. scared _____

2. happy _____

3. big _____

4. strong _____

5. tired _____

6. small _____

7. want _____

8. hit _____

9. fight _____

10. many _____

11. event _____

12. talk _____

13. look _____

14. kill _____

15. angry _____

1–13. SIMILES

Your writing can be more vivid and interesting with the use of **similes** (comparisons that use the connecting words *as* or *like*). Some similes, however, have been used so often that they have become trite and boring. Try to avoid overused similes such as *cold as ice* or *quiet as a mouse*. Use more original comparisons such as *cold as an Eskimo's backyard* or *quiet as a classroom during a final exam*.

DIRECTIONS: Complete the following similes. Try to be original and avoid trite comparisons.

as curious as _____

as tired as _____

as excited as _____

as furious as _____

as disgusting as _____

frightening like _____

as peaceful as _____

as brave as _____

as evil as _____

as unbelievable as _____

as difficult as _____

as hateful as _____

as loving as _____

as desperate as _____

as strange as _____

as common as _____

perfect like _____

1–14. METAPHORS

Metaphors are common in everyday life. We use them in our daily speech, hear them on television, and read them in magazines and newspapers. Metaphors make language exciting because they are shocking. They stand reality upside down by calling a thing something it is not. When we say, "*Tom struck out on his job interview,*" we don't mean that he was playing baseball. We call something easy a *piece of cake,* but we don't expect to eat it! Metaphors are fun to read and fun to write.

A. DIRECTIONS: Underline the metaphors in the following poem:

> A sunny morning at the beach,
>
> The sand sparkles with jewels glinting under the sun.
>
> Diamonds and pearls ride the white-crested waves,
>
> A girl stands at the edge of the water,
>
> She is blinded by the brilliance, but cannot look away.

B. DIRECTIONS: Write five original sentences containing metaphors. Choose from the suggestions below, or use your own ideas. **Note:** A metaphor does not use the words *as* or *like.*

> *A sentence describing a moment in a sport*
> *A sentence describing a car you would like to own*
> *A sentence about an embarrassing moment*
> *A sentence describing a visitor from outer space*
> *A sentence describing an angry person*
> *A sentence about a disappointing experience*

1. _____

2. _____

3. _____

4. _____

5. _____

1–15. SIMILES AND METAPHORS (REVIEW)

A *simile* is a comparison using the words *as* or *like*.
Example: as strange as a report card with all A's

A *metaphor* is a comparison between two unlike things.
Example: My Uncle Jesse is a piece of work.

Note: A metaphor does not use the words *as* or *like*.

DIRECTIONS: Make the following sentences more interesting by adding a metaphor or simile to each one. Write each new sentence on the line below the original.

1. New England can be cold in the winter.

   _____

2. My cousin Angelo is funny.

   _____

3. My favorite actor is very good-looking.

   _____

4. Maria's little brother is wild.

   _____

5. I don't like to visit Aunt Marisa because she is too strict.

   _____

6. Our classroom is very noisy today.

   _____

7. Matthew pitched well in the last Little League game.

   _____

8. It was a windy day.

   _____

1–16. SENSORY LANGUAGE (PART ONE)

The use of language that appeals to the senses (touch, taste, sight, sound, smell) can make your writing stronger and more vivid.

DIRECTIONS: Fill up the boxes below with as many sensory words as you can. Some words can be used for more than one sense. For example, *icy* could refer to taste, sight, or touch. Each list has been started for you.

TOUCH: rough, soft,

TASTE: peppery, salty,

SIGHT: yellow, bright,

SOUND: whisper, squeal,

SMELL: putrid, mouth-watering,

1–17. SENSORY LANGUAGE (PART TWO)

A. DIRECTIONS: For each sense, write two sentences containing words that refer to that sense.

1. Taste: _____

_____

2. Touch: _____

_____

3. Sight: _____

_____

4. Sound: _____

_____

5. Smell: _____

_____

B. DIRECTIONS: On the line next to each word, write all the sensory words that the word brings to mind. (**Example:** Turtle: <u>shy</u>, <u>green</u>, <u>hard shell</u>, <u>wet</u>)

1. Worm: _____

2. Ocean: _____

3. SUV: _____

4. Rap artist: _____

5. Sci-fi film: _____

6. Pizza: _____

7. Football stadium: _____

8. Dog: _____

Name _____ Date _____

1–18. STRONG, ACTIVE VERBS

Writing can be made more interesting with the use of strong, active verbs. *Rush* or *stumble* is more exciting than *go*. *Glare* or *squint* is more vivid than *see*. *Shout* or *whisper* is stronger than *say*.

DIRECTIONS: Circle the verbs in the following story. Then rewrite the story below, substituting active verbs wherever possible for passive ones. (Use the back of this sheet if you need more room.)

Jeff saw the mess in the kitchen. He went into the hall and took his jacket from the hook. Then he went outside. He got on his bike and went down the street to his friend Andy's house. Andy was in the front yard. Jeff got off his bike.

"Hi, Andy," he said.

"What's up, Jeff?" asked Andy.

Jeff moved closer to Andy. "I'm in big trouble," he said.

Andy looked at him. "You are?"

"Yeah," said Jeff. "I was going through the kitchen and I accidentally pushed over my mom's favorite china casserole. It went on the floor and is in a million pieces."

"Yeah," said Andy. "You're in big trouble.

_____

_____

_____

_____

_____

_____

_____

_____

1–19. TRANSITIVE AND INTRANSITIVE VERBS

1. Transitive verbs take a direct object.

    Examples: *I hit the ball.* (*Hit* is a transitive verb because it is doing something to the ball.)

    Alex drove the car. (*Drove* is a transitive verb because it is doing something to the car.)

2. **Intransitive verbs do not take direct objects.**

    Examples: *The movie was a good one.* (*Was* is the intransitive verb. There is no object.)

    Hudson left early today. (*Left* is an intransitive verb because it does not take an object.)

3. Some verbs can be used as either transitive or intransitive verbs.

    Examples: *The dog smells the flowers.* (*Smells* is **transitive** here. It takes the direct object *flowers.*)

    The dog smells bad. (*Smells* is **intransitive** here. There is no object.)

    Feel this silky material. (*Feel* is **transitive** here. The object is *material.*)

    My mom feels ill today. (*Feel* is **intransitive** here. There is no object.)

DIRECTIONS: Circle the verb in each sentence below. At the end of the line, indicate with a T if it is a transitive verb or an I if it is intransitive.

1. Sandy pitied the injured people in the newscast.   _____

2. Rose laid the book down on the desk.   _____

3. The children are complaining today.   _____

4. Your hair looks different in the sunlight.   _____

5. My sister and brother were happy at my birthday party.   _____

6. Nelson tasted the ice cream.   _____

7. The ice cream tasted too sweet.   _____

8. My cat purrs all day long.   _____

9. Your cat scratched me last week.   _____

10. She threw the leftovers in the garbage bin.   _____

1–20. LINKING VERBS

A **linking verb** is one type of intransitive verb. It does not express action, but it connects the subject with an adjective or noun in the predicate that describes or means the same as the subject.

Examples: Kim is the best shortstop on the team. (*Shortstop* describes the subject *Kim*. The linking verb is *is*.)

The students appear busy. (*Busy* describes the subject *students*. The linking verb is *appear*.)

The great white shark looks huge. (*Huge* describes the subject *shark*. The linking verb is *looks*.)

Some common linking verbs are *appear, be, become, feel, grow, look, remain, seem, smell, sound, taste.*

DIRECTIONS: Write two sentences using each linking verb listed below. You can use any tense. For example, the past tense of *be* would be *was* or *were,* as in "The boys were happy on the basketball court."

1. be _____

_____

2. sound _____

_____

3. look _____

_____

4. become _____

_____

5. feel _____

_____

6. taste _____

_____

7. smell _____

_____

8. appear _____

_____

1–21. IRREGULAR VERBS

Most verbs show the past tense by adding *d* or *ed*. (**Examples:** *jump, jumped; live, lived; toss, tossed.*) **Irregular verbs** end in irregular ways. (**Examples:** *awake, awoke; forgive, forgave; hide, hid.*) Here is a list of some common irregular verbs.

Present	Past	Past Participle (with *has, have, had*)	Present	Past	Past Participle (with *has, have, had*)
am	was	been	go	went	gone
become	became	become	grow	grew	grown
bring	brought	brought	ride	rode	ridden
buy	bought	bought	run	ran	run
break	broke	broken	see	saw	seen
choose	chose	chosen	sing	sang	sung
come	came	come	speed	sped	sped
do	did	done	steal	stole	stolen
drink	drank	drunk	swear	swore	sworn
drive	drove	driven	ring	rang	rung
eat	ate	eaten	take	took	taken
forget	forgot	forgotten	wear	wore	worn

DIRECTIONS: Write the correct past verb form in the blank spaces below.

1. When the warden _____ the bell, the prisoners came out of their cells. (**ring**)

2. Rachel has _____ her father's car many times. (**drive**)

3. Jonathan _____ in a deep, baritone voice. (**sing**)

4. I have _____ the bus to school twice during the past week. (**take**)

5. The tornado _____ the roofs off three houses on my block. (**blow**)

6. My aunt _____ two kinds of pies to Thanksgiving dinner. (**bring**)

7. I _____ to bring home the homework assignment in math. (**forget**)

8. I could have _____ that it was in my book bag. (**swear**)

9. The green sports car _____ away after the crash. (**speed**)

10. You were right to have _____ white shoes to wear with that outfit. (**choose**)

1–22. ADJECTIVES (PART ONE)

A sharp, clear photograph is better than a blurry one. A color picture is usually more exciting than one that is black and white. Adjectives are a handy tool for writers to use to make their work sharper and more exciting. **Adjectives** answer one of the following questions:

What kind?	*muscular* guy; *loving* family
Which ones?	*these* books; *various* houses
How much?	*few* people; *ten* dollars

DIRECTIONS: Take out your palette of colorful, vivid adjectives and use them to make these sentences clearer and more exciting. Rewrite each sentence on the line below it, adding at least one adjective.

1. The teacher came into the room.

   _____

2. He held books in his hands.

   _____

3. He put the books down on the desk.

   _____

4. He asked the students if they had read any books lately.

   _____

5. A student immediately raised his hand.

   _____

6. "I don't read books," he said. "I see the movie instead."

   _____

7. All the kids laughed, but the teacher's voice stopped them.

   _____

8. He gave the class an assignment.

   _____

9. Everyone had to read a book from a list he had prepared.

   _____

10. A report was due by the end of the week.

   _____

1–23. ADJECTIVES (PART TWO)

DIRECTIONS: For each item, write a sentence containing the two adjectives at the beginning of the line. (Use the back of this sheet if you need more room for your sentences.)

1. neat, small _____

2. furious, wild _____

3. lonely, sad _____

4. sweet, mouth-watering _____

5. red, large _____

6. scary, exciting _____

7. icy, frigid _____

8. orange, ugly _____

9. fifteen, brilliant _____

10. rare, green _____

11. rocky, enormous _____

12. impressive, short _____

13. thunderous, clear _____

14. bloody, brave _____

15. old-fashioned, funny _____

Name _____ Date _____

1–24. ILLITERACIES

The language you hear on the street is not always acceptable for written English. **Illiteracies** are words and phrases that are incorrect in formal spoken and written English. Here are some common illiteracies and how they can be corrected:

1. *Goes* indicates movement. It should NEVER be used to show speech.
   WRONG: Alan *goes,* "I didn't finish the math homework."
   RIGHT: Alan *says,* "I didn't finish the math homework."

2. The phrase *this here* should be *this.*
   WRONG: *This here* is an exciting computer game.
   RIGHT: *This* is an exciting computer game.

3. *Ain't* is incorrect in formal English. It should be *isn't, aren't,* or *am not.*
   WRONG: I *ain't* going to the prom this year.
   RIGHT: I *am not* going to the prom this year.

4. Other common **illiteracies** that should never be used in formal English are as follows:
   Drownded should be *drowned,* as in *A man drowned at the beach last summer.*
   Nowheres should be *nowhere,* as in *He seems to be going nowhere in his career.*
   Brung should be *brought,* as in *Tom brought me flowers on Mother's Day.*
   Alls should be *all,* as in *All I know is that I didn't see the crime being committed.*
   Nohow should be *at all,* as in *Patti did not understand the lesson at all.*

DIRECTIONS: Circle the illiteracy in each of the following sentences. Then write the sentences correctly on the lines below.

1. My dad often goes, "Watch out for cars when you are on your bike."

   _____

2. This here tennis racket is broken.

   _____

3. Luci ain't so smart as she thinks she is.

   _____

4. I almost drownded when that idiot pushed me into the pool.

   _____

5. My mom told me I was going nowheres until I cleaned up my room.

   _____

TENTH-GRADE LEVEL

CHOOSING THE RIGHT WORD
REVIEW TEST

REVIEW TEST: CHOOSING THE RIGHT WORD (PART ONE)

DIRECTIONS: The following paragraph contains **thirteen** errors in word usage. Can you find all thirteen? Circle the mistakes. Then copy the paragraph correctly on the lines below. (Continue on the back of this sheet, if necessary.)

My dad went to the hospital last week. He was having shortness of breathe and peculier pains in his chest. We were all worried, but Dad's moral was great. The family felt happyer after the tests were completed and we spoke to the docters. We implied from their reports that nothing was seriously wrong with Dad and that it was probible he had been doing too much exercise. We made arrangments with a neighbor who drived Dad home. He was told to rest and eat sensably. Everyone accept my sister, Rose, was there to greet him when he arrived. Mom even sung a song to him.

_____

_____

_____

_____

_____

_____

_____

_____

_____

REVIEW TEST: CHOOSING THE RIGHT WORD (PART TWO)

A. DIRECTIONS: Write a new word by adding a prefix or a suffix to each of the following words.

1. graduate _____   6. star _____

2. operate _____   7. popular _____

3. change _____   8. believe _____

4. forget _____   9. serve _____

5. manage _____   10. care _____

B. DIRECTIONS: Place a checkmark next to the correct sentence in each of the following groups.

1. ❏ a. It is regrettible that Marla did not dress formally for the dance.
   ❏ b. It is regrettable that Marla did not dress formally for the dance.
   ❏ c. It is regrettable that Marla did not dress formerly for the dance.

2. ❏ a. I wonder what kind of incredible life my ancestors will have in the future.
   ❏ b. I wonder what kind of incredable life my descendants will have in the future.
   ❏ c. I wonder what kind of incredible life my descendants will have in the future.

3. ❏ a. The New York baker exports olive oil into the United States.
   ❏ b. The New York bakor exports olive oil into the United States.
   ❏ c. The New York baker imports olive oil into the United States.

4. ❏ a. My mother goes, "You are going nowheres until you finish your homework."
   ❏ b. My mother says, "You are going nowhere until you finish your homework."
   ❏ c. My mother goes, "You are going nowhere until you finish your homework."

5. ❏ a. It is peaceful in my home accept when my brother is around.
   ❏ b. It is peaceful in my home except when my brother is around.
   ❏ c. It is peaceful in my home except when my brother is around.

MAKING MECHANICS AND USAGE WORK FOR YOU

Teacher Preparation and Lessons

The activities in Section 2 cover a wide variety of common mechanics and usage skills. Students need a solid foundation in these skills to become proficient writers. The concluding activity assesses your students' knowledge of the skills covered. Activities 2–1 through 2–14 focus on punctuation. Activities 2–15 through 2–21 concentrate on spelling. Common problems with grammar are addressed in the last group of activities. You may wish to use the REVIEW TEST as a pretest or posttest. Answer keys can be found on pages 39 to 44.

ACTIVITIES 2–1 and 2–2 review the use of **end marks.** Introduce this topic by writing on the board: *I feel tired after a long trip do you feel tired I'm exhausted* Ask the class to explain what is wrong with this. Elicit from them that there is no punctuation to mark the ends of the sentences. Have the students suggest end marks and locate where they should be placed. (Change the beginning of each new sentence so that it begins with a capital letter.) The sentences on the board should now read: *I feel tired after a long trip. Do you feel tired? I'm exhausted!* Point out that three types of sentences and end marks are illustrated here: a **period** at the end of a declarative sentence, a **question mark** following an interrogative sentence, and an **exclamation point** to indicate an exclamatory sentence. Distribute **Activity 2–1 End Marks (Part One).** Read and discuss the examples at the top of the page and then complete the activity. Distribute **Activity 2–2 End Marks (Part Two).** Read and discuss the directions at the top and complete the activity.

ACTIVITIES 2–3 through 2–5 review the use of **commas.** Ask the students to describe the difference between a red light and an amber light. Point out that an end mark is like a red light and signals the reader to stop, and a comma, like an amber light, indicates a pause. Distribute **Activity 2–3 Commas (Part One).** Read and discuss each of these five rules for the use of commas, and complete the activity. Distribute **Activity 2–4 Commas (Part Two).** Read and discuss the three ways that commas are used to clarify the meaning of sentences, and then complete the activity. Distribute **Activity 2–5 Commas (Part Three).** Read and discuss these four rules and examples for the use of commas, and complete the activity.

ACTIVITIES 2–6 through 2–8 review the use of **semicolons** and **colons.** Write the following sentences on the board:

> *I knocked at your door this morning, but nobody answered.*
> *I knocked at your door this morning; nobody answered.*

Ask the students to identify the marks of punctuation in these sentences (comma, semicolon, and two periods). Elicit from the class that each sentence contains two independent clauses, joined by a comma in the first and by a semicolon in the second. Point out that the colon is composed of a period and a comma and falls somewhere in between, indicating a stronger pause than a comma, but not a full stop like a period. Ask the students to identify the difference between these sentences: the clauses are joined by a conjunction in the first.

Distribute **Activity 2–6 Semicolons.** Read and discuss the rules for using semicolons, and then complete the activity. Ask students to write on the board the names of stop or pause signs that are used in sentences, including the period, exclamation point, question mark, comma, and semicolon. Add the word *colon* to this list. Point out that the colon is an abrupt stop, almost like a period. Unlike end marks, however, the colon does not indicate an end but the beginning of a presentation, such as a series, a statement, a quotation, or instructions. Write the following sentence on the board:

Farmer Jones grows three kinds of apples in the orchard: gala, winesap, and macintosh.

Discuss how the colon stops the sentence and also presents a series of words. Distribute **Activity 2–7 Colons (Part One).** Read and discuss the four rules presented here for the use of colons, and then complete the activity. Distribute **Activity 2–8 Colons (Part Two).** Read and discuss the four additional uses for the colon presented here, and complete the activity.

ACTIVITIES 2–9 through 2–11 review **parentheses, dashes,** and **hyphens.** Write the following sentences on the board:

She was horrified that her luggage (complete with the return ticket) was lost.
She was horrified that her luggage—complete with the return ticket—was lost.
She was horrified that her luggage was lost—gone forever.

Discuss how both the parenthesis and the dash serve as brief interruptions to the sentence. Point out that parentheses are always used in pairs—one at the beginning and another at the end of the inserted material. Dashes can also be used in pairs when the interruption occurs in the middle of the sentence (the second example above). However, when the interruption comes at the beginning or end of the sentence, one dash is used. Distribute **Activity 2–9 Parentheses.** Read and discuss the rules and examples, then complete the activity. Distribute **Activity 2–10 Dashes.** Read and discuss the rules at the top of the page, then complete the activity. Write the following sentence on the board:

The shoes you sold me—size seven and one-half—are the wrong size.

Point out the use of a dash to enclose the interruption to the sentence. Elicit that the stubbier line in *one-half* is called a hyphen. Ask for examples of other words that are hyphenated and write them on the board. Emphasize that the hyphen is not just a short dash but serves a different purpose entirely. Distribute **Activity 2–11 Hyphens.** Read and discuss the rules and examples for the use of hyphens, then complete the activity.

ACTIVITIES 2–12 and 2–13 review the use of **quotation marks.** Distribute **Activity 2–12 Quotation Marks (Part One).** Read and discuss the rules and examples for using **quotation marks,** then complete the activity. Distribute **Activity 2–13 Quotation Marks (Part Two).** Read the rules and examples at the top, and complete the activity.

ACTIVITY 2–14 reviews **punctuation.** Distribute **Activity 2-14 Punctuation Review.** When it has been completed, have the students work in small groups exchanging papers to correct and discuss each other's errors.

ACTIVITIES 2–15 to 2–21 focus on **spelling problems.** Write the following sentence on the board: *General George Washington led the Continental Army during the American Revolution and later became the first president of the United States.* Ask students to underline all the words that begin with capitals. These are *General, George Washington, Continental Army,*

American Revolution, United States. Discuss why capital letters are used in each of these cases as follows:

> *General:* title used as part of a name
> *George Washington:* proper name
> *Continental Army:* name of an army
> *American Revolution:* name of a war
> *United States:* name of a country

Discuss why the word *president* is not capitalized; although it is a title, it is not written as part of the name. Distribute **Activity 2–15 Capitalization (Part One).** Read and discuss the rules and examples for using capital letters, then complete the activity. Distribute **Activity 2–16 Capitalization (Part Two).** Read and discuss the rules for capitalization, then complete the activity.

Write the following sentences on the board:

> *My aunt's coat is in the den. Both of my aunts are in the den.*
> *The class's meeting time is 3 P.M. These two classes are starting late.*

Have the class read the first two sentences aloud. Point out that *aunt's* and *aunts* are pronounced the same. Elicit from the students the difference in meaning: *aunt's* means *belonging to the aunt* and *aunts* means *more than one aunt.* Point out that the apostrophe is used to show possession. Follow the same procedure with the words *class's* and *classes* in the second line. Distribute **Activity 2–17 Apostrophes (Part One).** Read and discuss the rules at the top of the page, then complete the activity. Ask the students to write the correct answers on the board and discuss the determining rule. Write these sentences on the board: *The Rooney's live in that house. There are three Allison's in my class.* Put a line through the words *Rooney's* and *Allison's,* and write the correctly spelled word (*Rooneys, Allisons*) above each one. Elicit from the class that an apostrophe + *s* shows possession and that *s* alone is used for the plural. Distribute **Activity 2–18 Apostrophes (Part Two).** Read and discuss the examples of contractions and the rules for their use. Complete the activity and have a sample of each sentence read aloud.

Say to the students "*i* before *e,*" and challenge them to recite the rest of the rule. Most of them will know it. Point out that even though everyone can recite the rule, many errors are still made with *ie* versus *ei.* Ask the students to write the following words on the board: *deceiver, frontier, reign, shriek, sheik, counterfeit.* Point out that the first four words follow the rule, but the final two words are exceptions. Distribute **Activity 2–19 Spelling Help (Part One).** Read the rule, examples, and exceptions, and then complete the activity. Ask the students to write the following words on the board: *occurred, noticeable, recommend, conscientious, coolly, rhythm, privilege, embarrassed.* Discuss and correct those words that have been misspelled. Point out that these words appear on lists of words most frequently misspelled. Distribute **Activity 2–20 Spelling Help (Part Two).** Read and discuss the directions with the class. Be sure the students understand that each sentence must contain *two* of the words on the list. When the activity has been finished, have the students read sample sentences out loud. Distribute **Activity 2–21 Spelling Review.** Read the directions aloud, and then complete the activity.

ACTIVITIES 2–22 through 2–28 address common **grammatical problems.** Write the following words as a list on the board: *phenomenon, alumnus, hanger-on, politics, economics, trout.* Elicit from the students that these are all *singular* nouns. Ask volunteers to write the plural on the board next to each word. It will probably take them several attempts to get all the words correct. The correct plurals are: *phenomena, alumni, hangers-on, politics, economics, trout.* Note that the last three words are the same in singular or plural form. Inform the students that the good news is that most plurals are not this difficult because they follow specific rules. Distribute **Activity 2–22 Plurals (Part One).** Read and discuss the rules and examples at the top of the page, then complete the lesson. Ask the students to exchange papers and discuss their answers. Distribute **Activity 2–23 Plurals (Part Two).** Read and discuss the rules and examples at the top of the page, then complete the assignment.

Write the following sentences on the board:

> *Look at Maria. She lost her bookbag. I gave her a new one. She put the new bookbag on her desk.*

Elicit from the class that the underscored words are all pronouns and that they all take the place of the noun *Maria,* except for *I* (also a pronoun, which refers to the speaker of the sentence). Point out that a pronoun can be a subject (*she*), an object (*gave her*), or a possessive (*her bookbag, her desk*). Ask for examples of other pronouns and write them on the board. Distribute **Activity 2–24 Pronouns (Part One).** Read and discuss the rules and examples at the top of the page, then complete the lesson. Divide the class into small groups, and have them share and discuss their answers. Distribute **Activity 2–25 Pronouns (Part Two).** Read and discuss the rules and examples, then complete the activity. Have the students read several examples of each sentence aloud. Distribute **Activity 2–26 Pronouns (Part Three).** Read and discuss the rules and examples, and complete the activity. Ask students to share their answers, and discuss. Distribute **Activity 2–27 Pronouns (Part Four).** Read and discuss the directions, then complete the activity.

Write the following words on the board: *to, from, in, into, up, down, before.* Elicit from the class that these words are all prepositions. Ask the students to contribute additional prepositions to the list and then to offer short sentences using these words. Point out that a preposition is a word that joins a noun or pronoun in a phrase and relates to some other part of the sentence. Distribute **Activity 2–28 Prepositions.** Read and discuss the rules and examples, then complete the activity. Have students read aloud several examples for each sentence.

ANSWER KEY

2–1. END MARKS (PART ONE)

1. period
2. question mark
3. question mark
4. period

5. question mark
6. exclamation point
7. period
8. question mark

9. exclamation point
10. period
11. exclamation point

2–2. END MARKS (PART TWO)

The corrected paragraph is shown below. (Note that some of the exclamation points could also be periods.)

   My neighbor, Mr. Arcaro, achieved some success as a detective. He was having dinner at a local restaurant. Mr. Arcaro was finishing his dessert when he heard a commotion at the cash register. People were shouting! Someone screamed! What was happening? Mr. Arcaro rushed over. The cashier was shouting, "Stop!" A thief was running out the door. Mr. Arcaro raced after him. The thief was big, but Mr. Arcaro was bigger. He caught up with the thief and held him until the police arrived. Now Mr. Arcaro can have a free lunch at that restaurant any time he wishes. Don't you agree that he deserves it?

2–3. COMMAS (PART ONE)

1. Because I got up late, everything went wrong.
2. Mr. James, my math teacher, is a computer whiz.
3. If it is properly maintained, a car can last a long time.
4. This book has an exciting plot, and it held my attention until the end.
5. After all, you can't expect me to do two jobs at once.
6. My father's boss, Mr. Franco, is coming to dinner on Sunday.
7. Before going out, you should check to see that the windows are closed.
8. When I saw my brother trying to dance, I laughed out loud.
9. Blushing with shame and embarrassment, Toni ran out of the room.
10. When John F. Kennedy was assassinated, the whole nation mourned.

2–4. COMMAS (PART TWO)

1. I ate two hamburgers, french fries, and ice cream at noon.
2. The music store is open evenings on Thursday, Friday, and Saturday.
3. Mr. Weems worked on the space program at NASA in 1998, 1999, and 2000.
4. It is obvious, therefore, that he is up-to-date on the latest space technology.
5. Our fast-food restaurant, which employs many teenagers, is open seven days a week.
6. The baseball game that I attended went into extra innings.
7. Jody belongs to the math club, the chorus, and the marching band.
8. The community college offers courses for paralegals, lab technicians, and computer programmers.
9. My brother, of course, will enter college in the fall.
10. Perelli's Shoe Store, which is closed on Sunday, is the only one that carries my size.

2–5.   COMMAS (PART THREE)

Dear Aunt Linda,

Mom told me, "You should write to Aunt Linda." That's what I'm doing now. Aunt Linda, I really miss you since you moved so far away. I know that you live in Dallas, Texas, but I wish you still lived near us in Bangor, Maine. Mostly, I miss the way you always helped me with homework. We are studying the Second World War in social studies. Did you know that Winston Churchill said, "We will never surrender!"

I hope I can visit you in Dallas, Texas, next summer.

Your loving niece,

2–6.   SEMICOLONS

1. I have studied the problem for three hours; however, I still don't understand it.
2. I don't like carrot cake; besides, I don't feel like having any dessert.
3. I have been working for a long time; I am tired.
4. Our neighbors are Mr. Mason, the plumber; Mrs. Gallo, the lawyer; and Jeni Orlando, the famous singer.
5. It is snowing hard; therefore, schools will be closed today.

2–7.   COLONS (PART ONE)

1. Thoreau wrote: "The mass of men live lives of quiet desperation. What is called resignation is confirmed desperation."
2. Add the ingredients in the following order: butter, sugar, salt, vanilla, nutmeg, and nuts.
3. Our family believes that only one thing is really important: love.
4. I have a big problem: what to buy my dad for his birthday.
5. Mr. Franklin stresses one rule in giving a test: no cheating.
6. My father had one basic principle: honesty is the best policy.
7. Don't forget this rule: safety first.

2–8.   COLONS (PART TWO)

1. The title of this book is *Shakespeare: A Writer for the Ages.*
2. The plane is scheduled to depart at 2:14 P.M.
3. The letter that began "Dear Mr. Jones:" was addressed to me.
4. The sign said "HELP WANTED: Inquire Within."
5. I always get out of bed at the same time: 6:30 A.M.
6. The store is open until 10:30 P.M. Monday through Saturday.

2–9.   PARENTHESES

1. In some states (New York and New Jersey, for example), the sale of firecrackers is illegal.
2. The sale of firecrackers is illegal in some states. (New York and New Jersey are examples.)
3. There is wildlife (deer, rabbits, squirrels, and bears) in the woods near my house.
4. The Daughters of the American Revolution (DAR) is a patriotic organization.
5. Amanda's father (he was the only one who couldn't attend) was sad to miss her performance.
6. Andrew Jackson (1767–1845) was the seventh president of the United States.

2–10. DASHES

1. Brian's luggage—two suitcases and a garment bag—was lost by the airline.
2. All of the professor's experiments—his entire life's work—were destroyed by the fire.
3. Bad luck—that's all it was.
4. Here is your dessert—chocolate cake.
5. She ran through the hall—her heels clattering on the hard floor—all the way to the end.
6. Don't forget my address—3 Willow Lane.
7. When I heard the banging on the door, I felt just one emotion—fear.

2–11. HYPHENS

The hyphenated words in each sentence are the following:

1. actor-director	4. twenty-six	7. well-known
2. anti-American	5. anti-pollution	8. syl-lables
3. blue-eyed	6. all-around	9. never-to-be

2–12. QUOTATION MARKS (PART ONE)

1. In his summation, the attorney instructed, "A defendant is presumed innocent unless proven guilty."
2. "You really aced this test," the teacher told Luke with a smile.
3. Rose was humming the new song "Moving On" under her breath.
4. Magda handed in a book report titled "Two Eerie Stories by Edgar Allan Poe."
5. Kim remarked, "I heard the teacher say, 'Quiet!' so I stopped talking."
6. Thomas Jefferson wrote, "All men are created equal."
7. Sean "Spike" McGuire was elected class president.

2–13. QUOTATION MARKS (PART TWO)

1. "That guy can talk for an hour without saying anything," the fellow near me complained.
2. I leaned over and whispered, "When do you think the lecture will end?"
3. "Are you listening?" asked the teacher.
4. Did she hear me say, "This is boring"?
5. I asked Mike, "Have you completed the English assignment?"

2–14. PUNCTUATION REVIEW

1. a	3. b	5. c	7. b
2. c	4. a	6. a	8. c

2–15. CAPITALIZATION (PART ONE)

The words that should be circled are as follows:

1. willis, baptist, tahiti
2. north carolina, South
3. gulf war, your
4. italy, renaissance
5. aunt, Summer
6. Aunt
7. Summer, august

2–16. Capitalization (part two)

1. Colby High School's chapter of the Drama Students of America will perform a new play in January.
2. The play is called, "All's Well That Ends Well."
3. It was written by William Shakespeare during England's Elizabethan era.
4. The adviser for the Drama Students of America is Vice Principal Morgan.
5. Sometimes the principal attends our rehearsals in the Packard Auditorium.
6. On Saturday, he told us, "This is going to be a great performance!"

2–17. Apostrophes (part one)

1. player's	5. wolves'	8. college's
2. players'	6. women's	9. Bess's
3. school's	7. Rolling Stones'	10. Megan's
4. schools'		

2–18. Apostrophes (part two)

Sentences will vary.

2–19. Spelling Help (part one)

1. a	3. b	5. a	7. a	9. a
2. b	4. b	6. a	8. b	10. a

2–20. Spelling Help (part two)

Sentences will vary.

2–21. Spelling Review

1. a	3. b	5. c	7. a
2. c	4. b	6. b	8. c

2–22. Plurals (part one)

1. topazes	5. parentheses	8. boxes
2. blueberries	6. bases	9. windows
3. speeches	7. attorneys	10. waltzes
4. Kennedys		

2–23. Plurals (part two)

fathers-in-law	2000s
tomatoes	plurals
moose	salesmen
banjos or banjoes	friends
oxen	stereos
children	heroes
aircraft	chiefs
assemblies	bunches
hoaxes	trout
sweepstakes	businesses
displays	inquiries
news	qualities
sheriffs	halves

2–24. PRONOUNS (PART ONE)
Pronouns to be underlined are as follows:

1. their (P)
2. their (P)
3. he (S)
4. I (S), him (O), he (S)
5. He (S)
6. They (S), him (O), he (S), his (P)
7. she (S)
8. we (S), hers (P)
9. They (S), their (P)
10. I (S), them (O)

2–25. PRONOUNS (PART TWO)
Sentences will vary.

2–26. PRONOUNS (PART THREE)

1. I	3. I	5. she	7. I
2. his	4. My	6. his	

2–27. PRONOUNS (PART FOUR)

1. b	4. a	7. a	10. b
2. a	5. b	8. b	
3. b	6. b	9. a	

2–28. PREPOSITIONS
Sentences will vary.

ANSWERS TO REVIEW TEST (PART ONE)
The paragraph with errors circled should look as follows:

Adam Fox a sophomore at Northeast high school, is tall and thin, with a ready smile. Born in Racine, Wisconsin, on July 23, 1988 Adam has three brothers; he says that they drive him crazy. Much to his releif, he has no sisters. Among Adam's hobbys are computor games, making car models, and cars in general. Adams friend Jim Wallis says "Adam can walk up to a car blindfolded, feel the tires, and tell you what kind of car it is." In school, Adam's favorite subjects are math, science, and reading. He says that hes not athletic, but does enjoy car racing of course he does, tennis, and soccer. When asked, "Who are your idols," he mentioned an ex-President, Jimmy Carter, and an entrepreneur, Bill Gates. Both of Adam's parents are attorney's, and he would like to follow in their footsteps.

The corrected paragraph appears below. The corrected portions are underlined.

> Adam <u>Fox,</u> a sophomore at Northeast <u>High School,</u> is tall and thin, with a ready smile. Born in Racine, Wisconsin, on July 23, <u>1988,</u> Adam has three brothers; he says that they drive him crazy. Much to his <u>relief,</u> he has no sisters. Among Adam's <u>hobbies</u> are <u>computer</u> games, making car models, and cars in general. <u>Adam's</u> friend Jim Wallis <u>says,</u> "Adam can walk up to a car blindfolded, feel the tires, and tell you what kind of car it is." In school, Adam's favorite subjects are math, science, and reading. He says that <u>he's</u> not athletic, but he enjoys car racing <u>(of course he does),</u> tennis, and soccer. When asked, "Who are your <u>idols?</u>" he mentioned an ex-<u>president,</u> Jimmy Carter, and an entrepreneur, Bill Gates. Both of Adam's parents are <u>attorneys,</u> and he would like to follow in their footsteps.

ANSWERS TO REVIEW TEST (PART TWO)

1. a	6. c
2. b	7. b
3. c	8. a
4. c	9. c
5. a	10. a

2–1. END MARKS (PART ONE)

End marks are signs that tell the reader to stop. In oral communication, the tones and inflections of the human voice indicate the nature of the stop—whether it is a statement (**declarative**), a question (**interrogative**), or an exclamation (**exclamatory**). In written language, there are three types of end marks that accomplish this.

> 1. The **period** follows the statement in a **declarative** sentence.
>   *I feel tired after a long trip.*
>   *Marci's family spends the summer traveling around the country in a van.*
>
> 2. The **question mark** follows the question in an **interrogative** sentence.
>   *Do you feel tired after a long trip?*
>   *Did you know that Marci's family travels around the country in a van?*
>
> 3. The **exclamation point** follows an exclamation or strong command.
>   *I'm exhausted!*
>   *Get ready for that trip right now!*

DIRECTIONS: Insert the correct punctuation mark at the end of each sentence.

1. Baseball and football are popular sports

2. What sport do you most enjoy playing

3. What is your favorite sport to watch

4. My brother and I are going to a football game on Sunday

5. Would you like to come with us

6. That would be great

7. We plan to leave the house at one o'clock

8. Can you be ready then

9. Don't forget

10. I'm going to wear a cap with my team's logo

11. That's awesome

2–2. END MARKS (PART TWO)

A paragraph without end marks would not make much sense. The reader would have no idea where one thought ends and the next begins. Read the paragraph below, and note how difficult it is to understand the meaning.

> My neighbor, Mr. Arcaro, achieved some success as a detective he was having dinner at a local restaurant Mr. Arcaro was finishing his dessert when he heard a commotion at the cash register people were shouting someone screamed what was happening Mr. Arcaro rushed over the cashier was shouting, "Stop" a thief was running out the door Mr. Arcaro raced after him the thief was big but Mr. Arcaro was bigger he caught up with the thief and held him until the police arrived now Mr. Arcaro can have a free lunch at that restaurant any time he wishes don't you agree that he deserves it

DIRECTIONS: Rewrite this paragraph on the lines below, putting in all the appropriate end marks. (Be sure to capitalize the beginning of each new sentence.)

_____

_____

_____

_____

_____

_____

_____

_____

_____

_____

2–3. COMMAS (PART ONE)

A **comma** signals a *pause within* a sentence, unlike an end mark, which indicates a *full stop* at the *end* of a sentence. Commas separate words or phrases within a sentence to make their meaning clearer.

Use a comma:
- After an **introductory adverbial clause**
  Since you are an experienced swimmer, you can help the beginners.
  If you have not studied, you will probably not do well on the test.
- After an **introductory participial phrase**
  Bowing and smiling, the singer acknowledged the audience's applause.
  Stumbling and falling, the explorer found his way out of the forest.
- After an **introductory word or phrase**, to set it off from the main part of the sentence
  After dinner, Leonardo usually takes a walk.
  For example, this comma is needed to set off the introductory phrase.
- With an **appositive** (a word or words that restate or identify a noun or pronoun)
  Tom's best friend, Tony, moved to a distant state.
  Jason, Mr. Frank's eldest son, is a freshman in college.
- When **independent clauses** are joined by a conjunction
  Melissa did not want to enter the room yet, but her aunt was expecting her.
  Bill decided to ride to the game with his folks, and I went with the other guys.

DIRECTIONS: Insert commas where needed in the following sentences.

1. Because I got up late everything went wrong.

2. Mr. James my math teacher is a computer whiz.

3. If it is properly maintained a car can last a long time.

4. This book has an exciting plot and it held my attention until the end.

5. After all you can't expect me to do two jobs at once.

6. My father's boss Mr. Franco is coming to dinner on Sunday.

7. Before going out you should check to see that the windows are closed.

8. When I saw my brother trying to dance I laughed out loud.

9. Blushing with shame and embarrassment Toni ran out of the room.

10. When John F. Kennedy was assassinated the whole nation mourned.

2–4. COMMAS (PART TWO)

The use of commas helps clarify the meaning of a sentence.

> 1. Use commas around clauses beginning with *which*. *Which* is used when the clause is optional, or nonrestrictive.
>   *The five o'clock train, which is usually on time, was late last Saturday.*
>   *The last game of the season, which I was hoping to attend, was canceled.*
>   > **Note:** *Do not* use commas around clauses beginning with *that*. *That* is used when the clause is essential to the meaning of the sentence, or restrictive.
>   > *The train that I usually take was late on Saturday.*
>   > *The game that I wanted to attend was canceled.*
>
> 2. Use commas around **conjunctive adverbs** and **transitional phrases** (*of course, therefore, however, moreover,* **and so on**) when they interrupt a sentence.
>   *This wallpaper, for example, would look perfect in the bedroom.*
>   *The red paint, however, is not appropriate.*
>
> 3. Use commas to separate words or phrases in **series**.
>   *Toni, Sean, Phil, and Zena have formed a band.*
>   *The film has exciting events, breathtaking scenery, and impressive special effects.*

DIRECTIONS: Insert commas where needed in the following sentences.

1. I ate two hamburgers french fries and ice cream at noon.

2. The music store is open evenings on Thursday Friday and Saturday.

3. Mr. Weems worked on the space program at NASA in 1998 1999 and 2000.

4. It is obvious therefore that he is up-to-date on the latest space technology.

5. Our fast-food restaurant which employs many teenagers is open seven days a week.

6. The baseball game that I attended went into extra innings.

7. Jody belongs to the math club the chorus and the marching band.

8. The community college offers courses for paralegals lab technicians and computer programmers.

9. My brother of course will enter college in the fall.

10. Perelli's Shoe Store which is closed on Sunday is the only one that carries my size.

2–5. COMMAS (PART THREE)

Here are some more situations that call for a comma.

1. Use a comma before (or after) a **quotation or dialogue**.
   Ben said, "I'll see you at the game this afternoon."
   "Give me liberty or give me death," said Patrick Henry.
   Note: *Do not* use a comma after a quote if there is a question mark or exclamation point at the end.
   "What time does the game begin?" asked Ben.

2. Use a comma after a **noun of direct address**.
   Mother, please open the door at once.

3. Use a comma between items in **addresses** and **dates** (but not before ZIP Codes).
   John Adams was born on October 19, 1735, in Braintree, Massachusetts.
   Glenn's address is 25 Elm Street, Malloy, OH 02457.

4. Use a comma after the **greeting** and after the **closing** in a friendly letter.
   Dear Aunt Linda,
   Your loving nephew,

DIRECTIONS: Insert commas where needed in the following letter.

Dear Aunt Linda

Mom told me "You should write to Aunt Linda." That's what I'm doing now. Aunt Linda I really miss you since you moved so far away. I know that you live in Dallas Texas, but I wish you still lived near us in Bangor Maine. Mostly I miss the way you always helped me with home-work. We are studying the Second World War in social studies. Did you know that Winston Churchill said "We will never surrender!"

I hope I can visit you in Dallas Texas next summer.

Your loving niece

Amelia

2–6. SEMICOLONS

A **semicolon** is a hybrid punctuation mark. It is made with a period and a comma, and its use falls somewhere in between. It shows a stronger pause than a comma, but not a full stop like a period.

Use a semicolon:

- **To separate closely linked independent clauses** when you don't want to come to a full stop between them and they are **not joined by a conjunction.**
  The plane was due to arrive at 6 o'clock; it came through heavy fog at 10.
  Sharks had been sighted; no swimmers were allowed in the water.
  But: *Sharks had been sighted, and no swimmers were allowed in the water.*

- **Between independent clauses** of a compound sentence when they are **joined by a conjunctive adverb** such as *however, moreover, therefore, besides,* and *then.*
  I want to come to your party; however, I need a new dress.
  I drove five hours to see Mr. Jensen; therefore, he must see me now.

- **Between items in a series** if they are particularly long or if they themselves contain commas.
  The committee included the company president, Mr. Perelli; the treasurer, Ms. Cantas; and the recording secretary, Mr. Franks.
  The menu includes an appetizer containing mushrooms, garlic, and onions; a main dish of leg of lamb, curried rice, and candied carrots; and a choice of strawberry shortcake, ice cream, or rice pudding for dessert.

DIRECTIONS: Insert semicolons where needed in the following sentences.

1. I have studied the problem for three hours however, I still don't understand it.

2. I don't like carrot cake besides, I don't feel like having any dessert.

3. I have been working for a long time I am tired.

4. Our neighbors are Mr. Mason, the plumber Mrs. Gallo, the lawyer and Jeni Orlando, the famous singer.

5. It is snowing hard therefore, schools will be closed today.

2–7. Colons (Part One)

A **colon** is made up of two periods. It also indicates a stop, but a different sort of stop: a stop that says, "Something else is on the way." Usually the word(s) that follow a colon are equivalent to the word(s) that precede it.

1. A colon introduces a word or phrase that explains or illustrates the preceding word, phrase, or sentence.
The 27th Regiment had its orders: to march to the next town and take it.

2. A colon is used to stress a word, phrase, or clause that follows.
There is only one reason for making such an error: stupidity.

3. A colon is used to introduce a series or list.
A successful dinner party needs three things: delicious food, pleasant surroundings, and good companions.

4. A colon may replace a comma before a long quotation.
The car dealer said: "You won't go wrong with this car. It is almost new, clean, runs well, and the previous owner always kept it well maintained. If you hesitate, someone else will buy it soon, probably today."

DIRECTIONS: Insert a colon where it belongs in the following sentences.

1. Thoreau wrote "The mass of men live lives of quiet desperation. What is called resignation is confirmed desperation."

2. Add the ingredients in the following order butter, sugar, salt, vanilla, nutmeg, and nuts.

3. Our family believes that only one thing is really important love.

4. I have a big problem what to buy my dad for his birthday.

5. Mr. Franklin stresses one rule when giving a test no cheating.

6. My father had one basic principle honesty is the best policy.

7. Don't forget this rule safety first.

2–8. Colons (Part Two)

Here are some additional uses for colons:

---

1. Use a colon to separate the title of a book, magazine, or movie from the subtitle.
    Transformations: A Quarterly of New Literature
    How to Become a Winner: The Ten Secrets of Success

2. Use a colon between the hour and minutes in writing the time.
    9:15 p.m.

3. Use the colon after the greeting in a business letter.
    Dear Mr. Fernandez:

4. Use a colon to separate a heading or introductory label from the words that follow.
    CAUTION: wet paint
    NOTICE: Do not go beyond this point

DIRECTIONS: Insert a colon where it belongs in the following sentences.

1. The title of this book is *Shakespeare A Writer for the Ages.*

2. The plane is scheduled to depart at 2 14 P.M.

3. The letter that began "Dear Mr. Jones " was addressed to me.

4. The sign said "HELP WANTED Inquire Within."

5. I always get out of bed at the same time 6 30 A.M.

6. The store is open until 10 30 P.M. Monday through Saturday.

2–9. PARENTHESES

Parentheses are used to enclose a brief interruption of a sentence or paragraph.

---

1. Parentheses are placed around a word or group of words within a sentence that are extra or explanatory. The sentence should be able to stand on its own and read as well without the material in the parentheses.
   We visited several European countries (Spain, Germany, Italy) on our trip.
   Eating vegetables (both green and yellow) is essential to health.

2. When a whole sentence is enclosed by parentheses within the main sentence, do not use capital letters or periods for the enclosed sentence.
   Your last report (see pages 10 and 12) contains several factual errors.

3. When a sentence is placed in parentheses after another sentence, capitalize the first letter and use an end mark at the end.
   Your last report contains several factual errors. (See pages 10 and 12.)

4. Use parentheses to enclose birth and death dates.
   William Grock (1840–1920) fought in the Civil War.

5. Use parentheses around the abbreviation of an organization after its name.
   National Organization for Women (NOW)
   Federal Bureau of Investigation (FBI)

DIRECTIONS: Insert parentheses where they belong.

1. In some states New York and New Jersey, for example, the sale of firecrackers is illegal.

2. The sale of firecrackers is illegal in some states. New York and New Jersey are examples.

3. There is wildlife deer, rabbits, squirrels, and bears in the woods near my house.

4. The Daughters of the American Revolution DAR is a patriotic organization.

5. Amanda's father he was the only one who couldn't attend was sad to miss her performance.

6. Andrew Jackson 1767–1845 was the seventh president of the United States.

2–10. DASHES

The **dash** is used to set off part of a sentence. It interrupts the sentence to insert another thought.

> 1. A single dash can be used at the beginning or end of a sentence to present information.
>   *Aunt Greta serves the food I like best—pizza.*
>   *Luck—it makes all the difference.*
>
> 2. Dashes can be used in pairs within a sentence to enclose an aside or explanation.
>   *Earning a good grade—an A is almost impossible—is my main goal this year.*
>   *Judd Hansen—he lives on the next block—will play quarterback next season.*
>
>   **Note:** Do not use too many dashes; they are often overused. A rule of thumb is to use dashes in only one sentence per paragraph.
>   **Note:** Most keyboards do not have dashes. Type two hyphens--no spaces before or after--to create a dash.

DIRECTIONS: Rewrite the sentences on the lines below. Insert dashes where needed.

1. Brian's luggage two suitcases and a garment bag was lost by the airline.

   _____

   _____

2. All of the professor's experiments his entire life's work were destroyed by the fire.

   _____

   _____

3. Bad luck that's all it was.

   _____

4. Here is your dessert chocolate cake.

   _____

5. She ran through the hall her heels clattering on the hard floor all the way to the end.

   _____

   _____

6. Don't forget my address 3 Willow Lane.

   _____

   _____

7. When I heard the banging on the door, I felt just one emotion fear.

   _____

   _____

2–11. HYPHENS

The **hyphen** is usually used as a combining mark.

---

1. Hyphens create compound words.
   forget-me-nots, mother-in-law, actor-director, attorney-at-law

2. A hyphen is used before a noun when either word in the description is not enough alone.
   Todd is a well-known actor.
   I saw the red-haired girl on the beach.

3. A hyphen is used after some prefixes.
   ex-president, self-sufficient, semi-invalid

4. A hyphen is used to join compound numbers and when spelling out fractions.
   twenty-four, ninety-nine, two-thirds, one-half

5. A hyphen is used between syllables if a word must be broken at the end of a line.
   I hope you do well on the fol-
      lowing exercise.

DIRECTIONS: Insert a hyphen where needed in the following sentences.

1. Woody Allen is a famous actor director.

2. The speaker's anti American attitude enraged the audience.

3. Elana's new baby sister is black haired and blue eyed.

4. There were twenty six students in the science class.

5. Sean is an activist in an anti pollution organization.

6. Jeff is an all around good student and popular guy.

7. My Uncle Jonathan is a well known inventor.

8. Consult a dictionary if you are not sure where to divide a word between syl lables.

9. It was a never to be forgotten experience.

2–12. QUOTATION MARKS (PART ONE)

Quotation marks are never lonely. They always come in pairs—one at the beginning and the other at the end.

---

1. Quotation marks are used to enclose **direct** (exact) **quotations.**
   "You're out!" called the umpire as the runner slid home.
   American patriot Nathan Hale said, "I regret that I have only one life to give for my country."

2. Quotation marks are used around **titles** of articles, poems, songs, reports, and chapters of books.
   "How to Help Your Team Win" is a great article in my sports magazine.
   "The Road Not Taken" is a well-known poem by Robert Frost.

3. Use quotation marks to enclose a **nickname** given with a formal name.
   Robert "Buck" Johnson is my father's cousin.

4. Use a single quotation mark (which looks like an apostrophe) to enclose a **quotation within a quotation.**
   Tom said, "I heard someone scream 'Help!' and rushed to see what was the matter."

DIRECTIONS: Place quotations marks where they belong in each sentence.

1. In his summation, the attorney instructed, A defendant is presumed innocent unless proven guilty.

2. You really aced this test, the teacher told Luke with a smile.

3. Rose was humming the new song Moving On under her breath.

4. Magda handed in a book report titled Two Eerie Stories by Edgar Allan Poe.

5. Kim remarked, I heard the teacher say, Quiet! so I stopped talking.

6. Thomas Jefferson wrote, All men are created equal.

7. Sean Spike McGuire was elected class president.

2–13. QUOTATION MARKS (PART TWO)

Using other punctuation with quotation marks can sometimes seem tricky, but the rules are quite simple.

---

1. The quotation mark is preceded by a comma when the quote comes midway or at the end of the sentence.
   Pat looked at the coach and whispered, "I'm going to steal second base."

2. When a quote comes at the beginning of a sentence, the comma is placed before the closing quotation.
   "I'm going to steal second base," Pat whispered to the coach.

3. Put periods inside quotation marks, whether or not they are part of the quotation.
   At their anniversary party, Mom and Dad sang their favorite song, "Forever."

4. Put question marks, exclamation points, and dashes inside quotation marks if they are part of the quotation; outside quotation marks if they are not.
   The philosopher asked, "Who has seen eternity?"
   Did the philosopher say, "I have seen eternity"?

DIRECTIONS: Rewrite each sentence on the line below with the correct punctuation.

1. That guy can talk for an hour without saying anything the fellow near me complained.

   _____

2. I leaned over and whispered When do you think the lecture will end

   _____

3. Are you listening asked the teacher.

   _____

4. Did she hear me say This is boring

   _____

5. I asked Mike Have you completed the English assignment

   _____

2–14. Punctuation Review

DIRECTIONS: Place a checkmark next to the sentence in each group that is punctuated correctly.

1. ❏ a. The sale begins December 3, 2004, and ends December 31, 2004, at 2:30 P.M.
   ❏ b. The sale begins December 3, 2004, and ends December 31 2004, at 2:30 P.M.
   ❏ c. The sale begins December 3, 2004, and ends December 31, 2004, at 2.30 P.M.

2. ❏ a. Gary won't you buy sweaters and gloves for me.
   ❏ b. Gary, won't you buy sweaters and gloves for me.
   ❏ c. Gary, won't you buy sweaters and gloves for me?

3. ❏ a. Unfortunately the best items have already been sold Gary said.
   ❏ b. "Unfortunately, the best items have already been sold," Gary said.
   ❏ c. "Unfortunately the best items have already been sold," Gary said.

4. ❏ a. Here is what we need for the hike: sturdy shoes, water, and an extra sweater.
   ❏ b. Here is what we need for the hike, sturdy shoes, water, and an extra sweater.
   ❏ c. Here is what we need for the hike: sturdy shoes; water; and an extra sweater.

5. ❏ a. Mark asked "Have you met our new coach, J. C. Rocky Arbuckle.
   ❏ b. Mark asked "Have you met our new coach, J. C. "Rocky Arbuckle."
   ❏ c. Mark asked, "Have you met our new coach, J. C. 'Rocky' Arbuckle?"

6. ❏ a. Did you hear Rocky say, "Our team will be first this year"?
   ❏ b. Did you hear Rocky say "Our team will be first this year?"
   ❏ c. Did you hear Rocky say, "Our team will be first this year?"

7. ❏ a. Huge waves pounded along the shore, no one was allowed on the beach.
   ❏ b. Huge waves pounded along the shore; no one was allowed on the beach.
   ❏ c. Huge waves pounded along the shore: no one was allowed on the beach.

8. ❏ a. Climbing halfway up the mountain, the top was inaccessible, was a struggle.
   ❏ b. Climbing halfway up the mountain: the top was inaccessible: was a struggle.
   ❏ c. Climbing halfway up the mountain—the top was inaccessible—was a struggle.

2–15. CAPITALIZATION (PART ONE)

An initial **capital letter** indicates that a word is a proper noun or adjective (or is to be considered as one), or that a new sentence or line of verse is beginning.

1. Use an initial capital letter to mark a proper noun or adjective.
   Thomas Jefferson was a Virginian and an American.
   Democracy is a Jeffersonian ideal.
2. Capitalize words that refer to ethnic groups, religions, and the people belonging to them.
   Many Japanese people are Buddhists.
3. Capitalize words that refer to wars, battles, and historical periods.
   Luke's grandfather fought at the Battle of the Bulge in World War II.
   Beautiful Catholic cathedrals were built during the Middle Ages.
4. Capitalize words that signify family relationships, but only when they are used as names.
   Jason said, "Let's go fishing, Dad."
   But: *Jason's dad took him fishing.*
5. Use an initial capital letter for geographical areas, but not when they refer only to points of the compass.
   He moved from California in the American West to the Middle Eastern country of Kuwait.
   But: *The car was traveling east on Route I-81.*
6. Capitalize the *first* word in a greeting or closing of a letter:
   Dear Susan,
   Yours truly,
7. Capitalize days of the week and months of the year, but not seasons.
   It was a snowy winter Monday in January.

DIRECTIONS: Circle the words that are not capitalized correctly in these sentences.

1. John willis was a baptist missionary in tahiti.

2. The north carolina countryside was lovely as we traveled South on Route I-95.

3. The letter from the soldier fighting in the gulf war ended, "your loving son."

4. Art flourished in italy during the renaissance.

5. Do you think that aunt Lucy will come to visit this Summer?

6. My Aunt lives in a big house near the seashore.

7. My favorite month of the Summer is august.

2–16. CAPITALIZATION (PART TWO)

1. Capitalize names of schools.
   My brother attends the University of Texas.
   Note: Do not capitalize the word when it is used as a general term and *not* with a specific name.
   My brother plans to attend a university in Texas.

2. Capitalize the first word, last word, and all important words in a title.
   Have you read the article called "How to Become a Millionaire"?

3. Capitalize the first word in a direct quotation.
   Dinah screamed, "There's a tornado coming this way!"

4. Capitalize names of companies, clubs, and official bodies.
   A representative from General Motors spoke to the U.S. Senate.
   Kara belongs to the Selby Bridge Club and is a member of the Selby Town Council.

5. Capitalize titles or positions when they refer to specific people, but not when they are used as a general, nonspecific term or preceded by a possessive pronoun.
   George Washington was the first president of the United States.
   President Washington was respected by everyone.
   Dr. Salinas is my family doctor.

DIRECTIONS: Rewrite each sentence on the line below using correct capitalization.

1. colby high school's chapter of the drama students of america will perform a new play in january.

   _____

2. The play is called "all's well that ends well."

   _____

3. It was written by william shakespeare during england's elizabethan era.

   _____

4. The adviser of the drama students of america is vice principal morgan.

   _____

5. Sometimes the principal attends our rehearsals in the packard auditorium.

   _____

6. On saturday, he told us, "this is going to be a great performance!"

   _____

2–17. APOSTROPHES (PART ONE)

The **apostrophe** has two distinct jobs: it indicates possession, and it is also used in contractions.

---

1. An apostrophe followed by the letter *s* is used at the end of a singular noun to show possession.
   My son's jacket (the jacket belonging to my son)
   The team's mascot (the mascot belong to the team)

2. An apostrophe followed by the letter *s* is used even if the singular noun ends with *s*.
   The boss's office has a magnificent view. (the office belongs to the boss)
   Keats's poetry is lyrical. (poetry written by Keats)
   Mr. Morris's cabin is in the woods. (The cabin belonging to Mr. Morris)
   The hostess's desk is in the front. (the desk belonging to the hostess)

3. Use an apostrophe alone after a plural noun ending in *s*.
   The two birds' nests are in the large oak tree. (more than one bird)
   Compare: *That bird's nest is in the large oak tree.* (one bird)
   The students' tests are on the teacher's desk. (more than one student; one teacher)

4. Use an apostrophe followed by *s* for a plural that does not end in *s*.
   We are installing new carpeting in the children's rooms.
   The men's room is down the hall.

DIRECTIONS: Fill in the blank with the correct possessive.

1. The umpire was ignoring the _____ request.   **(player)**

2. The baseball _____ new jackets arrived on time.   **(players)**

3. Our _____ dances are held every Friday evening.   **(school)**

4. All four _____ dances are held on Friday evenings.   **(schools)**

5. The _____ howling kept us up all night.   **(wolves)**

6. The _____ soccer team held tryouts yesterday.   **(women)**

7. Do you know the _____ travel plans?   **(Rolling Stones)**

8. What is the _____ position on affirmative action?   **(college)**

9. _____ team was the best in the league.   **(Bess)**

10. _____ team came in second.   **(Megan)**

2–18. APOSTROPHES (PART TWO)

An apostrophe is used to show the omission of one or more letters in a contraction. Some common contractions are shown below.

isn't (Stands for *is not;* the apostrophe takes the place of the letter *o* in *not*)
hasn't (Stands for *has not;* the apostrophe takes the place of the letter *o* in *not*)
wasn't (Stands for *was not;* the apostrophe takes the place of the letter *o* in *not*)
couldn't (Stands for *could not;* the apostrophe takes the place of the letter *o* in *not*)
he's (Stands for *he is* or *he has;* the apostrophe takes the place of the *i* in *is* or *ha* in *has.*)
they're (Stands for *they are;* the apostrophe takes the place of the *a* in *are.*)
I've (Stands for *I have;* the apostrophe takes the place of the *ha* in *have.*)

It's **vs.** *its*

1. *It's* is a contraction. It stands for *it is* or *it has.*
   Where is the dog? It's in the doghouse.   (it is)
   It's going to snow.   (it is)
   It's been nice meeting you.   (it has)
   It's felt like rain all day.   (it has)

2. *Its* is a possessive pronoun. It always shows possession.
   Did you read this book? Its theme is alien abduction. (the theme belongs to the book)
   Where is the dog? Here is its leash. (the leash belongs to the dog)

DIRECTIONS: Write a sentence using a contraction for each of the following phrases.

1. have not _____

2. were not _____

3. it is _____

4. could not _____

5. you are _____

6. she has _____

7. we are _____

8. who is _____

9. what is _____

10. they are _____

2–19. SPELLING HELP (PART ONE)

IE vs. EI: Everyone knows the cute rhyme that is supposed to tell us when to use *ie* and when to use *ei*. Yet words with these letter combinations are still spelled incorrectly by students and adults alike. When faced with this choice, you will find the rhyme helpful and completely accurate in most instances.

- *I BEFORE E:* This is the combination used in most cases.
  believe, belief, fierce, brief, debrief, tier, pier, bier, chief, mischief, hand-kerchief, piece, apiece, thief, yield, shield, frontier, lie

- EXCEPT AFTER *C:* Use *ei* after *c*.
  ceiling, conceited, receipt, receive, deceive, conceive, perceive

- OR WHEN SOUNDED LIKE *A* AS IN *NEIGHBOR* AND *WEIGH.*
  neighbor, weigh, sleigh, eight, chow mein, veil

  Exceptions: In most cases, using the rhyme will give you the correct spelling. There are, however, some exceptions to the rule: *ancient, caffeine, counterfeit, efficient, financier, foreign, forfeit, height, heir, leisure, neither, protein, seize, sheik, sleight, their, weird*

DIRECTIONS: Place a checkmark next to the correctly spelled word in each set below.

1. ❏ a. belief
   ❏ b. beleif

2. ❏ a. fronteir
   ❏ b. frontier

3. ❏ a. foriegn
   ❏ b. foreign

4. ❏ a. liesure
   ❏ b. leisure

5. ❏ a. deceive
   ❏ b. decieve

6. ❏ a. caffeine
   ❏ b. caffiene

7. ❏ a. financier
   ❏ b. financeir

8. ❏ a. mischeif
   ❏ b. mischief

9. ❏ a. sleigh
   ❏ b. sliegh

10. ❏ a. ceiling
    ❏ b. cieling

2–20. SPELLING HELP (PART TWO)

The words below are taken from a list of words most frequently misspelled by college freshmen. The only way to learn the correct spelling is to memorize and use these words in writing sentences.

absence	disappointed	noticeable
accidentally	eighth	occasion
aggravate	embarrassed	occurred
all right	environment	omitted
amateur	exercise	parallel
argument	friend	privilege
benefited	government	recommend
believed	grievance	rhythm
business	indispensable	schedule
cemetery	knowledge	separate
conscientious	laboratory	tragedy
coolly	maintenance	villain
criticism	mischievous	weird

DIRECTIONS: Write ten sentences on the lines below. Each sentence should contain **two** of the words on the list above.

1. _____

2. _____

3. _____

4. _____

5. _____

6. _____

7. _____

8. _____

9. _____

10. _____

Name _____ Date _____

2–21. SPELLING REVIEW

DIRECTIONS: Place a checkmark next to the correctly spelled sentence in each set below.

1. ❏ a. It is Professor Ryan's belief that amateur actors can never deceive the audience.
   ❏ b. It is Professor Ryan's belief that amateur actors can never decieve the audience.
   ❏ c. It is professor Ryan's belief that amateur actors can never deceive the audience.

2. ❏ a. He taught english at a College in the east.
   ❏ b. He taught English at a college in the east.
   ❏ c. He taught English at a college in the East.

3. ❏ a. Its his belief that the Drama Club has'nt performed up to it's potential.
   ❏ b. It's his belief that the Drama Club hasn't performed up to its potential.
   ❏ c. Its his belief that the drama club hasn't performed up to its potential.

4. ❏ a. Rehearsal's will take place the last week in january.
   ❏ b. Rehearsals will take place the last week in January.
   ❏ c. Rehearsals will take place the last week in january.

5. ❏ a. Some of the actors embarassed the group with their mischeif.
   ❏ b. Some of the actors embarassed the group with their mischeief.
   ❏ c. Some of the actors embarrassed the group with their mischief.

6. ❏ a. The play is about a General who is dissappointed during the Civil War.
   ❏ b. The play is about a general who is disappointed during the Civil War.
   ❏ c. The play is about a general who is disappointed during the civil war.

7. ❏ a. My friend told me that the play is called "General Morse's Revenge."
   ❏ b. My friend told me that the play is called "General Morses revenge."
   ❏ c. My freind told me that the play is called "General Morse's Revenge.

8. ❏ a. Pete Felcher, who plays the villian, is always conscientious about rehearsing.
   ❏ b. Pete Felcher, who plays the villain, is always conscientous about rehearsing.
   ❏ c. Pete Felcher, who plays the villain, is always conscientious about rehearsing.

2–22. PLURALS (PART ONE)

The letter *s* is added to most nouns to make them plural: *stereos, computers, books, desks, students, teachers, parents, automobiles, telephones, carpets,* and so on. Here are some exceptions to this general rule.

1. Add *es* to words that end with ***ch, sh, s, x,*** or ***z.***
   bunch/bunches, watch/watches, church/churches, wish/wishes, brush/brushes, mess/messes, business/businesses, fax/faxes, hoax/hoaxes, topaz/topazes

2. When a noun ends in *f* or *fe,* change the *f* to *v* and add *es.*
   thief/thieves, half/halves, leaf/leaves, knife/knives, life/lives
   Note: There are exceptions to this rule, including *chief/chiefs, roof/roofs, handkerchief/handkerchiefs, belief/beliefs, sheriff/sheriffs*
   And some can go either way: *scarf/scarfs* or *scarves, dwarf/dwarfs* or *dwarves*

3. When a word ends in a consonant followed by *y,* change the *y* to *ie* and add *s.*
   twenty/twenties, harpy/harpies, blackberry/blackberries, library/libraries
   Note: If the final *y* is preceded by a vowel, it usually does not change.
   donkey/donkeys, attorney/attorneys, birthday/birthdays, highway/highways
   Note: The final *y* does not change in proper names.
   the Kennedys, the Emmys, the Tonys

4. Words ending in *is* change to *es.*
   basis/bases, crisis/crises, parenthesis/parentheses, hypothesis/hypotheses

DIRECTIONS: Insert the correct plural in each sentence.

1. Ben gave his girlfriend two _____ for her birthday.   **(topaz)**

2. The campers went into the fields to pick _____.   **(blueberry)**

3. The politician made two _____ on the same day.   **(speech)**

4. I just read an interesting history of the _____.   **(Kennedy)**

5. You can put _____ around an aside in a sentence.   **(parenthesis)**

6. I have two main _____ for my opinion.   **(basis)**

7. Mr. Mason has already consulted two _____.   **(attorney)**

8. The post office delivered two large _____.   **(box)**

9. There are three _____ in her room.   **(window)**

10. The band played two _____ for the dancers.   **(waltz)**

2–23. PLURALS (PART TWO)

Here are additional rules for using the plural form of nouns.

> 1. With words ending in *o*, some add *s*, others add *es*, and some can go either way.
> *potato/potatoes, tomato/tomatoes, hero/heroes*
> *soprano/sopranos, piano/pianos, radio/radios, rodeo/rodeos, solo/solos*
> *banjo/banjos or banjoes, zero/zeros or zeroes, ghetto/ghettos or ghettoes,*
> *echo/echos or echoes, cargo/cargos or cargoes*
>
> 2. Add *'s* to most abbreviations or numbers.
> *CPA's, M.D.'s, IOU's, B.A.'s, PC's, but 1990s*
>
> 3. Some nouns have irregular plurals.
> *man/men, woman/women, child/children, mouse/mice, foot/feet, goose/geese,*
> *ox/oxen, tooth/teeth, mother-in-law/mothers-in-law, freshman/freshmen*
>
> 4. Some plurals are the same as the singular form.
> *deer/deer, moose/moose, sheep/sheep, aircraft/aircraft, series/series,*
> *sweepstakes/sweepstakes, trout/trout, news/news, spacecraft/spacecraft*

DIRECTIONS: Write the plural form of each of these singular nouns.

father-in-law	_____	2000	_____
tomato	_____	plural	_____
moose	_____	salesman	_____
banjo	_____	friend	_____
ox	_____	stereo	_____
child	_____	hero	_____
aircraft	_____	chief	_____
assembly	_____	bunch	_____
hoax	_____	trout	_____
sweepstakes	_____	business	_____
display	_____	inquiry	_____
news	_____	quality	_____
sheriff	_____	half	_____

2–24. PRONOUNS (PART ONE)

A **pronoun** can be used in place of a noun.

---

1. A personal pronoun can be a **subject**. (*I, you, he, she, it, we, they*)
   I enjoyed my trip to Puerto Rico last year. You should visit it, too.
   She plans to go next year. He is going, too.
   We can all go together. It will be a great adventure.
   They would all like to go.

2. A personal pronoun can be an **object**. (*me, you, him, her, it, us, them*)
   The secretary telephoned them and us.
   The property belongs to me and you together.
   Sophie voted for him. Julie voted for her.

3. Personal pronouns that show possession are called **possessive pronouns**. These
   pronouns are sometimes called **possessive adjectives** if they are used to modify
   nouns. (*my, mine, your, yours, his, her, hers, its, our, ours, their*)
   Is this your car? My car is in the garage. Our friend is coming to the party.

   Note: Never add an apostrophe to a personal pronoun. It already shows
   possession.
   WRONG: *The mad dog bared it's teeth.*
   RIGHT: *The mad dog bared its teeth.*

DIRECTIONS: Underline the pronouns in each sentence. Then write subject (S), object
(O), or possessive (P) above each underlined pronoun.

1. The manager and the staff worked hard for their pay.

2. The workers enjoy their jobs but would like to be paid better.

3. Nick applied for a job there once, but he was turned down.

4. I was sorry for him at the time, but he did not seem too disappointed.

5. He now works as a waiter at the Fairview Country Club.

6. They offered him a full-time job, but he needed time for his school work.

7. Nick's girlfriend, Lisa, works there, too; she is a chef.

8. The delicious lasagna we had yesterday was hers.

9. They are very ambitious about their futures.

10. I admire them very much.

2–25. PRONOUNS (PART TWO)

1. A personal pronoun should always agree with its **antecedent** (the noun to which it refers.)

   *The hikers tried to catch up with **their** group.*
   *The hiker tried to catch up with **his** group.*
   *Marla and I were in charge, so **we** led the way.*
   *Marla was in charge, so **she** led the way.*

2. A **demonstrative pronoun** points out something. It can be used by itself or with a noun. The demonstrative pronouns are *this, that, these, those.*

   *Take **this** away from me. Take **these** papers away from me.*

3. An **indefinite pronoun** does not define or stand for a particular person or thing. Some indefinite pronouns are *all, each, every, either, one, everyone, several, some, other, another, both, none, many, few.*

   ***Many** are called, but **few** are chosen.*
   ***Everyone** came to see the last game.*

   Indefinite pronouns are sometimes used as adjectives.

   *Not **every** fan enjoyed the game. **Several** people left early.*

4. A **reflexive pronoun** calls attention to itself. It ends with *self* or *selves* and is used for emphasis or to refer back to the subject.

   *The coach blamed **himself** for the loss of the game.*
   *They **themselves** will check into the matter.*

5. An **interrogative pronoun** asks a question. (*what, which, who, whom, whose*)

   ***What** is that book doing on my desk? **Who** put it there?*

DIRECTIONS: Write a sentence using each of the pronouns below.

1. himself _____

2. whose _____

3. none _____

4. these _____

5. what _____

6. several _____

7. everyone _____

8. myself _____

2–26. Pronouns (part three)

Some common pronoun errors can be avoided by following these rules.

> 1. Use a **subject pronoun** when it comes after a linking verb and describes the subject.
>   *It is he.* (follows the verb *is* and describes the subject *it*)
>   *Zena was in a play, but I didn't know that the leading character was she.*
>   *They thought it was he who caused the accident.*
>
> 2. Use a **possessive pronoun** when it modifies a gerund (a verb ending in *ing* that is used as a noun).
>   *The article told of his getting involved in an anti-war group.*
>   *Sheila's grade was low because of her coming to class late so often.*
>   *Dinner was easy for Mom because of our helping to prepare it.*
>
> 3. A pronoun following the word *than* can have different meanings. You must see what has been left out of the sentence to decide whether to use a subject or object pronoun.
>   *Dad loves pizza more than me* means Dad loves pizza more than he loves me.
>   *Dad loves pizza more than I* means Dad loves pizza more than I do.
>   *You know him as well as me* means you know him as well as you know me.
>   *You know him as well as I* means you know him as well as I do.

DIRECTIONS: Insert the correct pronouns in the blank spaces.

1. Mr. Alvarez speaks Spanish better than _____. (**I, me**)

2. Ray told me it was _____ playing that won the game. (**him, his**)

3. He knocked on the door and proclaimed, "It is _____." (**I, me**)

4. _____ learning computer skills could help get a job. (**My, Me**)

5. It is not _____ who caused all the trouble. (**she, her**)

6. Dad said that _____ leaving early could affect business. (**him, his**)

7. Jon is a better athlete than _____. (**I, me**)

2–27. PRONOUNS (PART FOUR)

DIRECTIONS: Place a checkmark next to the correct sentence in each of the sets below.

1. ❏ a. Students enjoy the course if he can get an interesting teacher.
   ❏ b. Students enjoy the course if they can get an interesting teacher.

2. ❏ a. A fascinating story was told to her.
   ❏ b. A fascinating story was told to she.

3. ❏ a. The team finished first in their league.
   ❏ b. The team finished first in its league.

4. ❏ a. Jenna and Rose spent their money as fast as they earned it.
   ❏ b. Jenna and Rose spent her money as fast as she earned it.

5. ❏ a. What was your best friend when you lived in Los Angeles?
   ❏ b. Who was your best friend when you lived in Los Angeles?

6. ❏ a. Shauna tried to board the bus, but she was too crowded.
   ❏ b. Shauna tried to board the bus, but it was too crowded.

7. ❏ a. He understands the difference between us.
   ❏ b. He understands the difference between we.

8. ❏ a. Three boys in our class gave a summary of his report.
   ❏ b. Three boys in our class gave a summary of their report.

9. ❏ a. You and she have the best grades in the school.
   ❏ b. You and her have the best grades in the school.

10. ❏ a. That book is her's.
    ❏ b. That book is hers.

2–28. PREPOSITIONS

A **preposition** is a word that joins a noun or pronoun in a phrase and shows a relation to some other part of the sentence. Some frequently used prepositions are shown below.

about	at	down	of	since	until
above	before	during	off	through	up
across	behind	for	on	till	upon
after	below	from	over	to	with
against	between	in	past	toward	within
among	by	into	round	under	without

1. Every preposition has a noun or pronoun as its **object.**
   This gift is for the bride. (*bride* is the object of *for*)
   The ball was wedged between two slats of the fence. (*two slats* is the object of *between*)
   Do you remember that I went to the circus with you last year? (*you* is the object of *with*)

2. **In** and **into** are both prepositions, but they have different meanings. *In* means within a place. *Into* means moving or going inside.
   *What are you doing **in** the garage?*
   *Are you putting the car **into** the garage?*

3. **Between** applies to two only. **Among** applies to more than two. The pronoun that follows either one is always in the objective case.
   This secret is between you and me.
   This secret is among the three of us.

DIRECTIONS: Write a sentence using each of the pronouns below.

1. into _____

2. in _____

3. among _____

4. between _____

5. toward _____

6. against _____

7. during _____

8. through _____

TENTH-GRADE LEVEL

MECHANICS AND USAGE
REVIEW TEST

Review Test: Mechanics and Usage (Part One)

DIRECTIONS: The following paragraph contains thirteen errors in mechanics and word usage. Can you find all thirteen? Circle the mistakes. Then copy the paragraph correctly on the lines below. (Continue on the back of this sheet, if necessary.)

Adam Fox a sophomore at Northeast high school, is tall and thin, with a ready smile. Born in Racine, Wisconsin, on July 23, 1988 Adam has three brothers; he says that they drive him crazy. Much to his releif, he has no sisters. Among Adam's hobbys are computor games, making car models, and cars in general. Adams friend Jim Wallis says "Adam can walk up to a car blindfolded, feel the tires, and tell you what kind of car it is." In school, Adam's favorite subjects are math, science, and reading. He says that hes not athletic, but he does enjoy car racing of course he does, tennis, and soccer. When asked, "Who are your idols," he mentioned an ex-President, Jimmy Carter, and an entrepreneur, Bill Gates. Both of Adam's parents are attorney's, and he would like to follow in their footsteps.

REVIEW TEST: MECHANICS AND USAGE (PART TWO)

DIRECTIONS: Place a checkmark next to the correct sentence in each group below.

1. ❑ a. "Who is there?" Sheila asked. "It is I," Jacob replied.
   ❑ b. "Who is there," Sheila asked. "It is I," Jacob replied.
   ❑ c. "Who is there?" Sheila asked. It is me," Jacob replied.

2. ❑ a. The Kennedy's include a senator and a President of the United States.
   ❑ b. The Kennedys include a senator and a president of the United States.
   ❑ c. The Kennedys include a senator and a President of the United States.

3. ❑ a. Roses mother says that the book about frontier life belongs to her.
   ❑ b. Rose's mother says that the book about fronteir life belongs to her.
   ❑ c. Rose's mother says that the book about frontier life belongs to her.

4. ❑ a. The red-haired waitress placed two knifes on the table.
   ❑ b. The red haired waitress placed two knives on the table.
   ❑ c. The red-haired waitress placed two knives on the table.

5. ❑ a. Ben made several inquiries; however, he couldn't get an answer.
   ❑ b. Ben made several inquiries, however, he couldnt get an answer.
   ❑ c. Ben made several inquirys; however, he couldn't get an answer.

6. ❑ a. Hes taking the following courses: english, spanish, and social studies.
   ❑ b. He's taking the following courses, English, Spanish, and Social Studies.
   ❑ c. He's taking the following courses: English, Spanish, and Social Studies.

7. ❑ a. The journalist asked, "What do you do in your liesure time."
   ❑ b. The journalist asked, "What do you do in your leisure time?"
   ❑ c. The journalist asked "What do you do in your leisure time?"

8. ❑ a. Theodore Roosevelt was born in New York on October 27, 1858.
   ❑ b. Theodore Roosevelt was born in New York on October 27 1858.
   ❑ c. Theodore Roosevelt was born in new york on October 27, 1858.

9. ❑ a. "Stop," shouted the police officer to the fleeing theif.
   ❑ b. "Stop!" shouted the police officer to the fleeing theif.
   ❑ c. "Stop!" shouted the police officer to the fleeing thief.

10. ❑ a. Bob ran into the house shouting, "It's starting to snow!"
    ❑ b. Bob ran in the house shouting, "It's starting to snow."
    ❑ c. Bob ran into the house shouting "It's starting to snow!"

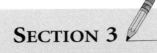

WRITING SENTENCES

Teacher Preparation and Lessons

Sentences are the building blocks of written communication. In oral discourse, gestures and voice inflections as well as words can convey meaning. Written language depends on sentences to achieve the same result. Skillful, grammatical use of sentence structure and style is essential to any type of student writing.

ACTIVITIES 3–1 through 3–4 discuss **subjects** and **predicates.** Write the following word on the board: *Jenkins.* Have the students identify this as a proper noun. Ask the class for the meaning of this word. They will be at a loss. Write on the board, under *Jenkins,* the word *ran.* The students will be able to identify *ran* as a verb. Ask the students exactly what message they are being given by this word. Beyond pointing out that it shows a certain action, they will be unable to define a message. Erase *ran* from the board and rewrite it next to *Jenkins.* Now when you ask the students to translate the message on the board, they will easily be able to identify it as a complete thought: *Jenkins ran.* Point out that this is the definition of a sentence: a group of words that express a complete meaning. Elicit the fact that two elements are necessary in a complete sentence: a **subject** (a person or thing to speak about) and a **predicate** (something to say about this person or thing). Show how the sentence can be expanded by enlarging the subject, as in *Jenkins, the star quarterback of the high school football team, ran.* Ask the students to suggest other ways to enlarge the subject. Then show how the sentence can be expanded by enlarging the predicate: *Jenkins, the star quarterback of the high school football team, ran forty yards for a touchdown.* Ask the students to suggest other ways to enlarge the predicate. Distribute **Activity 3–1 Subjects and Predicates (Part One).** Read and discuss the definitions and examples at the top of the page, then have the students complete the exercises. Have students read aloud several examples of each sentence.

Write the following on the board: *Ronnie Patel, my second cousin on my mother's side, who came to this country ten years ago.* Elicit from the students that this is *not* a sentence. Although the subject, *Ronnie Patel,* is named and described in great detail, the sentence is incomplete because the predicate is missing. Ask the students to suggest predicates that could be added to complete the thought, and write several of them on the board. Write the following on the board: *Sings folk songs of many nations to audiences in schools and community theaters.* Point out that although there are a lot of words here, it is not a sentence. Elicit that the subject is missing. Ask students to supply several examples of subjects that could be used to complete the thought. Distribute **Activity 3–2 Subjects and Predicates (Part Two).** Read and discuss the examples at the top, then have the students complete the activity. When students have finished, have several examples of each sentence read aloud. Distribute **Activity 3–3 Subjects and Predicates (Part Three).** Read and discuss the information and examples at the top, then have the students complete the exercises. Write the following sentence on the board: *My sister and her boyfriend are madly in love.* Elicit that both *My sister* and *her boyfriend* are subjects of the sentence and that they are joined by a conjunction (*and*). Point out that this is called a **compound subject.** Discuss the use of a plural verb following a compound subject.

77

Write on the board: *The emotional drama on the stage touched the hearts of the audience and made them rethink some of their ideas.* Elicit that this sentence contains two predicates (*touched the hearts of the audience* and *made them rethink some of their ideas*). Point out that a predicate containing two or more verbs or verb phrases joined by a conjunction is called a **compound predicate.** Distribute **Activity 3–4 Compound Subjects and Predicates.** Read and discuss the definitions and examples of compound subjects and predicates, then have the students complete the assignment. When they have finished, have them share and discuss their answers in small groups or with the entire class.

ACTIVITY 3–5 reviews the **three types of sentences.** Write the following sentences on the board: *George Washington slept here. Did George Washington sleep here? Come here!* Elicit that these three types of sentences are **declarative** (makes a statement), **interrogative** (asks a question), and **exclamatory** or **imperative** (expresses strong feelings or makes a command). Distribute **Activity 3–5 Types of Sentences.** Read and discuss the definitions and examples at the top, then have students complete the activity.

ACTIVITIES 3–6 to 3–9 review **agreement of subject and verb.** Write the following sentences on the board:

> *A new family is moving in next door.*
>
> *The Robinsons are moving in next door.*

Point out that *is* is a singular verb, and that *are* is a plural verb. Discuss why these verb forms are used and elicit that the singular verb agrees in number with the singular subject, *family,* while the plural verb agrees in number with the plural subject, *Robinsons.* Distribute **Activity 3–6 Subject-Verb Agreement (Part One).** Read and discuss the explanations and examples at the top. Be sure the students understand why verbs must agree with the subject in *person* as well as *number,* then have them complete the exercises.

Write the following sentence on the board: *The difficult journey undertaken by the six-member expedition and their ten local guides has ended successfully.* Elicit that the subject of this sentence is *journey,* a singular noun. Despite the many words in the description that follow, the predicate verb *has ended* agrees with the true subject, *journey.* Distribute **Activity 3–7 Subject-Verb Agreement (Part Two).** Read and discuss the explanation and examples at the top of the page, then have students complete the exercises.

Write on the board: *Either of them knows the answer. Both of them* <u>know</u> *the answer.* Discuss the fact that a singular verb is used in the first sentence while a plural verb is used in the second. Elicit the fact (or point out) that *either* and *both* are indefinite pronouns, but one takes a singular verb while the other takes a plural verb. Ask what verbs students would use with the following indefinite pronouns: *anybody, someone, many, several.* Distribute **Activity 3–8 Subject-Verb Agreement (Part Three).** Read and discuss the explanation and examples at the top, then have the students complete the assignment. Distribute **Activity 3–9 Subject-Verb Agreement (Part Four).** Read and discuss the rules and examples at the top of the page. Ask students to offer other examples for each rule, then have them complete the activity.

ACTIVITIES 3–10 and 3–11 review **simple, compound, and complex sentences.** Write the following sentences on the board:

> *Cara and I do our homework together.*
>
> *Cara and I do our homework together, and she brings her books to my house.*
>
> *When Cara and I do our homework together, she brings her books to my house.*

Elicit that the first sentence has one subject and one predicate. Point out that this is called a **simple sentence.** No matter how long it is, a sentence with one subject (even if it is a compound subject) and one predicate (even if it is a compound predicate) is still a simple sentence. Ask students to offer additional examples of simple sentences. Elicit that the second sentence consists of two simple sentences that are joined by the conjunction *and*. Point out that this is called a **compound sentence.** Ask students to offer additional examples of compound sentences, and discuss them. Elicit that the third sentence contains an independent clause with a subject and predicate that can stand alone as a sentence (*she brings her books to my house*) as well as a dependent clause, which by definition cannot stand by itself (*When Cara and I do our homework together*). Point out that this is called a **complex sentence.** Ask students to supply additional examples of **complex sentences,** and discuss them. Distribute **Activity 3–10 Simple, Compound, and Complex Sentences (Part One).** Read and discuss the explanations and examples at the top of the page, then have the students complete the exercises. Distribute **Activity 3–11 Simple, Compound, and Complex Sentences (Part Two).** Read and discuss the explanations and examples at the top of the page. Ask students to supply additional examples, then have them complete the activity.

ACTIVITIES 3–12 to 3–14 discuss the identification and avoidance of **misplaced words and phrases** in a sentence. Write this sentence on the board: *Walking up the stage steps, the audience cheered the winner of the prize.* Ask the students what is wrong with this sentence, and elicit the fact that, as written, it says that the audience is walking up the stage steps. Ask for alternative versions that are more accurate—perhaps one of these: *Walking up the stage steps, the winner of the prize was cheered by the audience.* Or *The audience cheered the winner of the prize as he walked up the stage steps.* Point out that misplaced words and phrases can give a sentence a completely different meaning from what was intended. Distribute **Activity 3–12 Misplaced Words and Phrases (Part One).** Read and discuss the examples and explanations at the top, then have students complete the assignment. Distribute **Activity 3–13 Misplaced Words and Phrases (Part Two).** Review the problem of misplaced words and phrases, then have students complete the activity. Distribute **Activity 3–14 Misplaced Words and Phrases (Part Three).** Read and discuss the examples and explanations at the top of the page. Ask students to supply additional examples for each rule, then have them complete the activity.

ACTIVITY 3–15 is about **double negatives.** Say to the class, "I am not giving you no homework today." The students will probably laugh. (If they don't, this lesson is desperately needed!) Elicit that the sentence contains a double negative, and, as written, suggests that homework will be given today. Elicit that you should have said, "I am not giving you homework today," or "I am giving you no homework today." Distribute **Activity 3–15 Double Negatives.** Read and discuss the explanations and examples at the top of the page, then have students complete the activity.

ACTIVITIES 3–16 and 3–17 review the identification and avoidance of **sentence fragments.** Write the following sentences on the board:

> *Whenever you visit a city and look at the skyline.*
> *Wondering how these tall skyscrapers were built.*

Elicit that these are not complete sentences. Analyze and discuss why they are only fragments, since each is just a dependent clause and does not contain a main subject and verb. Ask students to make suggestions for completing these fragments, such as *Whenever you visit a city, look at the skyline.* Or *Whenever you visit a city and look at the skyline, you will be amazed.* Or *You may wonder how these tall skyscrapers were built.* Or *Wondering how these tall skyscrapers were built, you may wish to read about the city's history.* Distribute **Activity 3–16 Recognizing Sentence Fragments (Part One).** Read and discuss the explanation and examples at the top, then have the students complete the activity. Distribute **Activity 3–17 Recognizing Sentence**

Fragments (Part Two). Read and discuss the explanation and examples at the top, then have students complete the exercises.

ACTIVITIES 3–18 to 3–20 discuss **run-on sentences.** Write the following sentence on the board: *Alex wants to go to the game tomorrow, Ben prefers to watch it on TV.* Ask the class how many complete thoughts are contained in this sentence. Elicit that an end mark should appear at the end of each complete thought. Therefore, there should be a period after *tomorrow,* since a comma is not an end mark. Point out that this is called a **run-on sentence** or a **comma splice,** since the comma is used incorrectly. Distribute **Activity 3–18 Recognizing Run-on Sentences (Part One).** Read and discuss the explanations and examples at the top of the page, then have students complete the exercises. Distribute **Activity 3–19 Recognizing Run-on Sentences (Part Two).** Read and discuss the explanation and examples at the top, then have students complete the exercises. Distribute **Activity 3–20 Recognizing Fragments and Run-on Sentences.** Read and discuss the directions, then have students complete the activity.

ANSWER KEY

3–1. SUBJECTS AND PREDICATES (PART ONE)
Part A.
Sentences will vary.

Part B.
Sentences will vary.

3–2. SUBJECTS AND PREDICATES (PART TWO)
Sentences will vary.

3–3. SUBJECTS AND PREDICATES (PART THREE)

1. Dorothy	3. students	5. I
2. Brad	4. Kara	6. people

3–4. COMPOUND SUBJECTS AND PREDICATES
Part A.
The following should be underlined:

1. Romeo and Juliet	4. the Murphys and the Arcaros
2. George Washington and John Adams	5. Mr. Sanchez and Ms. Sapirstein
3. Jon and Alex	

Part B.
The compound predicates will vary.

3–5. TYPES OF SENTENCES

1. exclamation point; IMP	5. question mark; INT	9. question mark; INT
2. period; DEC	6. exclamation point; EX	10. period; DEC
3. question mark; INT	7. question mark; INT	
4. period; DEC	8. period; DEC	

3–6. SUBJECT-VERB AGREEMENT (PART ONE)

1. are	3. want	5. thinks	7. are
2. hope	4. is	6. are	

3–7. SUBJECT-VERB AGREEMENT (PART TWO)

1. needs	4. hang	7. Are
2. is	5. was	
3. are	6. were	

3–8. SUBJECT-VERB AGREEMENT (PART THREE)

1. were	4. speaks	7. were
2. are	5. was	8. are
3. is	6. was	9. was

3–9. SUBJECT-VERB AGREEMENT (PART FOUR)

1. b	3. a	5. b
2. a	4. b	

3–10. Simple, Compound, and Complex Sentences (Part One)

1. simple	4. simple	7. complex
2. compound	5. simple	8. compound
3. complex	6. complex	

3–11. Simple, Compound, and Complex Sentences (Part Two)

1. c 2. a 3. b

3–12. Misplaced Words and Phrases in a Sentence (Part One)
Possible answers are as follows:

1. Lord Alderson's house in the valley is constructed of red brick.
2. When Brittany is sad, the television is a welcome distraction.
3. The test was a snap because I had studied my notes thoroughly.
4. After I watched the film version on television, the story seemed to come alive.
5. Happy with the audience's applause, the singer performed an encore.

3–13. Misplaced Words and Phrases in a Sentence (Part Two)
Possible answers are as follows:

1. To pass English this year, students must follow strict rules of grammar.
2. The Hermitage became a refuge for Andrew Jackson after he left the presidency.
3. Even though Ellie Masters was the best candidate for the job, the director chose Bruce Sabin.
4. Although he had never played baseball before, Ben scored a ninth-inning run.
5. Citing increases in the cost of gas, the trucking company told customers about higher fees.
6. After scoring high on the SAT, Sarah was accepted by the college.
7. When Evan was ten, his mother remarried.
8. Even after Mom had slaved all day over a hot stove, dinner was still not ready.
9. The party ended too quickly, since everyone was having a great time.

3–14. Misplaced Words and Phrases in a Sentence (Part Three)

1. b 2. b 3. a 4. b

3–15. Double Negatives

1. Josh ran out of the classroom because he didn't want any trouble with his teacher.
2. When he was caught, he insisted that he didn't do anything.
3. "I didn't cheat on the test either," he complained.
4. Josh hardly had any time at all before they called in his parents.
5. He decided it was hardly worth it to lie, so he told his parents the truth.

3–16. Recognizing Sentence Fragments (Part One)

1. fragment	4. fragment	7. fragment	10. fragment
2. complete	5. fragment	8. fragment	
3. fragment	6. complete	9. complete	

3–17. RECOGNIZING SENTENCE FRAGMENTS (PART TWO)
Some possible sentences are shown below:

1. He knew better than anyone else how the game should be played in order to win.
2. Complete
3. Striding up to home plate, smiling wickedly, and wielding his bat in a grandiose manner, he then waited for the pitch.
4. Brian wanted the job in the stadium and tried to hide his nervousness while being interviewed.
5. Complete

3–18. RECOGNIZING RUN-ON SENTENCES (PART ONE)
Some possible sentences are as follows:

1. He drove off in the truck, and Mike watched him go.
2. This book contains a lot of important information. Be sure to study it carefully.
3. Despite the storm, we attended the game. Happily, our team won.
4. This is the most important game of the season. Be sure to give it your best effort.
5. Greg couldn't get the helmet on his head; it was the wrong size.
6. The coach said, "Get out there on the field, and win the game for me."

3–19. RECOGNIZING RUN-ON SENTENCES (PART TWO)
Some possible answers are as follows:

1. I do not like Amy Brent; moreover, I do not like her whole family.
2. Correct
3. Brett is the most popular kid in our class. Besides, he is my best friend.
4. Mr. Santana is a good Spanish teacher; however, he is sometimes too strict.

3–20. RECOGNIZING FRAGMENTS AND RUN-ON SENTENCES

1. b, c	4. a, c	7. b, c
2. a, c	5. b	
3. b, c	6. c	

ANSWERS TO REVIEW TEST (PART ONE)
There are various ways in which the sentence structure in this paragraph could be corrected. Here is one of them.

The first typewriters were sold to the public in 1873. They were manufactured by the Remington Company, makers of guns and sewing machines. These early typewriters resembled old-fashioned sewing machines. They were mounted on sewing machine tables, and the carriage was returned by pressing a foot pedal. Christopher Sholes of Milwaukee, Wisconsin, had invented a workable typewriter the same year. Paying Sholes $6,000 and buying all rights, Remington produced one thousand of these new writing machines. They were immensely popular with the public and were quickly sold out. Many authors, including Mark Twain, were among the early purchasers. In fact, Twain wrote *Life on the Mississippi* on his Remington. Neither factories nor business was interested at first, but they soon saw the potential of this remarkable machine.

ANSWERS TO REVIEW TEST (PART TWO)

1. b	4. b	7. a
2. b	5. b	8. b
3. a	6. a	9. b

3–1. Subjects and Predicates (part one)

A **sentence** is a group of words that conveys a complete meaning. In order to do so, it must have two elements: a subject and a predicate.

> The **subject** is the person or thing that is spoken about. It is always a noun or a pronoun. The **predicate** tells what the subject is or does. It always contains a verb.
>
> **Example:** *Rose bought sneakers.*
> The **subject** of this sentence is *Rose.* She is the person spoken about. The rest of the sentence (*bought sneakers*) is the **predicate.** It describes what Rose did. Neither the subject nor the predicate can stand by itself.
>
> **Example:** *Rose, my sixteen-year-old cousin, bought three pairs of sneakers at the mall.* Subjects and predicates can be enlarged with greater detail. The **subject** of this sentence is still *Rose,* but it has been enlarged to include a description of Rose as *my sixteen-year-old cousin.* The **predicate** has been enlarged to *bought three pairs of sneakers at the mall.*

A. DIRECTIONS: Write a complete sentence with each of the following subjects.

1. My brother _____

2. The newspaper _____

3. You _____

4. The cat _____

5. The band _____

B. DIRECTIONS: Write a complete sentence containing each of the following predicates.

1. looked at me slyly _____

_____

2. pinned his opponent to the ground _____

_____

3. listened with great interest _____

_____

4. went camping last summer _____

_____

5. was the most frightening sight I have ever seen _____

_____

3–2. SUBJECTS AND PREDICATES (PART TWO)

Sometimes many words and details can obscure the fact that a sentence is incomplete. The easiest way to determine whether or not a sentence is complete is to ask, "Who or what is being or doing something?"

Example: *Scrabble®, my favorite game, also enjoyed by everyone in the family.* (The subject is *Scrabble®*. There are many details about *Scrabble®*, but there is nothing that tells what it is or does.)

Here are two ways that the sentence could be made complete:

Scrabble®, my favorite game, also enjoyed by everyone in the family, requires a good vocabulary. (A predicate is added: *requires a good vocabulary.*)
Scrabble®, my favorite game, is also enjoyed by everyone in the family. (A verb is inserted to show action, and the predicate now reads: *is also enjoyed by everyone in the family.*)

DIRECTIONS: The following items are not sentences. Each lacks either a subject or a predicate. Write a complete sentence below, adding a subject or predicate as needed.

1. Stuck in the house because he is grounded for a week.

   _____

   _____

2. The meeting of the Computer Club scheduled for Thursday afternoon.

   _____

   _____

3. The girl at the party wearing the funniest costume.

   _____

   _____

4. Brian, frustrated because he could not figure out the math homework.

   _____

   _____

5. Filled with examples of people who have worked hard and succeeded.

   _____

   _____

6. Not so great as our team will be in the playoffs.

   _____

   _____

3–3. Subjects and Predicates (part three)

The **subject** of a sentence should always be clear to the writer and the reader. This is easy when the subject is at the beginning. Sometimes, the subject does not appear until the middle of the sentence. This can cause confusion. To determine the subject, always ask the question, "To what person or thing is this happening?" Then the subject will become apparent.

Examples: *Even after applying a strong sunscreen, Bronwyn still got a severe sunburn.* (Who got the sunburn? Bronwyn did. Therefore, *Bronwyn* is the subject.)

When Brian was eight, his mother totaled the family car. (At first glance it might appear that the subject is *Brian*. This is wrong. The predicate tells about totaling the family car. Brian's mother did that. Therefore, the subject is *mother*.)

Citing skyrocketing medical insurance costs, Dr. Handel announced that he was raising his fees. (Although he does not appear until the middle of the sentence, Dr. Handel is the one raising his fees. Therefore, *Dr. Handel* is the subject.)

DIRECTIONS: Write the subject of each sentence.

1. After returning to Kansas from her fantastic journey to Oz, Dorothy said, "There's no place like home."   **Subject:** _____

2. Although he had never had much success at baseball, Brad scored the game-winning run.   **Subject:** _____

3. To pass science this year, all students must successfully complete three lab assignments.   **Subject:** _____

4. After shopping at the mall, Kara never comes home empty-handed.
   Subject: _____

5. When the warm rains of spring begin, I like to take long walks in the park.
   Subject: _____

6. Despite major campaigns by celebrities to encourage voting, many people do not go to the polls on Election Day.   **Subject:** _____

3–4. COMPOUND SUBJECTS AND PREDICATES

Compound Subjects: A compound subject means that the sentence has more than one subject. A compound subject often consists of two nouns joined by a conjunction.

> **Examples:** *The batter and the catcher disagreed about the umpire's call.* (The compound subject is *The batter and the catcher.*)
>
> *Jeni, Rose, and Zena agreed that they would always be friends.* (The compound subject is *Jeni, Rose, and Zena.*)

Compound Predicates: A compound predicate contains two or more verbs or verb phrases joined by a conjunction.

> **Examples:** *The falling climber slid and clawed his way to the bottom of the mountain.* (The compound predicate is *slid and clawed his way to the bottom of the mountain.*)
>
> *The horse kicked its heels and galloped away from its trainer.* (The compound predicate is *kicked its heels and galloped away from its trainer.*)

A. DIRECTIONS: Underline the compound subject in these sentences.

1. Romeo and Juliet were doomed lovers in a play by Shakespeare.

2. George Washington and John Adams were the first two presidents of the United States.

3. Though they did not live in the same neighborhood, Jon and Alex were close friends.

4. After more than a year of hard work, the Murphys and the Arcaros finished building the summer home they were sharing.

5. Mr. Sanchez and Ms. Sapirstein were my favorite teachers in the ninth grade.

B. DIRECTIONS: Complete each sentence with a compound predicate.

1. In the morning when I first wake up _____

2. When the teacher stepped out, the class _____

3. During the summer months, David often _____

4. The news bulletin told about _____

5. The guidance counselor told me to_____

3–5. TYPES OF SENTENCES

All sentences have one of these purposes: to state, to ask, to express strong feelings, or to command.

> 1. A **declarative sentence** makes a statement and ends with a period.
>   *This is an excellent pizza.*
>
> 2. An **interrogative sentence** asks a question and ends with a question mark.
>   *Is this an excellent pizza?*
>
> 3. An **exclamatory sentence** expresses strong feelings and ends with an exclamation point.
>   *What an excellent pizza!*
>
> 4. An **imperative sentence** expresses a command. It is followed by an exclamation point if it expresses strong feelings or by a period if it just makes a request.
>   *Deliver this pizza immediately!*
>   *Please deliver this pizza as soon as possible.*

DIRECTIONS: Put the correct end mark after each sentence, then write DEC if it is declarative, INT if it is interrogative, EX if it is exclamatory, or IMP if it is imperative.

1. Stop that fight immediately _____

2. The community has united to fight pollution _____

3. Do you know who made the first successful flight _____

4. The city's skyscrapers define its skyline _____

5. What kind of building would be best at that location _____

6. No, I won't do it _____

7. Can you give an example to support that theory _____

8. I have already given three excellent examples _____

9. Does this sentence have both a subject and a predicate _____

10. I think that Ross wants to be the class comedian _____

3–6. SUBJECT-VERB AGREEMENT (PART ONE)

A verb should agree with its subject in number and person.

Number:

1. A **singular** subject takes the singular form of a verb.
   My cousin, Tony, always wins first prize in the rodeo. (singular subject, *Tony;* singular verb, *wins*)

2. A **plural** subject takes the plural form of a verb.
   Tony and Rory always win prizes in the rodeo. (plural subject, *Tony and Rory;* plural verb, *win*)

Person:

1. A **first-person** subject refers to the person speaking and takes a first-person verb.
   I am a contestant in the rodeo. (first-person singular subject, *I;* first-person singular verb, *am*)
   We are contestants in the rodeo. (first-person plural subject, *we;* first-person plural verb, *are*)

2. A **second-person** subject refers to the person spoken to and takes a second-person verb.
   You are a TV addict. (second-person singular subject, *you;* second-person singular verb, *are*)
   You are TV addicts. (second-person plural subject, *you;* second-person plural verb, *are*)

3. A **third-person** subject refers to the person, place, or thing spoken about and takes a third-person verb.
   Shauna is a well-known journalist. (third-person singular subject, *Shauna;* third-person singular verb, *is*)
   They are well-known journalists. (third-person plural subject, *They;* third-person plural verb, *are*)

DIRECTIONS: Complete the sentences by filling in the correct verb.

1. Mark and Dana _____ reporters for the school newspaper. (**is, are**)

2. They _____ to be on the TV news some day. (**hope, hopes**)

3. Marla and I _____ to be reporters, too. (**want, wants**)

4. Mark _____ one of the reporters who may be an editor. (**is, are**)

5. Dana _____ she will write a music column. (**think, thinks**)

6. Jazz musicians _____ among the world's great artists. (**is, are**)

7. You and your sister _____ good writers, too. (**is, are**)

3–7. SUBJECT-VERB AGREEMENT (PART TWO)

A verb must always agree with its subject even when extra information is inserted between them. For example, a singular subject might be separated from the verb by a plural modifier describing the subject. That doesn't alter the verb. It must still be singular like the subject. Do not make the mistake of using a verb that agrees with the modifier instead of the subject.

Examples: *The swimmer on the diving board, as well as many of his teammates, is dressed in black.* (The **singular verb,** *is,* agrees with the **singular subject,** *swimmer,* not with its **modifier,** *as well as many of his teammates.*)

The glory of autumn, with its reds, browns, and yellows, is always impressive. (The **singular verb,** *is,* agrees with the **singular subject,** *glory,* not with its **modifier,** *reds, browns, and yellows.*)

DIRECTIONS: Complete these sentences by filling in the correct verb.

1. Every part of me—my neck, back, and arms—desperately _____ a massage. (**need, needs**)

2. Mr. Savage, not any of the other teachers, _____ in charge of the Science Club. (**is, are**)

3. Mr. Savage and the new student teacher _____ working on extra projects with the students. (**is, are**)

4. Paintings by Vincent Van Gogh _____ in many museums. (**hang, hangs**)

5. John Adams, one of the founders of America, _____ a great patriot. (**was, were**)

6. Spaniards _____ among the early explorers in the Americas. (**was, were**)

7. _____ you familiar with the French language? (**Is, Are**)

3–8. SUBJECT-VERB AGREEMENT (PART THREE)

When an indefinite pronoun is used as the subject of a sentence, the verb must agree in number with the subject. Some indefinite pronouns are used with a singular verb. Others are used with a plural verb.

---

1. Indefinite pronouns used with a **singular verb**:

another	either	nobody
anybody	everybody	one
anyone	everyone	somebody
each	neither	someone

   One of his friends lives next door. (Singular verb *lives* agrees with singular subject *one.*)

   Everybody knows the answer to that question. (Singular verb *knows* agrees with singular subject *everybody.*)

2. Indefinite pronouns used with a **plural verb**:

both	many	several
few	others	

   Few are able to attain great success. (Plural verb *attain* agrees with plural subject *few.*)

   Many of them agree that I am right. (Plural verb *agree* agrees with plural subject *many.*)

3. Indefinite pronouns that can be used with **either a singular or a plural verb**:

all	any	none	some

   When indicating *how much,* use a singular verb. When indicating *how many,* use a plural verb.

   None of them are prepared. (Plural verb *are* indicates *how many.*)

   None of the food was eaten. (Singular verb *was* indicates *how much.*)

DIRECTIONS: Insert the correct verb in the following sentences.

1. Few of the applicants _____ selected. (**was, were**)

2. All of the jobs _____ filled. (**is, are**)

3. Everybody _____ happy to be on a winning team. (**is, are**)

4. Neither of them _____ clearly. (**speak, speaks**)

5. Each of the applicants _____ interviewed. (**was, were**)

6. Some of my jewelry _____ taken by the burglar. (**was, were**)

7. Several players _____ injured during the game. (**was, were**)

8. None of them _____ playing tomorrow. (**is, are**)

9. None of the cake _____ eaten. (**was, were**)

3–9. SUBJECT-VERB AGREEMENT (PART FOUR)

1. *There* is never used as the subject of a sentence. When a sentence begins with *there,* look for the subject after the verb.
   There is a broken key on this computer. (Singular verb *is* agrees with singular subject *key.*)
   There are two broken keys on this computer. (Plural verb *are* agrees with plural subject *keys.*)

2. When *or* or *nor* is used to describe two or more subjects, use a singular verb if the subject nearest the verb is singular. Use a plural verb if the subject nearest the verb is plural.
   Neither the eggs nor the meat was fresh. (Singular verb *was* agrees with singular subject *meat.*)
   Neither the meat nor the eggs were fresh. (Plural verb *were* agrees with plural subject *eggs.*)

3. **Collective nouns** refer to groups or collections. When they mean the group as a whole, they are singular and take a singular verb. When they refer to individual members of the group, they are plural and take a plural verb.
   The couple lives in the next condo. (This refers to the whole couple and takes the singular verb *lives.*)
   A couple of unfriendly people live in the next condo. (This refers to a *couple* of individual people and takes the plural verb *live.*)

DIRECTIONS: Place a checkmark next to the correct sentence in each of the following sets.

1. ❑ a. A pencil or a pen are required for this test.
   ❑ b. A pencil or a pen is required for this test.

2. ❑ a. Special skills or a willingness to work is required for the job.
   ❑ b. Special skills or a willingness to work are required for the job.

3. ❑ a. That group of players is staying in the bullpen.
   ❑ b. That group of players are staying in the bullpen.

4. ❑ a. The majority of the committee agrees with me.
   ❑ b. The majority of the committee agree with me.

5. ❑ a. This year's football team are the best ever.
   ❑ b. This year's football team is the best ever.

3–10. SIMPLE, COMPOUND, AND COMPLEX SENTENCES
(PART ONE)

1. A **simple sentence** has one complete subject and one complete predicate.
   My friend Elmo headed for the beach. (The complete subject is *My friend Elmo.* The complete predicate is *headed for the beach.*)
   My friends Maria and Bree put on their swimsuits and headed for the beach. (This sentence has one complete subject, *My friends Maria and Bree,* and one complete predicate, *put on their swimsuits and headed for the beach.* Therefore, it is a simple sentence.)

2. A **compound sentence** consists of **two simple sentences** that are joined by a coordinating conjunction such as *and, but,* or *or.* A comma usually precedes the conjunction.
   My friend Elmo telephoned me, and we headed for the beach. (This contains two simple sentences: *My friend Elmo telephoned me* and *we headed for the beach,* which are joined into one sentence by the conjunction *and.*)

3. A **complex sentence** contains an **independent clause**, which has a subject and verb and can stand by itself as a sentence, as well as a **dependent clause**, which cannot stand alone.
   As soon as Sean saw the weird lights in the sky, he knew it was a spaceship. (The independent clause, which can stand by itself, is *he knew it was a spaceship.* The dependent clause, which cannot stand by itself, is *as soon as Sean saw the weird lights in the sky.*)

DIRECTIONS: Next to each sentence below, indicate whether it is simple, compound, or complex.

1. Ben was determined to study hard and ace the Spanish test. _____

2. He worked hard for an hour, but there were still many pages left to review. _____

3. When he noticed it was time for his favorite TV sitcom, Ben decided to take some time off from studying. _____

4. His mom saw him watching TV and asked if he had finished studying. _____

5. Ben shook his head and admitted that he had not finished. _____

6. As soon as the program ended, Ben went back to his room. _____

7. By the time he finished studying, Ben felt completely prepared. _____

8. The next day, Ben took the test, and he got an A without any trouble. _____

3–11. SIMPLE, COMPOUND, AND COMPLEX SENTENCES (PART TWO)

There are several types of **dependent clauses** that are used in sentences.

---

1. A dependent clause used as an adjective is called an **adjective clause**. It describes a noun or pronoun and is usually introduced by *who, whom, that,* or *which*.
   The pitcher who threw the final out was the hero of the game. (The adjective clause *who threw the final out* describes *the pitcher*.)

2. **Adverbial clauses** modify verbs, adjectives, or other adverbs by answering the questions "How?" "Where?" or "When?" They are usually introduced by subordinating conjunctions such as *after, although, as, because, before, if, since, though, unless, until, when, where, while*.
   Because we arrived at the theater late, we missed the first act. (The dependent adverbial clause *because we arrived at the theater late* modifies the verb *missed*.)
   He practiced pitching against the stone wall until it got dark. (The dependent adverbial clause *until it got dark* modifies the verb *practiced*.)

3. **Noun clauses** can be used as subjects or objects of the sentence. They consist of a group of words with a subject and verb that is used as a single noun and are usually introduced by *that, how, why, whatever, whoever,* or *whether*.
   The coach was asked how the team was doing. (*How the team was doing* is a dependent clause used as a noun. It is the object of the verb *was asked*.)

DIRECTIONS: Place a checkmark next to the correct answer in each set.

1. In the sentence, "The burglar *who terrorized our block for a month* was never caught," the italicized words are:
   - ❏ a. a noun clause
   - ❏ b. an adverbial clause
   - ❏ c. an adjective clause

2. In the sentence, "They were told *that the merchandise would arrive late,*" the italicized words are:
   - ❏ a. a noun clause
   - ❏ b. an adverbial clause
   - ❏ c. an adjective clause

3. In the sentence, "They will go shopping *if the stores are open late,*" the italicized words are:
   - ❏ a. a noun clause
   - ❏ b. an adverbial clause
   - ❏ c. an adjective clause

3–12. MISPLACED WORDS AND PHRASES IN A SENTENCE
(PART ONE)

Misplaced words and phrases in a sentence can give it a completely different meaning.

WRONG: *The Taj Mahal is one of the Seven Wonders of the World in India.* (This says that the Seven Wonders of the World are all in India.)

RIGHT: *The Taj Mahal, in India, is one of the Seven Wonders of the World. OR One of the Seven Wonders of the World is the Taj Mahal in India.*

WRONG: *Advancing across the field, the hot sun burned down on the regiment.* (This says that the hot sun was advancing across the field.)

RIGHT: *The hot sun burned down on the regiment as it advanced across the field. OR The regiment advanced across the field under the burning sun.*

WRONG: *Having come late, the lecture was incomprehensible.* (This says that the lecture came late.)

RIGHT: *Having come late, I found the lecture incomprehensible. OR I found the lecture incomprehensible, since I got there late.*

DIRECTIONS: Rewrite each sentence, correcting the misplaced words or phrases.

1. The house in the valley constructed of red brick is the home of Lord Alderson.

   _____

2. When feeling sad, the television is a welcome distraction.

   _____

3. Having studied my notes thoroughly, the test was a snap.

   _____

4. After watching the film version on television, the story seemed to come alive.

   _____

5. Happy with the audience's applause, an encore was performed by the singer.

   _____

3–13. MISPLACED WORDS AND PHRASES IN A SENTENCE
(PART TWO)

DIRECTIONS: The meaning of each sentence below is obscured because of misplaced words or phrases. Rewrite each sentence correctly.

1. To pass English this year, strict rules of grammar must be followed.

   _____

2. After leaving the presidency, the Hermitage became a refuge for Andrew Jackson.

   _____

3. Even though she was the best candidate for the job, the director chose Bruce Sabin over Ellie Masters.

   _____

4. Although he had never played baseball before, a ninth-inning run was scored by Ben.

   _____

5. Citing increases in the cost of gas, customers were told about higher trucking fees.

   _____

6. After scoring high on the SAT, the college accepted Sarah's application.

   _____

7. At the age of ten, Evan's mother remarried.

   _____

8. After slaving all day over a hot stove, dinner was still not ready.

   _____

9. Having a great time, the party ended too quickly.

   _____

3–14. MISPLACED WORDS AND PHRASES IN A SENTENCE
(PART THREE)

1. An **adverbial phrase or clause** is a legitimate way to begin a sentence, but it cannot be used as a noun.
   WRONG: *In its attempt to increase sales, special discount days were offered.* (There is no subject noun in this sentence.)
   RIGHT: *In its attempt to increase sales, the Muffin Shoppe offered special discount days.* (A subject noun, *Muffin Shoppe*, has been added.)

2. When using clauses beginning with the pronouns *which, that, it,* and *this,* be sure it is perfectly clear what the pronoun refers to.
   WRONG: *The substitute teacher knew nothing about the subject, which the students picked up on immediately.* (This says that the students picked up on the subject immediately.)
   RIGHT: *The students immediately picked up on the fact that the substitute teacher knew nothing about the subject.*

3. Avoid **confusing comparisons.**
   WRONG: *The principal favors after-school activities more than her teachers.* (This indicates that the principal likes after-school activities more than she likes her teachers.)
   RIGHT: *The principal favors after-school activities more than her teachers do.*

DIRECTIONS: Place a checkmark next to the correct sentence in each set.

1. ❏ a. The history teacher knows more about this topic than the class.
   ❏ b. The history teacher knows more about this topic than the class does.

2. ❏ a. The new coach wanted to spend extra hours on training and exercise, but it was not necessary.
   ❏ b. It was not necessary for the new coach to spend extra hours on training and exercise.

3. ❏ a. Brian tried to practice the piano one hour each day, but it did not work out.
   ❏ b. In trying to practice the piano one hour each day did not work out.

4. ❏ a. Maria put a dozen roses into a planter that her parents did not like in the house.
   ❏ b. Maria put a dozen roses into a planter, but her parents did not like flowers in the house.

3–15. DOUBLE NEGATIVES

A **double negative** can change the meaning of a sentence in unintended ways.

WRONG: *The student was unable to offer no reasons for his lateness.* (Contains two negatives: *unable* and *no. Unable to offer no reasons* suggests that the student was able to offer some reasons, just the opposite of the desired meaning.)

RIGHT: *The student was unable to offer any reasons for his lateness.*

WRONG: *Brian complained that his family didn't do nothing interesting during vacations.* (This suggests that Brian's family did something interesting.)

RIGHT: *Brian complained that his family didn't do anything interesting during vacations.*

Remember that words such as *hardly, scarcely,* and *barely* are negative.

WRONG: *Pat was so surprised that he was hardly able to say nothing at all.* (If he was *hardly* able to say *nothing,* then he was able to say something. This is the opposite of the desired meaning.)

RIGHT: *Pat was so surprised that he was hardly able to say anything at all.*

DIRECTIONS: The following sentences contain double negatives. Rewrite each sentence correctly on the line below.

1. Josh ran out of the classroom because he didn't want no trouble with his teacher.

   _____

2. When he was caught, he insisted that he didn't do nothing.

   _____

3. "I didn't cheat on the test neither," he complained.

   _____

4. Josh hardly had no time at all before they called in his parents.

   _____

5. He decided it wasn't hardly worth it to lie, so he told his parents the truth.

   _____

3–16. RECOGNIZING SENTENCE FRAGMENTS (PART ONE)

> A **sentence fragment** fails to be a sentence because it is unable to stand by itself. It does not contain even one independent clause. Usually this is because either the subject or the verb to which it relates is missing.
>
> **Examples:** *Maxwell, telling jokes, making faces, and being class clown.* (There are three verbs here—*telling, making,* and *being*—but none of them completes a thought relating to the subject *Maxwell.*)
> *Even though Josh was the youngest kid in his class.* (This fragment begins with the dependent phrase *even though.* It is, therefore, a dependent clause, not a complete sentence.)
>
> These fragments can be made into complete sentences:
>
> *Maxwell, telling jokes, making faces, and being class clown, kept us entertained all semester.*
> *Even though Josh was the youngest kid in his class, he was very popular.*

DIRECTIONS: Next to each sentence below, write "complete" if it is a complete sentence or "fragment" if it is not a complete sentence.

1. Working far into the night in an effort to complete the assignment. _____

2. Brian worked hard. _____

3. Some of the students in my summer school class. _____

4. My best friend's sister, Amy, who has long black hair and brown eyes. _____

5. Realizing that I was acting foolishly, but unable to stop. _____

6. Running to the door, she tripped over a protruding nail. _____

7. In the American colonies just before the Revolution began. _____

8. The nineteenth century, a time of amazing industrial growth. _____

9. Exploring outer space may become routine in the near future. _____

10. Rushing to make the plane and dropping her purse along the way. _____

3–17. Recognizing Sentence Fragments (Part Two)

Just because a sentence is long, that does not mean that it is a complete sentence. A complete sentence could be very short, as in these examples:

His grandmother sobbed. (subject: *grandmother*, predicate verb: *sobbed*)
The bird soared. (subject: *bird*, predicate verb: *soared*)

A fragment could be long, containing lots of information, and still not be a complete sentence, as in these examples:

Although the old soldier fought many bloody battles during two wars, was decorated for bravery, and served his community and country in various positions. (There are several verbs here telling us what the old soldier did, but it is not a complete sentence since the word *although* introduces everything that follows as a dependent clause.)

The professor, spending many hours studying and taking notes on volume after volume of detailed information about the nineteenth century and its greatest literary figures. (This sentence contains a subject: *the professor*, but everything that follows is part of a dependent clause.)

DIRECTIONS: Can you recognize which of the following are complete sentences and which are only fragments? For each item below, if it is a complete sentence, write "complete" on the line below. If it is a fragment, rewrite it on the line below as a complete sentence.

1. Knowing better than anyone else how the game should be played in order to win.

   _____

2. She turned.

   _____

3. Striding up to home plate, smiling wickedly, and wielding his bat in a grandiose manner.

   _____

4. Brian, wanting the job in the stadium and trying to hide his nervousness while being interviewed.

   _____

5. Hold it.

   _____

3–18. RECOGNIZING RUN-ON SENTENCES (PART ONE)

A **run-on sentence** has at least two parts, either of which can stand alone. When the two parts are not properly connected, it becomes a run-on sentence. Since a comma is often used incorrectly here, this error is often called a comma splice. Here are three ways to fix run-on sentences:

1. An end mark can be used at the end of each sentence.
   WRONG: *I am here, now we can begin.* (A comma alone cannot be used to connect two independent clauses.)
   RIGHT: *I am here. Now we can begin.* (An end mark [period] correctly appears at the end of each sentence.)

2. The two independent clauses can be joined with a comma accompanied by a coordinating conjunction such as *and, but, so, for, or, nor,* or *yet.* The sentence above could be written correctly as follows:
   RIGHT: *I am here, so now we can begin.*

3. The two independent clauses can be joined with a semicolon.
   RIGHT: *I am here; now we can begin.*

DIRECTIONS: Rewrite each of these run-on sentences correctly on the line below.

1. He drove off in the truck, Mike watched him go.

   _____

2. This book contains a lot of important information, be sure to study it carefully.

   _____

3. Despite the storm, we attended the game, happily, our team won.

   _____

4. This is the most important game of the season, be sure to give it your best effort.

   _____

5. Greg couldn't get the helmet on his head, it was the wrong size.

   _____

6. The coach said, "Get out there on the field, win the game for me."

   _____

3–19. RECOGNIZING RUN-ON SENTENCES (PART TWO)

Two independent clauses may be correctly joined by coordinating conjunctions such as *and, but, or, nor, for, so,* and *yet.* The words listed below look like coordinating conjunctions, but they are not. They are **conjunctive adverbs** and should not be used to join two independent clauses.

also	however	otherwise
besides	indeed	then
consequently	moreover	therefore
further/furthermore	nevertheless	thus

WRONG: Jeff wanted to go to the party, however, he had no transportation.
RIGHT: Jeff wanted to go to the party. However, he had no transportation.
RIGHT: Jeff wanted to go to the party, but he had no transportation.
RIGHT: Jeff wanted to go to the party; however, he had no transportation.

WRONG: The evidence was overwhelming, nevertheless, the jury found the defendant not guilty.
RIGHT: The evidence was overwhelming; nevertheless, the jury found the defendant not guilty.
RIGHT: The evidence was overwhelming. Nevertheless, the jury found the defendant not guilty.
RIGHT: The evidence was overwhelming, but the jury found the defendant not guilty.

DIRECTIONS: Rewrite correctly each run-on sentence below. If the sentence is not a run-on, write the word "Correct" on the line below.

1. I do not like Amy Brent, moreover, I do not like her whole family.

_____

_____

2. I would like to try out for the football team, but I do not think I am good enough.

_____

_____

3. Brett is the most popular kid in our class, besides, he is my best friend.

_____

_____

4. Mr. Santana is a good Spanish teacher, however, he is sometimes too strict.

_____

_____

3–20. RECOGNIZING FRAGMENTS AND RUN-ON SENTENCES

DIRECTIONS: Place a checkmark next to all the correct sentences in each set below. (Each set may have more than one correct sentence.)

1. ❏ a. Although Jon had enough money in his pocket when he went to the mall.
   ❏ b. Jon had enough money in his pocket when he went to the mall.
   ❏ c. Although Jon had enough money in his pocket when he went to the mall, he did not buy anything.

2. ❏ a. He went into three shoe stores; none of them carried his favorite brand.
   ❏ b. He went into three shoe stores, none of them carried his favorite brand.
   ❏ c. He went into three shoe stores, but none of them carried his favorite brand.

3. ❏ a. He drove carefully when he neared the bridge, it had been the site of a recent crash.
   ❏ b. He drove carefully when he neared the bridge. It had been the site of a recent crash.
   ❏ c. He drove carefully when he neared the bridge, since it had been the site of a recent crash.

4. ❏ a. We are not going to the mall; we are going to the library.
   ❏ b. We are not going to the mall, we are going to the library.
   ❏ c. We are not going to the mall. We are going to the library.

5. ❏ a. During the Civil War, members of the same family fighting on different sides.
   ❏ b. During the Civil War, members of the same family fighting on different sides sometimes faced one another in battle.
   ❏ c. During the Civil War, members of the same family fought on different sides, they sometimes faced one another in battle.

6. ❏ a. We live in the same city as the Andrettis, our house is on the other side of town.
   ❏ b. Living in the same city as the Andrettis, our house on the other side of town.
   ❏ c. We live in the same city as the Andrettis, but our house is on the other side of town.

7. ❏ a. My father's job in market research causing him to travel fifty percent of the time.
   ❏ b. My father's job in market research caused him to travel fifty percent of the time.
   ❏ c. My father's job in market research, causing him to travel fifty percent of the time, kept him away from home a lot.

Tenth-Grade Level

Writing Sentences Review Test

Name _____   **Date** _____

REVIEW TEST: WRITING SENTENCES (PART ONE)

DIRECTIONS: The following paragraph contains many errors in sentence structure. Rewrite the paragraph correctly on the lines below. (Continue on the back of this sheet, if necessary)

The first typewriters were sold to the public in 1873, It was manufactured by the Remington Company. Makers of guns and sewing machines. These early typewriters resembled old-fashioned sewing machines. Mounted on sewing machine tables. The carriage was returned by pressing a foot pedal. Christopher Sholes of Milwaukee, Wisconsin, had invented a workable typewriter the same year. Paying Sholes $6,000 and buying all rights. Remington produced one thousand of these new writing machines, they were immediately popular with the public and was quickly sold out. Many authors, including Mark Twain, was among the early purchasers, in fact, Twain wrote *Life on the Mississippi* on his Remington. Neither factories nor business were interested at first, however, they soon saw the potential of this remarkable machine.

Name _____ Date _____

Review Test: Writing Sentences (part two)

DIRECTIONS: Place a checkmark next to the correct sentence in each group below.

1. ❏ a. Neither my parents nor my teacher are able to figure out why I'm failing math.
   ❏ b. Neither my parents nor my teacher is able to figure out why I'm failing math.

2. ❏ a. The report issued by the corporate treasurer acting in place of the chief executive officer.
   ❏ b. The report is issued by the corporate treasurer acting in place of the chief executive officer.

3. ❏ a. Most of the Board of Directors had hardly any interest in hearing the details of the report.
   ❏ b. Most of the Board of Directors hardly had no interest in hearing the details of the report.

4. ❏ a. Food production has decreased, even though the number of people needing to be fed have increased.
   ❏ b. Food production has decreased, even though the number of people needing to be fed has increased.

5. ❏ a. Although both authors on the panel have new books on the market, only one of them are successful.
   ❏ b. Although both authors on the panel have new books on the market, only one of them is successful.

6. ❏ a. Karen waited until the last minute to write out all the invitations, and she mailed them immediately.
   ❏ b. Karen waited until the last minute to write out all the invitations, however, she mailed them immediately.

7. ❏ a. Neither of us wants to go to that movie.
   ❏ b. Neither of us want to go to that movie.

8. ❏ a. Because their class was going on a field trip that day and everybody needed to bring a lunch.
   ❏ b. Because their class was going on a field trip that day, everybody needed to bring a lunch.

9. ❏ a. Desktop publishing is the latest thing, in fact, there is a conference about it at the high school.
   ❏ b. Desktop publishing is the latest thing. In fact, there is a conference about it at the high school.

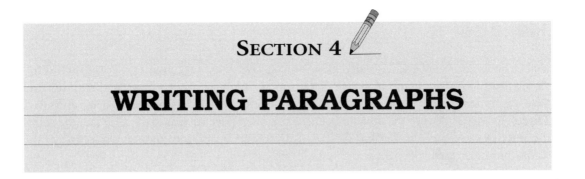

WRITING PARAGRAPHS

Teacher Preparation and Lessons

Recognizing and writing paragraphs is a necessary prerequisite to essay writing. The paragraph is an essay in miniature. Like an essay, it contains a statement of topic, development, and conclusion. A student who has mastered the paragraph form will find it easy to slip into its expanded form, the essay. The activities in Section 4 help students to organize their thinking as well as their writing, and to communicate thoughts and ideas clearly to the reader. These skills are an important component of the scoring process in both state and national standardized assessment tests for writing. Selected answers are given on pages 113 to 115. The PRACTICE TEST on pages 146 to 148 assesses students' ability to apply their knowledge of language and writing skills in a sample writing passage. The rubric and student samples can be used in assessing students' writing.

ACTIVITIES 4–1 through 4–3 deal with **organizing a paragraph.** Write the following short paragraph on the board:

> *Being involved in an automobile accident was the most frightening experience of my life. The incident occurred on July 3. My whole family was in the car, and Dad was driving. As we headed south on I-56, a big van passed on the right, then suddenly cut in front of us, connecting with the front end of our Camry. The front bumper was ripped from the body. Fortunately, no one was hurt, and we were able to continue driving to our destination. It was an experience I won't soon forget.*

Point out that, like a story, a paragraph has a beginning, middle, and end. Ask students to identify the **topic sentence,** and discuss how it introduces the subject. Examine the **concluding sentence** with the class and discuss how it brings the story to an end. Discuss how the middle section of the paragraph **develops** the story or topic. Distribute **Activity 4–1 Organizing a Paragraph (Part One).** Read and discuss the explanation, examples, and questions at the top. Have the students complete the activity, and then have a selection of their paragraphs read aloud. Write the following short paragraph on the board:

> *There were only a few people on the slopes due to icy conditions. Yesterday, I went skiing with my friend, Matt. He chickened out and went back to the lodge, but I was determined to fly those slopes despite the ice. That taught me not to ski under icy circumstances. That was a mistake, as I ended up with a broken leg.*

Discuss this paragraph and bring out the fact that it reads in a confusing, disorganized way. Ask students to select the sentence that should be at the beginning, since it states the topic. (*Yesterday, I went skiing with my friend, Matt.*) Ask students to identify the sentence that best sums up the story in this paragraph. (*That taught me not to ski under icy circumstances.*) Rewrite the paragraph with these changes and have it read aloud so the students can see how it now flows smoothly and logically. Distribute **Activity 4–2 Organizing a Paragraph (Part Two).** Read and discuss the material at the top of the page. Then read the directions and have the students complete the activity. Distribute **Activity 4–3 Organizing a Paragraph (Part Three).** Read and discuss the directions at the top, then have the students complete the activity. Since this exercise is somewhat difficult, it would be a good idea to read a selection of the solutions aloud, then compare and discuss them.

ACTIVITIES **4–4 through 4–6** deal with **topic sentences.** Distribute **Activity 4–4 Writing a Topic Sentence (Part One).** Read and discuss the explanation at the top. Then read the directions and have students complete the exercise. Follow up with a discussion of the topic sentence in each of the three paragraphs of the exercise. Distribute **Activity 4–5 Writing a Topic Sentence (Part Two).** Read and discuss the purposes of a good topic sentence, then discuss the three types of sentences that can be used—declarative, interrogative, and exclamatory. Read the directions, then have students complete the activity. Have a selection of the topic sentences used in each paragraph read aloud and discuss their effectiveness. Distribute **Activity 4–6 Writing a Topic Sentence (Part Three).** Read and discuss the directions. When students have completed the activity, have several examples of each topic sentence read aloud.

ACTIVITIES **4–7 and 4–8** deal with **concluding sentences.** Distribute **Activity 4–7 Writing a Concluding Sentence (Part One).** Read and discuss the material at the top of the page. Be sure that students understand the purpose of the concluding paragraph. Read the directions and have students complete the activity. Have several samples of each concluding sentence read aloud and discussed. Distribute **Activity 4–8 Writing a Concluding Sentence (Part Two).** Review the use of concluding sentences. Read and discuss the directions. When the students have completed the activity, have them read aloud and discuss several examples of each set of topic sentences and concluding sentences.

ACTIVITIES **4–9 through 4–17** deal with **developing a topic.** Distribute **Activity 4–9 Developing the Topic.** Discuss in detail each of the purposes and methods of presenting supporting details listed at the top of the page. Read and discuss the directions. Be sure students understand that the sentences in the second paragraph are scrambled. When students have completed the exercise, have them read aloud and discuss some of their solutions. Distribute **Activity 4–10 Developing the Topic in a Definition Paragraph.** Read the list of eight types of paragraphs, and tell students that they will concentrate on only one type at a time. Read and discuss the explanation and example of a definition paragraph. Read and discuss the directions, then have students complete the activity. Distribute **Activity 4–11 Developing the Topic in a Description Paragraph.** Read and discuss in detail the explanation and example of a description paragraph. Ask the students to write down the adjectives and similes in the sample, and have them share their answers aloud. Read and discuss the directions, then have students complete the activity. Organize the class into small groups and instruct the students in each group to share and discuss the paragraphs they wrote. Distribute **Activity 4–12 Developing the Topic in a Classification Paragraph.** Read and discuss the definition and example of a classification paragraph. Read and discuss the directions, then have students complete the activity. Collect the papers and read aloud several student paragraphs, then discuss them. Distribute **Activity 4–13 Developing the Topic in a Compare and Contrast Paragraph.** Read and discuss the definition and example of a compare and contrast paragraph. Be sure students understand how this kind of paragraph is organized. Point out, in particular, the use of words that are useful in this type of paragraph, such as *but, also, while, however,* and the others listed on the worksheet. Encourage students to use these words in their paragraph. Read and discuss the directions, then have students complete the activity. Collect the papers and read aloud several student paragraphs; discuss their effectiveness. Distribute **Activity 4–14**

Developing the Topic in a Sequence Paragraph. Read and discuss the definition and example of a sequence paragraph. Be sure students understand the purpose of a sequence paragraph. Discuss the list of words that are effective in this type of paragraph, and encourage the students to use them in their own writing. Read and discuss the directions, and have students complete the activity. Divide the class into small groups to share and discuss the effectiveness of the paragraphs they have written. Distribute **Activity 4–15 Developing the Topic in a Choice Paragraph.** Read and discuss the definition and example of a choice paragraph. Read and discuss the list of words that are useful in a choice paragraph; ask students to identify the ones that appear in the example, as required in the activity. Read and discuss the directions, then have students complete the activity. Have several students read their paragraph aloud, and discuss how well they work as choice paragraphs and why. Distribute **Activity 4–16 Developing the Topic in an Explanation Paragraph.** Read and discuss the definition and example of an explanation paragraph. Point out the words and phrases that are useful when writing this type of paragraph. Read the directions, then have students complete the activity. Collect the papers and read several examples aloud for class discussion and criticism of their effectiveness. Distribute **Activity 4–17 Developing the Topic in an Evaluation Paragraph.** Read and discuss the definition and example of an evaluation paragraph. Read the list of words that can be helpful in this type of writing, and encourage the students to use these words in their own writing. Read and discuss the directions. When students have completed the activity, collect the papers and read several examples aloud, so that the class can discuss and critique their effectiveness.

ACTIVITIES 4–18 and 4–19 deal with **consistency of tense.** Write the following short paragraph on the board:

> *Last summer, Brooke got a job as junior counselor at a camp. It was a perfect job for Brooke, and she is happy to be working with little kids. The children in her charge are seven and eight years old. Brooke loves being a counselor.*

Ask the students what is wrong with this paragraph. Elicit that the tense changes in the middle of the second sentence. Point out how confusing this is for the reader and how important it is to keep the time consistent unless there is a logical reason for changing it. Distribute **Activity 4–18 Using Tense Consistently (Part One).** Read and discuss the sample paragraph and explanation. Read and discuss the directions, then have students complete the exercises. Distribute **Activity 4–19 Using Tense Consistently (Part Two).** Read and discuss the sample paragraph; ask students to supply other examples of cases where tense is correctly shifted during a paragraph. Read and discuss the directions, and have students complete the exercises.

ACTIVITIES 4–20 and 4–21 deal with **transitional words and phrases.** Distribute **Activity 4–20 Using Transitional Words and Phrases (Part One).** Read the explanation and examples. Discuss how and why the second example paragraph is stronger and smoother than the first one. Have students locate and write down the transitional words and phrases in the second paragraph as directed in the activity, then share the results aloud. Read and discuss the directions, and have students complete the activity. Divide the class into small groups; direct the students to share and discuss the rewritten paragraphs. Distribute **Activity 4–21 Using Transitional Words and Phrases (Part Two).** Discuss the list of common transitional words and phrases. Ask students to add to the list. Read and discuss the directions, then have the students complete the activity by writing their own sentences.

ACTIVITY 4-22 deals with **coherence within a paragraph.** Distribute **Activity 4–22 Staying on the Subject.** Read the explanation and example with the class, then follow directions on the worksheet for discussing the importance of staying on the subject. Read and discuss the directions, then have students complete the activity.

ACTIVITY 4–23 also helps students achieve coherence within a paragraph by showing them how to **avoid irrelevant details.** Distribute **Activity 4–23 Avoiding Irrelevant Details.** Read the explanation and first example paragraph. Guide students through the explanation of irrelevant details in the first example. Then read the second example aloud, and discuss why it is a better paragraph. Read the directions, and have the students complete the activity.

ACTIVITIES 4–24 through 4–26 deal with using a **variety of sentences** in a paragraph. Distribute **Activity 4–24 Using Variety in Sentence Length.** Read the first example aloud and elicit from the students that the paragraph seems choppy because it contains only short sentences. Read the second example aloud and discuss how the writer produced a better paragraph by varying the length of sentences. Read and discuss the directions, and have students complete the writing activity. Have some of the students' examples read aloud and discussed. Review simple, compound, and complex sentences by asking students to write an example of each on the board. Distribute **Activity 4–25 Using Variety in Sentence Structure.** Read and discuss the explanation and examples. Read and discuss the directions. After students have completed their paragraphs, have each student exchange papers with a partner and discuss their paragraphs. Review declarative, interrogative, and exclamatory sentences by asking students to write an example of each on the board. Distribute **Activity 4–26 Using a Variety of Sentence Types.** Read and discuss the explanation at the top. Read and discuss the directions, and have students complete the activity. Have samples of the students' rewritten paragraphs read aloud.

ACTIVITIES 4–27 through 4–29 review the **writing process.** Distribute **Activity 4–27 Using the Writing Process: Prewriting.** Read the explanation and discuss why prewriting activities are necessary. Read and discuss the directions for preparing a **brainstorming list,** and have students complete the activity. Divide the class into small groups so that students can compare their lists as well as their topic sentences and concluding sentences. Distribute **Activity 4–28 Using the Writing Process: Writing the First Draft.** Discuss the directions. Be sure that students understand that this is a first draft and they should just concentrate on getting their thoughts down on paper, with the help of their brainstorming list. Distribute **Activity 4–29 Using the Writing Process: Revising and Writing a Final Copy.** Discuss the importance of revisions. Read and discuss the directions and the specific suggestions for revision. Have students complete the activity by writing their own final paragraph.

Practice Test: Writing Paragraphs

The sample student paragraphs A and B on page 148 are rated a 2 and a 6, respectively.

Paragraph A states the topic in both the topic sentence and the closing sentence. The development, however, is sketchy and unfocused. Sentences are short and choppy, and the writer goes completely off the subject in sentences five through seven. This paragraph received a score of 2.

Paragraph B introduces the topic with two strong and striking sentences. The development is focused and logical and contains relevant and well-expressed details. There is an interesting variety in sentence structure, type, and length. Sentences are punctuated correctly, with consistency of tense. Spelling and word usage is appropriate throughout. The concluding sentence neatly sums up the topic. This paragraph was rated a 6.

ANSWER KEY

4–1 ORGANIZING A PARAGRAPH (PART ONE)
Paragraphs will vary.

4–2 ORGANIZING A PARAGRAPH (PART TWO)

Yesterday was a busy day at my house. While I was at school, several repair people arrived. These included the plumber, the carpenter, and the electrician. Two of them had left by the time I got home, but the plumber was still there. I was able to watch him install the new fixtures in our bathroom. At the end of the day, our house was in much better shape than it had been before.

4–3 ORGANIZING A PARAGRAPH (PART THREE)

The structure of a violin is cleverly designed to produce sounds that are beautiful and unique. The main part of the violin is a hollow, oval body. The top and bottom of this body are curved. Two sound holes are cut on either side of the bridge. These holes are f-shaped. A neck that contains the pegs is fixed to the upper part of the body. A fingerboard is then glued to the neck of the violin. Strings are stretched across this fingerboard. The construction of a violin is the secret of its sweet, pleasing voice.

4–4 WRITING A TOPIC SENTENCE (PART ONE)
The topic sentences are as follows:

1. There was one painting in the room that caught my attention immediately.
2. My first day on the job was a disaster.
3. Last night, I tried to straighten up my room.

4–5 WRITING A TOPIC SENTENCE (PART TWO)
Topic sentences will vary.

4–6 WRITING A TOPIC SENTENCE (PART THREE)
Topic sentences will vary.

4–7 WRITING A CONCLUDING SENTENCE (PART ONE)
Concluding sentences will vary.

4–8 WRITING A CONCLUDING SENTENCE (PART TWO)
Topic sentences and concluding sentences will vary.

4–9 DEVELOPING THE TOPIC
Circle the following sentences:
Paragraph 1:   Did you know that there are three basic types of Floridians? These three types are what make this state so unique.

Paragraph 2:   Habits are not easily broken. It is an uphill battle, but I am determined to win in the end.

All the other sentences should be underlined as part of the development.

4–10 DEVELOPING THE TOPIC IN A DEFINITION PARAGRAPH
Paragraphs will vary.

4–11 DEVELOPING THE TOPIC IN A DESCRIPTION PARAGRAPH

Adjectives: English, good-looking, lean, muscular, interesting, angular, wide, deep-set, blue, shy, polite, precise, clipped, interesting

Similes: like a movie star, polite and precise as a professor

Paragraphs will vary.

4–12 DEVELOPING THE TOPIC IN A CLASSIFICATION PARAGRAPH
Paragraphs will vary.

4–13 DEVELOPING THE TOPIC IN A COMPARE AND CONTRAST PARAGRAPH
Paragraphs will vary.

4–14 DEVELOPING THE TOPIC IN A SEQUENCE PARAGRAPH
Paragraphs will vary.

4–15 DEVELOPING THE TOPIC IN A CHOICE PARAGRAPH
Words and phrases: like, enjoy, I think, I would like, it seems to me, love, I feel, on the other hand, I believe

Paragraphs will vary.

4–16 DEVELOPING THE TOPIC IN AN EXPLANATION PARAGRAPH
Paragraphs will vary.

4–17 DEVELOPING THE TOPIC IN AN EVALUATION PARAGRAPH
Paragraphs will vary.

4–18 USING TENSE CONSISTENTLY (PART ONE)
The following verbs should be underlined:

1. calls   2. are shocked   3. take

4–19 USING TENSE CONSISTENTLY (PART TWO)

1. Correct   2. Incorrect   3. Correct

4–20 USING TRANSITIONAL WORDS AND PHRASES (PART ONE)

Transitional words and phrases in the example are: After all, However, For example, also, On the other hand, All in all, however

Paragraphs will vary. One possible answer is as follows:
There are several reasons why I enjoyed reading *My Summer with Frankie*. First, the writing is vivid and colorful. Second, the characters, good and bad, seem like real people. Also, the plot is exciting till the very end. Of course, it was a bit long. However, it is one of the best books I have ever read.

4–21 USING TRANSITIONAL WORDS AND PHRASES (PART TWO)
Sentences will vary.

4–22 STAYING ON THE SUBJECT
Paragraphs will vary.

4–23 AVOIDING IRRELEVANT DETAILS
The sentences that have irrelevant details and should be crossed out are as follows:

April is often a rainy month, but the rain is good for flowers.
I like red eggs best, but yellow are nice, too.
Several different kinds of matzos can be found in the supermarkets.

4–24 USING VARIETY IN SENTENCE LENGTH
Paragraphs will vary.

4–25 USING VARIETY IN SENTENCE STRUCTURE
Paragraphs will vary.

4–26 USING A VARIETY OF SENTENCE TYPES
Paragraphs will vary.

4–27 USING THE WRITING PROCESS: PREWRITING
Answers will vary.

4–28 USING THE WRITING PROCESS: WRITING THE FIRST DRAFT
Paragraphs will vary.

4–29 USING THE WRITING PROCESS: REVISING AND WRITING A FINAL COPY
Paragraphs will vary.

4–1. ORGANIZING A PARAGRAPH (PART ONE)

A sentence is a group of words expressing a complete thought. A **paragraph** is a group of sentences that not only expresses a thought, but expands on it. The parts (sentences) of a paragraph all focus on the same topic. They **state** or **define** that topic, then **amplify** and **explain** or **defend** that topic. These details must be arranged in a logical way. The amount of detail included in a paragraph is up to the writer, but every detail must be related to the single topic.

A paragraph is usually short, but it must be long enough to clarify the topic. Compare these two paragraphs:

> Young people, more than many others, understand what a vital part music plays in their lives. It helps them get in touch with their feelings and with themselves. It plugs them into the currents, ideas, and language of their generation. It brings pleasure, magic, and excitement into their day-by-day existence. Music is essential to them in so many ways.
>
> Music is essential to young people in many ways. It is an important part of their lives. Listening to music can make a real difference. Many teenagers have large collections of CD's, and play them often. Music means a lot to them.

Here are some questions to discuss with your teacher and class:

1. Both paragraphs are about the same topic. What is it?

2. Why is the first paragraph so much more satisfying than the second?

3. In the first paragraph, which sentences explain and amplify the topic?

4. Do any of the sentences in the second paragraph amplify the topic?

5. Why does much of the second paragraph fail to amplify the topic?

DIRECTIONS: Choose one of the following topic sentences and copy it on the lines below. Then complete the paragraph by expanding and explaining the topic in a logical way. The paragraph should have at least four but no more than eight sentences. Use the back of this paper if you need more writing space.

Some sports are more fun to watch than to play.
Don't you love a picnic in the park in the summertime?
My mother follows the same routine every morning.

_____

_____

_____

_____

_____

4–2. ORGANIZING A PARAGRAPH (PART TWO)

The sentences in a paragraph should be arranged in a logical order that makes the meaning clear. It is like a very short story, with a beginning, a middle, and an end.

- A **topic sentence** usually comes first.
- The **middle sentences** offer details that expand and explain the topic in a logical order.
- The **concluding sentence** brings the topic to a close.

DIRECTIONS: The sentences in the box can be combined into one paragraph, but they are not in a logical order. Unscramble these sentences and copy them in the correct order on the lines below, creating a paragraph that makes sense. The topic sentence should come first, the concluding sentence last, and the other sentences should be in the middle.

---

1. I was able to watch him install the new fixtures in our bathroom.

2. At the end of the day, our house was in much better shape than it had been before.

3. These included the plumber, the carpenter, and the electrician.

4. Yesterday was a busy day at my house.

5. Two of them had left by the time I got home, but the plumber was still there.

6. While I was at school, several repair people arrived.

_____

_____

_____

_____

_____

_____

_____

_____

_____

_____

4–3. ORGANIZING A PARAGRAPH (PART THREE)

DIRECTIONS: Here is a scrambled paragraph that will be a challenge! The sentences below can be combined into one paragraph, but they are not in a logical order. Unscramble these paragraphs and copy them in the correct order on the lines below. Remember:

- The **topic sentence** should come first.
- The **middle sentences** should be arranged in a logical order.
- The **concluding sentence** brings the topic to a close.

1. Strings are stretched across this fingerboard.

2. The structure of a violin is cleverly designed to produce sounds that are beautiful and unique.

3. The top and bottom of this body are curved.

4. The main part of the violin is a hollow, oval body.

5. These holes are f-shaped.

6. Two sound holes are cut on either side of the bridge.

7. The construction of a violin is the secret of its sweet, pleasing voice.

8. A neck that contains the pegs is fixed to the upper part of the body.

9. A fingerboard is then glued to the neck of the violin.

4–4. Writing a Topic Sentence (Part One)

> The **topic sentence** introduces the main idea of a paragraph. It states or summarizes the theme and forms the basis of a well-written paragraph. It is useful to both the reader and the writer, because it
>
> - Tells the reader what to expect
> - Helps the writer to clarify the subject in his or her own mind and to stay focused throughout the writing of the paragraph
>
> The topic sentence is usually the first sentence of a paragraph. Occasionally, to achieve a particular effect, it may come later. This works only for experienced writers. For others, it is best to begin with the statement of topic to avoid confusion for both the writer and the reader.

DIRECTIONS: The topic sentence of each paragraph below is hidden in the middle. It doesn't belong there. Find each topic sentence and circle it.

1. It was a large seascape in vivid colors. I was drawn to the crashing blue-green surf rolling in toward shore. There was one painting in the room that caught my attention immediately. The largest breaker was breathtaking as it curled and plunged downward into the sea. A single surfer was poised at the top of the wave, his surfboard pointed to the sky. I stood there for a long time unable to look away.

2. Everything went wrong. The person who was supposed to train me was home sick. My first day on the job was a disaster. There was nobody who had time to show me what to do, so I was on my own. I tried my best, but I seemed to make one mistake after another. I think I'll do better tomorrow. I know I wouldn't want to repeat this horrible day.

3. First, I picked up everything that was on the floor and set it on the bed. Then, I tackled the items one at a time, trying to decide where each one belonged. Some things went into the closet. Last night, I tried to straighten up my room. Others were put into drawers. I found some papers I had been meaning to post on my bulletin board, so I tacked them up. It was a lot of work, but at the end I was satisfied that my room looked like a human abode once more.

4–5. Writing a Topic Sentence (part two)

A good **topic sentence**:

- Introduces the main idea of the paragraph
- Gives the reader an idea of what the rest of the paragraph is about
- Appears somewhere at the beginning of the paragraph
- Gets the reader's attention in an interesting way

A topic sentence can be:

- Declarative   *I like my English teacher, Ms. Santana.*
- Interrogative   *Did you ever have Ms. Santana for English?*
- Exclamatory   *My English teacher, Ms. Santana, is great!*

DIRECTIONS: Insert a topic sentence at the beginning of each paragraph below. Use one declarative topic sentence, one interrogative sentence, and one exclamatory sentence.

1. _____.

We got him when he was a tiny kitten, and he is now two years old. Marlon is devoted to me more than anyone else in the family. When it is time for me to come home from school, he suddenly appears from where he has been hiding and rushes to the door to wait for me. I am always greeted by an affectionate purring and rubbing against my ankles. It is so nice to have a devoted friend like Marlon.

2. _____.

Mrs. Manheim told the students about her experiences during the Holocaust of World War II. When her country was attacked, she had to flee from German soldiers. She hid in people's barns and basements, and came close to death six times. Mrs. Manheim's story was exciting and interesting and kept her listeners in suspense.

3. _____.

Citizens were given a chance to express their opinions about a proposed indoor pool. Those in favor say it will be a safe, healthful place for kids to hang out in the winter and will benefit all residents. The opposition asks, "Where is the money coming from?" No decision had been reached by the time the meeting ended.

Name _____ **Date** _____

4–6. WRITING A TOPIC SENTENCE (PART THREE)

DIRECTIONS: Write a topic sentence for a paragraph on each of the subjects listed below. Try to make your topic sentence interesting enough to get the reader's attention. Be sure it introduces the main idea of the paragraph.

(You do not have to write a complete paragraph—just the topic sentence.)

1. How to get the most out of your computer

   Topic sentence:_____

   _____

   _____

2. A celebrity I admire

   Topic sentence:_____

   _____

   _____

3. A recent movie or TV show

   Topic sentence:_____

   _____

   _____

4. The truth behind UFO's

   Topic sentence:_____

   _____

   _____

5. The American form of government

   Topic sentence:_____

   _____

   _____

4–7. WRITING A CONCLUDING SENTENCE (PART ONE)

A good **concluding sentence (closing)** should accomplish three things:

1. Restate the main idea of the paragraph using different words than were previously used.

2. Remind the reader of the writer's feelings about the subject.

3. Appear at the end of the paragraph, bringing it to a satisfying close.

The concluding sentence is underlined in the following example:

> Spring is amazing because everything comes to life at that time of the year. Even before the snow has melted, crocuses poke up their heads to say hello. Daffodils and tulips follow in colorful profusion. Green buds appear overnight on trees that have been stark and bare all winter. The chirping of birds fills the morning air. <u>Spring is nature's delicious gift to the Earth.</u>

DIRECTIONS: Write a concluding sentence for each paragraph.

1. Most kids in our school fit into one of three categories. There is the popular "in" group of jocks, party-givers, and cut-ups. Then, there are the serious, hard-working "good" students. Last are the "different" ones—the outsiders and nerds. _____

   _____

   _____

2. Don't you think it is time for our country to have a woman president? Women are successful in many areas. Their efforts contribute to success in business, education, government, health professions, research, and entertainment. Very often, they do all this while running a household and raising a family. _____

   _____

   _____

Name _____   **Date** _____

4–8. WRITING A CONCLUDING SENTENCE (PART TWO)

> The **concluding sentence** brings a paragraph to a satisfying end. It restates the main idea that was introduced in the topic sentence but uses different words.

DIRECTIONS: Write a topic sentence and a concluding sentence for a paragraph about each subject. (Do not write a complete paragraph, just the topic sentence and concluding sentence.)

1. How my town or city has changed in the past few years

   Topic sentence:_____

   _____

   Concluding sentence:_____

   _____

2. Planning a party

   Topic sentence:_____

   _____

   Concluding sentence:_____

   _____

3. A favorite TV program

   Topic sentence:_____

   _____

   Concluding sentence:_____

   _____

4–9. DEVELOPING THE TOPIC

After the topic sentence opens the paragraph, the rest of the sentences expand on the topic and **develop** the paragraph. These **supporting details** should:

- Be relevant to the main idea as stated in the topic sentence.
- Give specific details, facts, or examples to support, prove, or explain the main idea.
- Be as descriptive and interesting as possible.
- Explain or define any terms the reader may not know.
- Be presented in a sensible, concise, and natural order.

DIRECTIONS: In each paragraph below, circle the topic sentence and the concluding sentence. Underline the sentences that develop the idea with supporting details. (The sentences in the first paragraph are arranged correctly. In the second paragraph, they are scrambled.)

1.   Did you know that there are three basic types of Floridians? First, there are the native-born. These are in the minority and take pride in their birthplace. Next, there are those transplanted from other states and countries. They love their new surroundings in a subtropical "paradise" and contribute to the community, but they also enjoy reminiscing about "back home." Finally, there are Floridians who come to visit or do a job. No matter how many months or years they remain, they always consider it a temporary home. These three types are what make this state so unique.

2.   I know this well, because I have been trying to cure myself of eating too fast. Habits are not easily broken. It is a nasty habit. It looks unattractive to others and is bad for the digestion. It is an uphill battle, but I am determined to win in the end. The utmost concentration is required, and I am constantly backsliding.

4–10. Developing the Topic in a Definition Paragraph

There are eight types of paragraphs: definition, description, classification, compare and contrast, sequence, choice, explanation, and evaluation.

The first of these types, a **definition paragraph,** takes a thing or an idea and explains what it is. Some phrases that can be helpful in writing this kind of paragraph are *is defined as* and *is a kind of.*

> Do you know about the different varieties of pests in our country? One type of pest is an animal or plant that damages crops, forests, or property. Some examples of this sort of pest are mice, rats, locusts, and rabbits. There is also another kind of pest—the human variety. These pests annoy and irritate other people. They can be found in school, at home, on the ball field, or at the mall. All pests, whatever their type, are undesirable to have around.

DIRECTIONS: Check one of the subjects below, and write a definition paragraph about it.

- ❑ *National parks*
- ❑ *Science fiction*
- ❑ *A marching band*
- ❑ *Rap music*

_____

_____

_____

_____

_____

_____

_____

_____

_____

_____

4–11. DEVELOPING THE TOPIC
IN A DESCRIPTION PARAGRAPH

In a **description paragraph,** you are writing about what a person, place, location, or thing is like. Adjectives, sensory language, similes, and metaphors are especially suited to this type of writing, as in the following description paragraph:

> My English cousin, Clive, is staying with us for the summer. He is sixteen and good-looking, almost like a movie star. He has a lean, muscular build and an interesting, angular face with a wide mouth and deep-set blue eyes. He seems a bit shy and doesn't talk a lot, but when he does, he is always as polite and precise as a professor. I adore his clipped English accent. It should be an interesting summer with Clive around.

Can you find all the adjectives in this description paragraph? List them below.

_____

_____

There are two similes in this description. Copy them below.

_____

_____

DIRECTIONS: Write a description paragraph about a person, place, or thing on the lines below. Introduce the topic in the first sentence. Develop the paragraph with three or four sentences, then end with a concluding sentence. (Continue on the back of this sheet, if necessary.)

_____

_____

_____

_____

_____

_____

_____

_____

4–12. DEVELOPING THE TOPIC
IN A CLASSIFICATION PARAGRAPH

A **classification paragraph** groups things, people, or ideas into specific categories, as in the following example:

> There are eight basic types of paragraphs. The definition paragraph takes a thing or idea and explains what it is. If you want to tell what a person, place, or thing is like, you can use a description paragraph. A classification paragraph groups things or ideas into specific categories. A compare and contrast paragraph discusses the similarities and differences between two or more things. If you are writing to describe a series of events or a process in some kind of order, use a sequence paragraph. A choice paragraph will offer your opinion on a choice that you need to make, while an explanation paragraph explains how or why something happens. Finally, in an evaluation paragraph, you make judgments about people, ideas, and actions. Almost all paragraph writing fits into one of these categories.

DIRECTIONS: On the lines below, write a classification paragraph in which things or ideas are grouped into categories. You can write about types of houses, cars, schools, sports activities, or any other topic of your choice. Include a topic sentence at the beginning, then two to four sentences in the development, and a concluding sentence at the end. (Continue on the back of this sheet, if necessary.)

_____

_____

_____

_____

_____

_____

_____

_____

4–13. DEVELOPING THE TOPIC IN A COMPARE AND CONTRAST PARAGRAPH

In a **compare and contrast paragraph**, you write about the similarities and differences between two or more people, places, things, or ideas, as in the example that follows.

My friend Sandy and I like to compare our families. They are alike in many ways, but there are also some important differences. There are two kids in each family, but I have an older brother, while Sandy has a younger sister. Both of our mothers are teachers. However, Sandy's dad is a lawyer, while mine is in construction. Our families are both religious, but I am Jewish and Sandy is Catholic. One thing both sets of parents agree on is the importance of school and getting good grades. Sandy and I believe that our families are similar in most ways that are important.

Notice the use of the words *but, also, while, however,* and *similar*. Other words and phrases that are useful in this type of paragraph are *too, as well, in contrast, differs from, alike,* and *unlike.*

DIRECTIONS: Write a compare and contrast paragraph about one of the following:

- The weather in Massachusetts and Florida (or any other two states)
- Your current class and the one you were in last year
- Two TV shows or films you have recently seen
- Two of your friends
- Any other topic of your choice

_____

_____

_____

_____

_____

_____

_____

(Continue on the back of this sheet, if necessary.)

4–14. DEVELOPING THE TOPIC IN A SEQUENCE PARAGRAPH

A **sequence paragraph** describes a series of events or a process in some sort of order. The sequence is usually based on time (*First, we did this. After that, we did that. Finally, we did the last thing.*), but it can be sequenced differently. The following example uses a time sequence.

> Anyone can produce a good paragraph by following these steps. First, you write a dynamite topic sentence. Then, you develop the topic in a logical and interesting manner. Finally, you sum it all up with your concluding sentence. Writing a paragraph is a remarkably simple task.

Time-specific words can be helpful when writing a sequencing paragraph. Those used in the example are *first, then,* and *finally.* Other words and phrases that are useful are *in the beginning, before, after, at last, subsequently, recently, previously, afterward, when,* and *after.*

DIRECTIONS: Write a sequence paragraph on one of the following topics:

- How to play a game (for example, Monopoly®, Scrabble®, or chess)
- How a person becomes president of the United States
- How to become a successful business executive
- How to cook pasta (or any other food)
- How to give the dog a bath
- Your after-school routine
- Any other topic of your choice

Write your sequencing paragraph below (and continue on the back of this sheet, if necessary). Write a topic sentence. Develop the sequence in three or four additional sentences. End with a satisfying concluding sentence.

_____

_____

_____

_____

_____

_____

4–15. DEVELOPING THE TOPIC IN A CHOICE PARAGRAPH

In a **choice paragraph,** you express your opinion by choosing which object, idea, or action you prefer from two or more possibilities, as in this example:

> I have to make a choice between playing in the band or being on the soccer team, since there is a conflict in practice times. It is a tough decision, because I like both activities. Soccer is a fun game, and I enjoy physical activity. Also, I think that I would like playing with my friends on the team. On the other hand, it seems to me that I can't ignore my love of music and my eight years of lessons and practice on the clarinet. I believe that I might even major in music in college. Therefore, the band is the choice that I feel I must make.

Here are some words and phrases that are useful when writing a choice paragraph: *I believe, idea, I think that, I consider, I prefer, it seems to me, enjoy, like, dislike, feel, hope, understanding, in my opinion, on the other hand.* How many of these words can you find in the example? List them on the lines below.

_____

_____

DIRECTIONS: Write a choice paragraph on one of these topics:

- A choice between taking a course in art or music
- A choice between attending a private school or a public school
- A choice between a trip to Washington, D.C. or a trip to Walt Disney World
- Which is more important, intelligence or perseverance?
- Another topic of your choice

Write your choice paragraph below, beginning with a topic sentence, then developing the topic, and ending with a concluding sentence.

_____

_____

_____

_____

_____

(Continue on the back of this sheet, if necessary.)

4–16. DEVELOPING THE TOPIC IN AN EXPLANATION PARAGRAPH

An **explanation paragraph** tells how or why something happens. It can be personal, such as an explanation of why you failed to turn in a term paper on time, or it can be something broader such as explaining how or why a historical event came to occur. Here is an example of an **explanation paragraph:**

> The American Revolution can be explained to some extent in terms of the differences that had developed between the people of the American colonies and their English cousins. There were strong, long-held traditions in England as well as rigid classes. It was almost impossible for anyone born into one class to rise to another. In the colonies, generations were born and raised in a society where independence and self-reliance were prized, and anyone who was willing to work hard might achieve great success. As a result, when the English king and parliament imposed taxes that seemed unfair to the colonists, the Americans were ready to demand justice or independence.

Some words and phrases that are useful when writing an explanation paragraph are *because, since, as a result, due to, therefore, hence, consequently,* and *it follows that.*

DIRECTIONS: Write an explanation paragraph on one of these topics:

- The causes of the American Civil War
- Why Native Americans lost most of their tribal lands
- Why you are doing exceptionally well (or exceptionally poorly) in a school subject
- How computers have changed society
- Any other topic of your choice

Write your explanation paragraph below (and continue on the back of this sheet, if necessary). Begin with a topic sentence. Develop the topic logically in two to four sentences. End with a concluding sentence.

_____

_____

_____

_____

_____

4–17. DEVELOPING THE TOPIC IN AN EVALUATION PARAGRAPH

In an **evaluation paragraph,** you make judgments about people, actions, or ideas. A good evaluation paragraph develops the evaluation with facts and criteria that support it, as in this example:

> The food service at our school needs improvement. Right now, scheduling is so inefficient that some lunch periods are uncomfortably overcrowded, while others are practically empty. Most cafeteria employees are pleasant, but there are one or two who are mean and nasty to students. Perhaps they are not happy in their jobs, but that is no excuse for being impolite. I suggest that they be reprimanded. The food itself is edible, but just barely so. Meat is often undercooked and vegetables are always overcooked and mushy. Proper nutrition is important to active teenagers. I recommend that the administration do the right thing and correct these problems.

Some words that can be used to write a good evaluation paragraph are *good, bad, correct, incorrect, moral, immoral, right, wrong, important, trivial, suggest, recommend, advise,* and *argue.*

DIRECTIONS: Write an evaluation paragraph on one of the following topics:

- The policies of the current administration in Washington
- Prayer in public schools
- Your school newspaper
- Facilities for after-school activities at your school and/or in your town
- Any other topic of your choice

Write your evaluation paragraph below (and continue on the back of this sheet, if necessary). Begin with a topic sentence. Develop your supporting details in two to four sentences. Write a concluding sentence at the end.

_____

_____

_____

_____

_____

4–18. Using Tense Consistently (Part One)

Last week, our class went on a field trip to the science museum. The trip on the bus was a blast. The driver completely ignored what was going on behind her, so things got out of hand. Sean Meara does his loud clown act at the back, and everyone is laughing hysterically. Papers, pencils, and other missiles are flying all over the bus. The museum is okay, but the ride is the high point of the trip.

A **verb tense** establishes the **time** of action of a piece of writing. The paragraph above is confusing because the writer switches tenses in the middle. Can you find the sentence where the tense shifts? It is the one beginning *Scott Meara does his . . .* Up to this point, the paragraph is in the past tense. From this point on, it is in the present tense.

DIRECTIONS: Each paragraph below suddenly switches verb tenses in the middle. <u>Underline</u> the <u>verb</u> where the incorrect shift occurs.

1. The town hall was filled to capacity by eight o'clock. The meeting began when the chairperson calls the members to order. First, the minutes are read. Then old business is discussed. After that, new business is taken up. That's what everyone in the audience is there to hear.

2. Today, everyone has heard of the painter Vincent van Gogh. This was not true in his lifetime. He worked hard to achieve success, but it always eluded him. The people of the time are shocked by his work and do not appreciate it. He never sells a single painting. The strain on the painter is so great that eventually he goes mad and cuts off his own ear. Fame is denied him during his lifetime.

3. Until he was seventeen years old, James K. Polk could barely read or write. Since early childhood, he had suffered with constant terrible stomach pain. It was so disabling that he could not go to school. Finally, his parents take him to a doctor who diagnoses his illness as a gallbladder problem. The gallbladder is removed during a painful surgery without anesthesia. When James recovers from the operation, he is cured. At eighteen, he goes to school and not only learns to read and write, but becomes a top student. He completes college and eventually becomes president of the United States.

4–19. Using Tense Consistently (Part Two)

It is inadvisable to switch verb tenses during a paragraph unless there is a logical reason to do so. Here is an example of a paragraph in which the change of tense is appropriate.

> Last Saturday, Althea and her mom went shopping. The mall was not crowded, so they were able to make their purchases and be back home in less than two hours. Now Althea plans to wear a new outfit to school every day this week.

The first two sentences in this paragraph tell of an event in the past (*last Saturday*) and are in the past tense. The third sentence describes an event in the present (*Now Althea plans*). This is a case, therefore, in which it is correct to change to the present tense.

DIRECTIONS: Each of the following paragraphs contains a change of verb tense. Write "Correct" below the paragraph if the change is logical and correct. Write "Incorrect" next to the paragraph if the tense is switched without a logical reason.

1. Valentine's Day is a time to think about the people who are important to us. It is the perfect occasion to let these special folks know how we feel. Last year on February 14, I bought my mom a gold heart for her chain bracelet. It was small, but it represented my love for her.

   _____

2. Luke felt the sharp bite of the March wind. It blew his baseball cap right off his head and he had to run a long way to catch it. Sharp blasts lashed him from behind and pushed him along the street. He is thankful when those icy gusts finally blow him right to his front door.

   _____

3. On December 1, 1955, Rosa Parks, an African American woman, sat on a front bus seat in Montgomery, Alabama. These seats were usually reserved for white people. Mrs. Parks's brave action was the spark that started the civil rights movement led by Dr. Martin Luther King, Jr., whose birthday is now a national holiday.

   _____

4–20. Using Transitional Words and Phrases
(Part One)

Transitional words and phrases are useful writing tools. They help make smooth transitions from one sentence or thought to another. Without them, a paragraph could be choppy and unpleasant to read, as in this example.

> Social studies can be a boring subject. Most of the things we study happened a long time ago. Mrs. Potter, my social studies instructor, has a way of making our class interesting. She acts out historical events. She relates fascinating, little-known facts about famous people. She gives us a lot of homework. I think she is the best teacher in the school.

See how much more smoothly this paragraph reads when transitional words and phrases are used:

> Social studies can be a boring subject. After all, most of the things we study happened a long time ago. However, Mrs. Potter, my social studies instructor, has a way of making our class interesting. For example, she acts out historical events. She also relates fascinating, little-known facts about famous people. On the other hand, she gives us a lot of homework. All in all, however, I think she is the best teacher in the school.

Can you find all the transitional words and phrases in the above paragraph? Write them below.

_____

_____

DIRECTIONS: Rewrite the following paragraph, adding transitional words and phrases to make it smoother and clearer. (Continue on the back of this sheet, if necessary.)

> There are several reasons why I enjoyed reading *My Summer with Frankie*. The writing is vivid and colorful. It is easy to read. The characters, bad and good, seem like real people. The plot is exciting till the very end. It was a bit long. It is one of the best books I have ever read.

_____

_____

_____

_____

4–21. USING TRANSITIONAL WORDS AND PHRASES
(PART TWO)

Here is a list of some common transitional words and phrases:

at that time	certainly	in fact	on the other hand
also	even though	in other words	of course
although	finally	in the first place	since
all in all	first	lately	so far
after all	for instance	likewise	soon
afterward	for example	moreover	then
at last	furthermore	next	therefore
again	however	now	to summarize
besides	in conclusion	on the whole	though

DIRECTIONS: Write ten sentences using transitional words and phrases.

1. _____

2. _____

3. _____

4. _____

5. _____

6. _____

7. _____

8. _____

9. _____

10. _____

4–22. STAYING ON THE SUBJECT

A paragraph is not just a collection of sentences. It is a **unified, coherent group of sentences built around one point.** Every sentence must relate in some way to the point that was made in the topic sentence. Sentences that do not stay on the subject confuse the reader and show that the writer has lost focus, as in the following example:

> Business has been bad at our family store during the past six months. Sales are off by twenty percent. Even during the holiday season, there were no long lines at the cash register as is usual at that time. There were many customers browsing, but few purchases were made. I went to the men's shop next door and found a wonderful tie for my father with the logo of his favorite football team. We are hoping that the projected upturn in the economy will mean increased business for us.

Do you see which sentence is unrelated to the topic? You should! It stands out like a sore thumb! *I went to the men's shop next door . . .* has nothing to do with the subject and is confusing to any reader who is trying to make sense of it. It takes attention away from the subject of bad business at the family store.

DIRECTIONS: The following paragraph changes subject in the middle. Cross out the sentences that do not relate to the topic. Next, rewrite and complete the paragraph on the lines below. Be sure you stick to the topic.

> In 1492, it was commonly believed that the Earth was flat. Christopher Columbus said it was round. Lots of people thought he was crazy. It is not right to call anyone crazy. Mental illness is a disease. Sometimes it can be cured or controlled by drugs.

_____

_____

_____

_____

_____

_____

4–23. Avoiding Irrelevant Details

It is important to include details that support the topic of a paragraph. It is equally important *not* to add irrelevant details that shift the focus away from the subject. Can you find the irrelevant details in the following paragraph?

> Do you know how the celebration of Mother's Day got started? In 1907, a woman named Anna Jarvis campaigned to set aside a day to recognize mothers. It is hard to imagine what life in this country was like in 1907. Anna Jarvis believed that mothers deserve this honor. Fathers deserve their own day, too. Mrs. Jarvis fought to make her dream a reality. Some people give up too soon when trying to achieve a dream. In 1914, the president designated the second Sunday in May as a day to honor the nation's mothers.

This paragraph is about how the celebration of Mother's Day got started, but it contains a few sentences that are irrelevant:

It is hard to imagine what life in this country was like in 1907.
Fathers deserve their own day, too.
Some people give up too soon when trying to achieve a dream.

See how much more effective the paragraph is without these irrelevant sentences:

> Do you know how the celebration of Mother's Day got started? In 1907, a woman named Anna Jarvis campaigned to set aside a day to recognize mothers. Anna Jarvis believed that mothers deserve this honor. Mrs. Jarvis fought to make her dream a reality. In 1914, the president designated the second Sunday in May as a day to honor the nation's mothers.

DIRECTIONS: Cross out the irrelevant details in the following paragraph:

> The Christian celebration of Easter and the Jewish festival of Passover usually occur in April. April is often a rainy month, but the rain is good for flowers. Both holidays include treasure hunts. Brightly colored eggs are hunted at Easter. I like red eggs best, but yellow are nice, too. At Passover, the children search for a hidden piece of matzo called the *afikomen*. Several different kinds of matzos can be found in the supermarket. These holidays are a joyful time of year for both children and adults.

4–24. USING VARIETY IN SENTENCE LENGTH

A paragraph that consists of only short sentences can seem brusque and choppy, as in this example:

> I have a cousin named Brian. He is an unusual teenager. Brian is smart. But he does not do well in school. Brian will not work hard at things that do not interest him. He has amazing knowledge about some things. Brian is an expert on the history of baseball. He knows the name of every player on every team from the beginning. He spouts little-known statistics. They will astound you. So will Brian.

This paragraph would flow more smoothly and be more readable with some long sentences interspersed among the short ones.

> I have a cousin named Brian, who is an unusual teenager. Brian is smart, but he does not do well in school. Brian will not work hard at things that do not interest him, but he has amazing knowledge about some things. Brian is an expert on the history of baseball and knows the name of every player on every team from the beginning. He spouts little-known statistics that will astound you. So will Brian.

DIRECTIONS: The following paragraph consists mostly of short, choppy sentences. Rewrite the paragraph on the lines below (and continue on the back of this sheet, if necessary). Combine and rearrange some of the sentences so that there is a variety of short and long sentences.

> Competition is both good and bad. It can motivate people. They will try harder. They will achieve greater goals. Standards will become higher. Too much emphasis on competition can be destructive. People become enemies. They try to outdo one another. This can lead to insensitivity toward others. Competition is helpful. It should be retained. It should also be kept under control.

_____

_____

_____

_____

4–25. USING VARIETY IN SENTENCE STRUCTURE

A paragraph can be improved by using a variety of sentence structures.

> • A **simple sentence** contains one independent clause.
>   *Frankie's baseball team is called the Pirates.*
> • A **compound sentence** contains more than one independent clause.
>   *The Pirates just had their best season ever, but they fell one game short of winning first place in the league.*
> • A **complex sentence** contains one independent clause and at least one dependent clause.
>   *Although they are happy with their showing this season, the Pirates are determined to do even better next year.*

These examples can be combined into a paragraph that contains all three types of sentences.

> Frankie's baseball team is called the Pirates. The Pirates just had their best season ever, but they fell one game short of winning first place in the league. Although they are happy with their showing this season, the Pirates are determined to do even better next year.

DIRECTIONS: Write a paragraph that contains all three types of sentence structure: simple, compound, and complex. Choose one of the following topic sentences:

- There are some things about myself that I would like to change.
- There are some things about my family that I would like to change.
- There are some things about my school that I would like to change.
- There are some things about my country that I would like to change.

Copy the topic sentence you have chosen on the lines below. Then write a paragraph developing that topic. Your paragraph should include all three kinds of sentence structure as well as a variety of long and short sentences. (Continue your paragraph on the back of this sheet.)

_____

_____

_____

_____

_____

4–26. Using a Variety of Sentence Types

You can use a variety of sentence types to make your paragraphs more interesting and more fun to read.

- **Declarative sentences** make a statement.
    Pat is going to eat spaghetti and meatballs for dinner.
- **Interrogative sentences** ask questions. These can sometimes be used effectively in the topic sentence to spark the reader's interest.
    Can you guess what we are having for dinner tonight?
- **Exclamatory sentences** make an exclamation or command. This type of sentence can be used effectively to stimulate reader interest.
    Eat your dinner!

DIRECTIONS: The paragraph that follows contains only declarative sentences. Can you make it more interesting for a reader by changing some of these declarative sentences to interrogative and exclamatory sentences? Rewrite the paragraph on the lines below (and continue on the back of this sheet).

High school students often work after school. Some kids have to get jobs because they or their families desperately need the money. For others, it is a choice—a chance to earn extra cash. Surveys show, however, that on the average, teens who work after school do not perform so well in their classes and get poorer grades. Students should evaluate the possible negative effects of after-school employment before they make a decision to look for a job.

_____

_____

_____

_____

_____

_____

_____

4–27. Using the Writing Process: Prewriting

Most people wouldn't think of taking a trip without advance planning. Any project requires preparation if it is to succeed. The same is true of writing. Even experienced writers who have been producing written products for many years usually do some sort of **prewriting activity,** even if it just involves organizing the material in their minds. Student writers, however, will find written planning much more helpful. A **brainstorming list** is useful for compiling and organizing the information in a paragraph.

DIRECTIONS:

1. Prepare a **brainstorming list** for a paragraph describing a piece of sports or musical equipment, such as a football, hockey stick, tennis racket, piano keyboard, or snare drum. Write the item you will be describing on the line below.

    _____

2. In the first column below, write words and phrases you can use to describe the physical appearance of the object, such as its shape, size, color, or what it is made of. Include some **sensory words** and at least one **simile.**

3. In the second column below, write words and phrases you can use to describe how the item is used.

BRAINSTORMING LIST	
Description of Item	**How It Is Used**

4. Write a **topic sentence** for the beginning of the paragraph. Try to make it original and interesting. Sometimes a question will catch the reader's attention.

    _____

5. Write a **concluding sentence** for the end of your paragraph that sums up the topic or restates it in a different way.

4–28. USING THE WRITING PROCESS: WRITING THE FIRST DRAFT

DIRECTIONS: Write the **first draft** of a paragraph describing a piece of sports or musical equipment.

1. Copy the **topic sentence** from your brainstorming list.

2. Begin to **develop the topic.** Describe the appearance of the object in two or three sentences. Use descriptive words and phrases from your brainstorming list.

3. **Develop the topic further** by describing how the item is used in one or two sentences. Use the words and phrases on your brainstorming list.

4. Copy the **concluding sentence** from your brainstorming list.

Write your paragraph below. This is just a first draft, so don't be too concerned about spelling or grammar at this point. Concentrate on getting your thoughts down on paper.

_____

_____

_____

_____

_____

_____

_____

_____

_____

_____

(Continue on the back of this sheet, if necessary.)

4–29. USING THE WRITING PROCESS: REVISING AND WRITING A FINAL COPY

DIRECTIONS: Correct and revise the first draft of your paragraph. Make the corrections right on your draft copy. If you know proofreading symbols, use them wherever they would be helpful.

1. Does your **topic sentence** correctly state the subject? Can you make it more exciting with vivid language or a question?

2. Do you **develop the topic** in a logical sequence, first describing the appearance of the object and then its use?

3. Does the paragraph **stay on the topic**? Take out anything that does not relate to the subject.

4. Can you add **adjectives and sensory words** to make the description more vivid?

5. Does your description contain at least one **simile**? If not, add one.

6. Does your **concluding sentence** sum up or restate the topic?

7. Is your **spelling** correct? Consult a dictionary if necessary.

When your paragraph is as good as you can make it, write the final copy below. Indent at the beginning of the paragraph.

_____

_____

_____

_____

_____

_____

_____

_____

(Continue on the back of this sheet, if necessary.)

WRITING PARAGRAPHS PRACTICE TEST

Name _____ Date _____

Practice Test: Writing Paragraphs

DIRECTIONS: Everyone has dreams and goals for the future. You are going to write a paragraph about one such dream—something you would like to be or accomplish or have. It could be something you have a good chance of getting, but it might also be a goal that doesn't seem possible, at least right now. Either one would be fun to write about.

To write your paragraph, follow these four steps:

1. On the page labeled "Prewriting," brainstorm ideas for your paragraph as follows:

   a. Make a list of words and phrases that describe this goal.

   b. Make a list of words and phrases that explain why it is important to you.

   c. Make a list of words and phrases that tell what you need to do to achieve it.

   d. Write a topic sentence and a concluding sentence.

2. On a separate sheet of paper, write the first draft of your paragraph. Be sure to use the middle portion of the paragraph to develop the topic.

3. Revise and edit your first draft, using the following checklist:

CHECKLIST

❑ Does your topic sentence introduce the subject? Can you make it more interesting with vivid language or as a question or exclamation?

❑ Do you develop the topic in a logical sequence, describing the goal, explaining why it is important to you, and then telling what you need to do to achieve it?

❑ Can you add more adjectives and sensory words to make your writing vivid?

❑ Can you add one simile to create interest?

❑ Do you stay on the subject throughout the paragraph? Are there any irrelevant details that should be cut?

❑ Do you vary your sentences in length and structure?

❑ Correct any run-on sentences or fragments.

❑ Do your subjects and verbs agree?

❑ Do you use tense consistently?

❑ Are all words spelled correctly? Consult a dictionary if necessary.

---

4. When your paragraph is as perfect as you can make it, write the final copy on a separate sheet of paper.

PRACTICE TEST: WRITING PARAGRAPHS *(continued)*

Prewriting

DIRECTIONS:

1. Brainstorm ideas for your paragraph on the lines below. You may do this in any way that works for you. One good idea is to write a list of words and phrases that describe your goal, another list to use in explaining its importance to you, and a third list of words and phrases that tell what you must do to reach the goal.

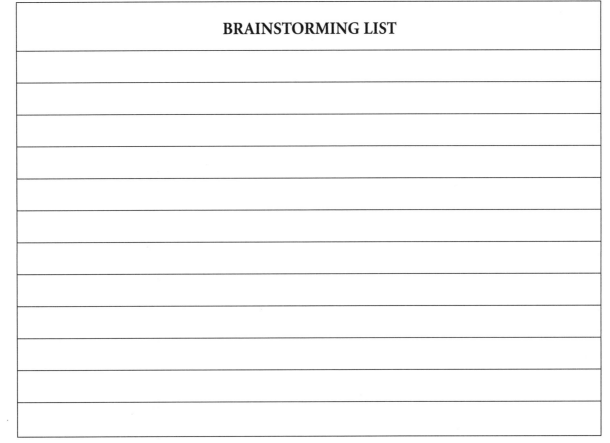

BRAINSTORMING LIST

2. Write a topic sentence on the lines provided below.

_____

_____

3. Write a concluding sentence on the lines provided below.

_____

_____

PRACTICE TEST: WRITING PARAGRAPHS (continued)

Student Samples

DIRECTIONS: Rate the paragraphs with a score from 1 (lowest) to 6 (highest).

PARAGRAPH A

I'd like to be a dentist. That's what my Uncle Joe does. A dentist has lots of cool equipment. There are Xray machines and drills. Uncle Joe has a condo in Florida. I like to go there in the winter. It's fun to hang out at the beach. That's my secret goal—to be a dentist.

Score _____

PARAGRAPH B

Are you one of those people who are afraid to visit the dentist? You won't be fearful at my office when I become a dentist. I've learned that dentistry today is as pain-free as a stroll in the park. Dentists have all sorts of modern equipment and drugs that make regular dental care easy and comfortable. I long to do something with my life that benefits humanity. Dentists provide a valuable service to the public. I understand that the path to becoming a doctor of dentistry is difficult and requires intense study as well as years of preparation in college and dental school. I am prepared to work hard to achieve my goal of becoming a dentist.

Score _____

PRACTICE TEST: WRITING PARAGRAPHS *(continued)*

Scoring Guide

SCORE	Unsatisfactory—1	Insufficient—2
Content	Attempts to respond to prompt, but provides few details; may only paraphrase prompt	Presents fragmented information OR may be very repetitive OR may be very undeveloped
Organization	Has no clear organization OR consists of a single statement	Is very disorganized; ideas are weakly connected OR the response is too brief to detect organization
Sentence Structure	Little or no control over sentence boundaries and sentence structure; word choice may be incorrect in much or all of the response	Little control over sentence boundaries and sentence structure; word choice may often be incorrect
Grammar, Usage, and Mechanics	Many errors in grammar or usage (such as tense inconsistency, lack of subject-verb agreement), spelling, and punctuation severely interfere with understanding	Errors in grammar or usage (such as inconsistency, lack of subject-verb agreement), spelling, and punctuation interfere with understanding in much of the response

SCORE	Uneven—3	Sufficient—4
Content	Presents some clear information, but is list-like, undeveloped, or repetitive OR offers no more than a well-written beginning	Develops information with some details
Organization	Is unevenly organized; the paragraph may be disjointed	Is organized with ideas that are generally related but has few or no transitions
Sentence Structure	Exhibits uneven control over sentence boundaries and sentence structure; may have some incorrect word choices	Exhibits control over sentence boundaries and sentence structure, but sentences and word choices may be simple and unvaried
Grammar, Usage, and Mechanics	Errors in grammar or usage (such as tense inconsistency, lack of subject-verb agreement), spelling, and punctuation sometimes interfere with understanding	Errors in grammar or usage (such as tense inconsistency, lack of subject-verb agreement), spelling, and punctuation do not interfere with understanding

SCORE	Skillful—5	Excellent—6
Content	Develops and shapes information with details in parts of the paragraph	Develops and shapes information with well-chosen details across the paragraph
Organization	Is clearly organized, but may lack some transitions and/or have lapses in continuity	Is well organized with strong transitions
Sentence Structure	Exhibits some variety in sentence structure and some good word choices	Sustains variety in sentence structure and exhibits good word choice
Grammar, Usage, and Mechanics	Errors in grammar, spelling, and punctuation do not interfere with understanding	Errors in grammar, spelling, and punctuation are few and do not interfere with understanding

ESSAY-WRITING TECHNIQUES

Standardized Testing Information

Standardized writing tests evaluate students on their ability to state a theme and develop it in a clear and logical manner, leading to a satisfactory conclusion. Three types of essays are required: **expository/informational, narrative/imaginative,** and **persuasive.** Some tests require students to write samples of each of these; most tests ask for only one.

Most standardized tests encourage students to use the steps of the writing process: **prewriting** (brainstorming, clustering, outlining, and so forth), writing a **first draft,** making **revisions,** and writing a **final copy.** Even where these steps are not specified on the test itself, students who are well trained in their use will be able to achieve a higher-scoring product than those who are not.

Standardized writing tests usually present one or more topics on which to write (sometimes called prompts or strands). Students are expected to produce a final copy that meets grade standards for achievement. Scorers are given a rubric that lists the points on which the samples should be evaluated. Among the items usually listed are the following:

- Clear beginning, middle, and end
- Logical progression of writing
- A response that stays on topic
- Use of details to support that topic
- Use of a variety of word and sentence patterns with correct spelling and usage of high-frequency, grade-appropriate language
- Correct, grade-appropriate capitalization and punctuation

Due to nationwide concern about the inability of students to write clearly and grammatically, many school districts now mandate regularly scheduled writing assignments. This is all to the good, but writing without guidance and instruction has only limited results. The worksheets and teacher lesson plans in Sections 5 through 9 of this resource provide the instruction and guidance necessary to prepare every student to write a competent essay and offer a wealth of suggestions and activities to augment the teacher's own writing instruction. Use of the four-step writing process is emphasized at all times.

Teacher Preparation and Lessons

The activities in Section 5 provide students with practice in developing an essay. The activities cover the following topics: (1) organizing thoughts logically through prewriting activities, (2) writing an introductory paragraph, (3) developing the topic, (4) staying on the subject, and (5) writing a concluding paragraph. Students are given practice in writing simple three-paragraph essays as well as five-paragraph essays. You may wish to precede this section with definitions of the three types of essays—narrative, informative, and persuasive. The PRACTICE TEST on pages 184 to 187 assesses students' ability to apply their language and writing skills in an essay similar to one they might be asked to write on a standardized test.

ACTIVITIES 5–1 through 5–6 focus on organizing thoughts and ideas with **prewriting activities.** Ask the class for examples of activities where planning is necessary. Elicit items such as taking a vacation or trip, cooking a meal, choosing a college, going shopping, preparing a strategy for a football game, and so on. Elicit some advantages of planning, such as saving time, avoiding errors, not forgetting items or steps, and being more efficient. Discuss the types of lists and notes that are made beforehand. Point out that this sort of preparation is advantageous when writing an essay, too. Elicit the kinds of prewriting activities that can be helpful, such as making lists, doing research, creating outlines, discussing your topic, and conducting interviews. Distribute **Activity 5–1 Brainstorming (Part One).** Read and discuss the description of brainstorming, then read and discuss the directions for preparing a brainstorming list. When students have completed their brainstorming lists, have them share their lists aloud with the class, exchange them, or pass them around. Distribute **Activity 5–2 Brainstorming (Part Two).** Read and discuss the directions for preparing each brainstorming list. When students have completed their lists, have them work in small groups to share and discuss their lists.

Distribute **Activity 5–3 Clustering (Part One).** Read and discuss the description of clustering and the example. Read and, if necessary, clarify the directions. When students have completed the activity, have them share their clusters aloud or exchange papers. Distribute **Activity 5–4 Clustering (Part Two).** Review the definition of clustering and discuss the suggestions set forth. Read the directions. When students have completed the activity, have them share and discuss their clusters in small groups.

Ask which students have ever written an outline for an essay or composition. Write the structure of an essay on the board, as follows:

> Planning a Trip
> I. Deciding on a destination
>   a. Read brochures
>   b. Research the Internet
>   c. Visit a travel agent
> II. Deciding on a method of travel
>   a. Car
>   b. Train
>   c. Bus
>   d. Plane
> III. Packing
>   a. Number and sizes of suitcases
>   b. Clothes and personal items
>   c. Other items

Point out that the title of the outline is the subject of the essay and will be presented in the introductory paragraph. Each of the three Roman numerals represents a supporting point, and the lettered items underneath each supporting point are the details that will be used to present that point. Distribute **Activity 5–5 Outlining (Part One).** Read and discuss the explanation and example of a simple outline. Read and discuss the directions. When students have completed their outlines, collect the papers, read several aloud, and discuss them. Distribute **Activity 5–6 Outlining (Part Two).** Read and discuss the description and example of a more formal outline. Read and discuss the directions. When students have completed the activity, have each student exchange papers with another student for reading and discussion.

ACTIVITIES 5–7 through 5–12 deal with **writing an introductory paragraph.** Review the purpose of a topic sentence in a paragraph. Point out that in an essay, the topic is stated in the first (introductory) paragraph. Read the following paragraph to the class:

> *Are you a movie buff? I am the emperor of movie fans. Believe it or not, I'd rather see a film than play even the most exciting computer game. That's why I can offer some good advice on how to choose the next movie you attend.*

Identify this as the introductory paragraph (topic paragraph) of an essay. Elicit that the subject of this essay is "how to choose a movie." Point out that while the topic is often stated in the first sentence, it can sometimes, as in this example, be effective to delay stating the topic until the end of the paragraph. Distribute **Activity 5–7 Introductory Paragraphs (Part One).** Read and discuss the explanation and directions. Stress that only introductory paragraphs, not complete essays, are required. When students have completed their paragraphs, collect the papers. Read aloud several examples of each paragraph, and discuss them. Distribute **Activity 5–8 Introductory Paragraphs (Part Two).** Read and discuss the directions. When students have completed their paragraphs, have samples read aloud and discussed.

Review that the purpose of an introductory paragraph is to state the topic. Point out that there are ways to use the introductory paragraph to generate interest for the reader. Read the following paragraph aloud to the class:

> *Are you strong and courageous? Do you like excitement and adventure? If so, you will have a chance to test yourself at one of the adventure summer camps that are located around the country.*

Identify this as the introductory paragraph of an essay. Ask what technique the writer uses to provoke the reader's interest, and elicit that it is the use of a question. Distribute **Activity 5–9 Introductory Paragraphs Beginning with a Question.** Read and discuss the explanation, example, and directions for completing the activity. When the students have finished writing their introductory paragraphs with a question, have samples read aloud and discussed.

Tell students that a second way to attract the reader's attention is to begin with a startling statement or exclamation. Distribute **Activity 5–10 Introductory Paragraphs Beginning with an Exclamation.** Read aloud the sample paragraph. Discuss how the exclamation at the beginning sparks reader interest. Read and discuss the directions. When the assignment has been completed, have each student exchange papers with a partner to share and discuss paragraphs.

Tell students that another way to attract the reader's attention is to begin with an anecdote (story) in the introductory paragraph. Distribute **Activity 5–11 Introductory Paragraphs Beginning with an Anecdote.** Read the sample paragraph aloud and discuss how the use of the anecdote sparks reader interest. Read and discuss the directions. When students have completed their paragraphs, have samples read aloud and discussed.

Read a familiar quotation to the class and ask them to identify the author or speaker (for example, "We hold these truths to be self-evident; that all men are created equal" by Thomas Jefferson). Point out that such a quote or a bit of dialogue (for example, "I'll never go there again") can be an interesting and attention-getting way to begin an essay. Distribute **Activity 5–12 Introductory Paragraphs with a Quote.** Read and discuss the sample paragraph. Read and discuss the directions. When students have completed the two paragraphs of the activity, have samples of each read aloud and discussed.

ACTIVITIES 5–13 through 5–16 focus on developing the topic. Write the following on the board:

Topic
Supporting Point #1
Supporting Point #2
Supporting Point #3

Circle the word *Topic* and point out that this refers to the subject of the essay, which is presented in the introductory paragraph. Circle *Supporting Point #1, Supporting Point #2,* and *Supporting Point #3.* Elicit that these are used to develop the topic and that these can be included in one middle paragraph in a short essay or by using two, three, or more developmental paragraphs in a more detailed essay. Point out that various methods can be used to develop the topic. Distribute **Activity 5–13 Developing the Topic: Description.** Read and discuss the information and sample developmental paragraph. Read and discuss the directions. Read the introductory paragraph aloud, then instruct students to develop the topic in a middle paragraph. When the activity has been completed, read several samples aloud and discuss them.

Tell the students that listing and detailing examples is another excellent way to develop a topic. Distribute **Activity 5–14 Developing the Topic: Examples.** Read and discuss the explanation and sample developmental paragraph. Read and discuss the directions. When the activity has been completed, have students work in small groups to share and discuss their developmental paragraphs.

Distribute **Activity 5–15 Developing the Topic: Classification.** Read the explanation and sample paragraph. Discuss how the topic is classified by sections of town to develop the topic. Read and discuss the directions. When the students have completed their paragraphs, have several samples read aloud and discussed.

Distribute **Activity 5–16 Developing the Topic: Choosing the Right Technique.** Other techniques can be used to develop a topic, including definition, sequence, and comparison and contrast. Discuss the examples of which essay topics lend themselves to which type of development technique. If necessary, refer back to the detailed descriptions and examples of these techniques in Section 4. Read and discuss the directions. When the students have completed the two developmental paragraphs, have several samples of each paragraph read aloud.

ACTIVITIES 5–17 and 5–18 focus on **concluding paragraphs.** Distribute **Activity 5–17 Concluding Paragraphs (Part One).** Read aloud and discuss the definition and purposes of a concluding paragraph. Read the example of a concluding paragraph, and discuss how it is successful in meeting the objectives that are listed. Read and discuss the directions. When students have completed the exercise, have several of the paragraphs read aloud and discussed. Distribute **Activity 5–18 Concluding Paragraphs (Part Two).** Review the objectives of a concluding paragraph. Read and discuss the directions. When students are finished with the activity, read several of the paragraphs aloud and discuss their effectiveness.

ACTIVITIES 5–19 and 5–20 focus on the structure and organization of a complete essay. Distribute **Activity 5–19 Organizing Your Essay: Focus.** Read the explanation of how to focus on the specific topic being discussed in an essay. Discuss how topics can sound similar but actually have different purposes and need a different focus. Here are some examples of similar but different subjects that you can present to the students in addition to the one used on the worksheet.

An Unusual Day vs. An Unusual Day at School
The Civil War vs. Great Battles of the Civil War
Types of Bicycles vs. Types of Mountain Bikes

Discuss the differences in each pair of topics and how these differences might affect the focus of each essay. Read and discuss the directions. Point out that this assignment calls for just a list of details, not a paragraph. When students have completed the assignment, have several examples of each list read aloud.

Distribute **Activity 5–20 Organizing Your Essay: Order.** Read and discuss the most common types of order used in essay writing. Emphasize the importance of using the same type of order throughout the essay. Read and discuss the directions. Point out that the directions call for a single paragraph. When students have completed their paragraphs, have several samples read aloud and discussed for each category of order.

ACTIVITIES 5–21 through 5–26 focus on writing three-paragraph and five-paragraph essays. Distribute **Activity 5–21 Writing a Three-Paragraph Essay (Brainstorming).** Review the structure of a three-paragraph essay (introductory paragraph, middle developmental paragraph, and concluding paragraph). Read and discuss the list of essay topics. Read and discuss the directions for completing the brainstorming list. When students have completed their lists, have them work in small groups to share and discuss their lists. Distribute **Activity 5–22 Writing a Three-Paragraph Essay (First Draft).** Read and discuss the directions; point out to students the usefulness of referring to their brainstorming list when writing the essay. Emphasize that this is a first draft. When students have completed their first drafts, have several samples read aloud and discussed. Distribute **Activity 5–23 Writing a Three-Paragraph Essay (Revising and Writing a Final Copy).** Discuss the methods and purposes of the revision process. Distribute a list of proofreading symbols (page 307). Read the specific suggestions for revision on the worksheet and instruct students to check off each one as they complete it. Read the directions for completing the final copy of the essay. When students have completed their essays, have several samples read aloud and discussed, focusing on possible additional revisions. Distribute **Activity 5–24 Writing a Five-Paragraph Essay (Outline).** Read and discuss the directions for organizing an essay in five paragraphs. Read and discuss the directions for preparing an outline for the essay "An Appealing Career." Point out that one possible format for the outline is presented on the worksheet. When students have completed their outlines, have each student exchange papers with a partner to share and discuss outlines. Distribute **Activity 5–25 Writing a Five-Paragraph Essay (First Draft).** Read and discuss the directions, emphasizing the explanation and purpose of each paragraph. Point out that this writing will be only a first draft. When students have completed their first drafts, have several samples read aloud and discussed. Distribute **Activity 5–26 Writing a Five-Paragraph Essay (Revising and Writing a Final Copy).** Read the directions for revising and suggest that students use proofreading symbols. Read the checklist carefully, and discuss how each point is important to a successful essay. Read the directions for writing the final copy. When students have completed the assignment, have students meet in small groups to read and discuss their essays.

Practice Test: Essay-Writing Techniques

The sample student essays A and B on page 186 are rated 6 and 2, respectively.

Essay A focuses on the topic with ample supporting ideas and examples, and it has a logical structure. The five paragraphs convey a sense of wholeness and completeness. The essay is well organized and demonstrates a mature command of language. A few errors in spelling do not interfere with understanding. This essay scored a 6.

Essay B states a topic and offers some supporting ideas and examples, but the development is uneven and disorganized, and many of the details are irrelevant to the subject. Errors in sentence structure, punctuation, and spelling interfere with understanding in much of the response. This essay scored a 2.

Name _____   Date _____

5–1. Brainstorming (Part One)

Wouldn't it be nice to sit down at the computer and tap out a fine piece of writing off the top of one's head? Sorry, but it just doesn't work that way! Planning is an essential ingredient for success in any undertaking, and writing is no exception. A good essay or story does not just happen. It is the result of careful prewriting activities that help you organize your thoughts and ideas before you begin to write. Brainstorming is an excellent method for organizing ideas, and it works for most people. One way to brainstorm is to engage in a group discussion in which everybody can share ideas about a topic. When working alone, a brainstorming list will help you prepare for a writing assignment.

There are various ways to set up a brainstorming list. Here is one useful model.

DIRECTIONS: Complete a **brainstorming list** for an essay on the subject "The Perfect School," as follows:

1. Next to "Main topic," write *The Perfect School.*

2. In the first column, list three different aspects of a school (for example, *building, location, classrooms, teachers, administration, students, courses, after-school programs*). These are the subtopics you will use for your supporting details.

3. In the second column, next to each subtopic, write words and phrases you can use to describe this item.

4. In the third column, list reasons why each item is important. (You don't need to write sentences here—just words and phrases.)

Main topic: _____

Aspects of a School	Description	Importance
1.		
2.		
3.		

5–2. BRAINSTORMING (PART TWO)

A. DIRECTIONS: Prepare a **brainstorming list** for an essay on the subject "Careers That Interest Me." In the first column, list three careers that you find interesting. In the second column, write words and phrases that describe that career. In the third column, write words and phrases that describe things about yourself that make this a good career choice.

Career	Description of Career	Description of Myself
1.		
2.		
3.		

B. DIRECTIONS: Prepare a **brainstorming list** for an essay on the subject "Keeping Up with the News." In the first column, list three sources for current news (for example, *newspapers, magazines, radio, TV, word of mouth*). In the second column, list words and phrases that can be used to describe the advantages of this news source. In the third column, list words and phrases that describe the disadvantages of this news source.

News Source	Advantages	Disadvantages
1.		
2.		
3.		

Name _____   Date _____

5–3. Clustering (part one)

Clustering is a popular method to use when preparing to write an essay. It helps a writer identify, organize, and focus on the main topic, subtopics, and supporting details. It is even fun to do. Just follow these easy steps:

1. Draw a large circle on a piece of paper. Write the **subject** of the essay or story in the middle of the circle in big letters.

2. Think about the **main points** you want to make about this subject. Using somewhat smaller print, jot down these main points (supporting details) in different parts of the circle around the subject.

3. Near each of the main points, use even smaller lettering to write **words and phrases that describe it.**

Here is an example of clustering for an essay called "Weight Control."

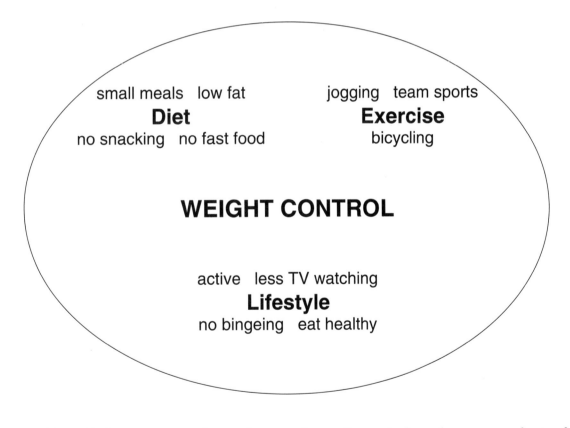

DIRECTIONS: On a separate sheet of paper, draw a large circle and prepare a cluster for an essay called "Baseball." Use different sizes of lettering or different-colored pens for the subject, the main points, and the descriptions.

5–4. CLUSTERING (PART TWO)

Planning is essential to good writing. **Clustering** is an enjoyable technique that helps a writer focus on the subject and organize supporting details. Here are some useful points for clustering:

1. Clustering is an exercise in free association. Put down *all* the ideas that come into your head as you think about the subject. You won't use them all, but the more you have, the better your choice will be.

2. Don't stop too soon! Give yourself at least five to ten minutes to prepare a cluster. Some great ideas could be just around the corner in your mind, and you don't want to miss them by stopping prematurely.

3. Set the subject in the middle of the cluster. Write the main points or supporting facts around it. Then, put down as many descriptive words and phrases as you can think of that relate to each main point.

4. Use different-sized lettering (or different-colored pens) for subject, main points, and descriptive words.

DIRECTIONS: In the circle below, prepare a cluster for an essay called "Life in the Twenty-Second Century."

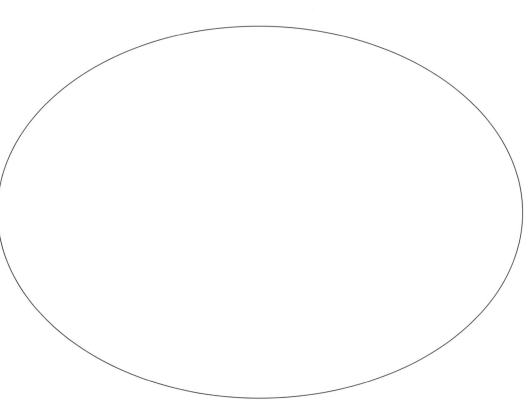

5–5. Outlining (Part One)

A simple **outline** is easy to develop and helps to organize an essay in a clear and logical way. Here is an example of a simple outline for an essay called "Positive Results from Negative Experiences."

1. Topic statement: It is possible for negative experiences to have positive results.
   a. Opening sentence: Good can come out of bad!
2. Types of negative experiences
   a. In the family
   b. In school
   c. With friends
   d. Other situations
3. Causes
   a. Unrealistic expectations—your own or those of others
   b. Carelessness—your own or that of others
   c. Insensitivity—your own or that of others
   d. Unlucky coincidences
4. Positive results
   a. Learning to modify expectations
   b. Not making the same mistake twice
   c. Gaining more insight into yourself or others
   d. Learning to evaluate a situation better
5. Conclusion

In the essay, point 1 will be developed as an introductory paragraph. Points 2, 3, and 4 state main points, each of which will be developed as a paragraph. A concluding paragraph can be developed from point 5.

DIRECTIONS: On a separate sheet of paper, write simple outlines for each of the following essays, using the model shown above.

1. City Life vs. Suburban Living

2. My Favorite Spectator Sport

5–6. Outlining (part two)

A formal **outline** takes time to prepare, but it can make essay writing much easier since it provides the writer with form, structure, and details that can then be smoothly incorporated into a well-written essay. Here is an example of a formal outline for an essay on the American Revolution.

I. Causes
   A. Economic
      1. Growth of farms and industry in the American colonies
      2. British merchants' desire for exclusive colonial markets
   B. Social
      1. Development of a distinctly American culture
      2. Growth of a desire for independence in the colonies
   C. Political
      1. Taxation without representation
         a. The Stamp Act
         b. The Townshend Acts
      2. American refusal to comply with British regulations
         a. Boston Tea Party
      3. Stationing of British troops in American cities
         a. Boston Massacre
      4. Convening of Continental Congress
         a. Declaration of Independence
II. Major Battles
   A. Lexington and Concord
   B. Bunker Hill
   C. Saratoga
   D. Trenton
   E. Yorktown
III. Results
   A. Treaty of Paris
   B. Recognition of the United States as a nation
   C. Establishment of a democratic government
      1. The Constitutional Convention

DIRECTIONS: On a separate sheet of paper, write a formal outline for an essay on each of the following subjects:

1. Immigrants in America

2. How to Stay Healthy

5–7. Introductory Paragraphs (Part One)

The introductory paragraph of an essay tells the reader what to expect. An effective introductory paragraph should fulfill the following purposes:

- Get the readers' attention and make them want to find out more.
- State the main idea immediately.
- Set the tone of the essay (for example, humorous, serious, exciting).

DIRECTIONS: Keeping the points listed above in mind, write an introductory paragraph for each of the topics below. (Do not write a complete essay; write only an introductory paragraph.)

National Sports of Different Countries

_____

_____

_____

_____

_____

_____

_____

_____

The Purposes of Political Parties

_____

_____

_____

_____

_____

_____

_____

_____

5–8. INTRODUCTORY PARAGRAPHS (PART TWO)

DIRECTIONS: Write an introductory paragraph for each of the topics below. (Do not write a complete essay; write only the opening paragraph.) When writing your paragraph, remember that an introductory paragraph should do the following:

- Get the readers' attention and interest.
- Introduce the main topic.
- Set the tone of the essay.

Books That Made a Difference in My Life

_____

_____

_____

_____

_____

_____

_____

The Current Music Scene

_____

_____

_____

_____

_____

_____

_____

5–9. INRODUCTORY PARAGRAPHS WITH A QUESTION

One time-tested technique that essay writers can use to spark a reader's attention and interest is beginning with a question, as in the opening paragraph shown below. Notice the provocative, attention-getting question that begins the paragraph.

> Would you like to be a leader instead of just a follower? It is easier than you think. All you need do is learn a few proven techniques.

DIRECTIONS: Write an introductory paragraph beginning with a question for an essay on each of the topics below. (Do not write the complete essay; just write the introductory paragraph.)

How to Protect the Environment

_____

_____

_____

_____

_____

_____

_____

An Interesting Time in History

_____

_____

_____

_____

_____

_____

_____

5–10. INTRODUCTORY PARAGRAPHS WITH AN EXCLAMATION

An effective way to grab the attention of the reader is to begin the introductory paragraph with an exclamation—perhaps a startling or surprising statement, as in this example:

> Break a leg! That doesn't sound like a kindly wish, but it is what actors routinely say to one another when it is time to step onto the stage. There are other statements that people commonly use that don't mean what they seem to suggest.

"Break a leg!" is a startling statement, one that is sure to make the reader want to read on.

DIRECTIONS: Write an introductory paragraph that begins with an exclamation—a startling or surprising statement—for each of the essay topics below. (Do not write the complete essay; just write the introductory paragraph.)

Following a Dream

_____

_____

_____

_____

_____

How to Stop Being a TV Addict

_____

_____

_____

_____

_____

5–11. INTRODUCTORY PARAGRAPHS WITH AN ANECDOTE

Everybody loves to hear a story. Beginning an essay with a brief story or anecdote can spark a reader's interest, as in this example:

> He was a poor, sickly boy who was always in pain. He did not learn to read well until he was eighteen years old. Yet, he grew up to become president of the United States. His name was James Knox Polk.

The anecdote in this introductory paragraph makes the reader want to know more.

DIRECTIONS: Write an introductory paragraph beginning with an anecdote for an essay on each of the topics below. (Do not write a complete essay; just write the opening paragraph.)

Memories of My Childhood

_____

_____

_____

_____

_____

_____

An Exciting Journey

_____

_____

_____

_____

_____

_____

5–12. Introductory Paragraphs with a Quote

A quotation or a bit of dialogue is an interesting and attention-getting way to begin an introductory paragraph, as in the following example:

> "Give me liberty or give me death!" These passionate words rang out in St. John's Church in Richmond, Virginia, on March 30, 1775. The person making this defiant call for freedom was named Patrick Henry. His speech was one of many exciting incidents that led to the American Revolution.

This powerful quotation will surely grab the interest of a reader, but any sort of quote can have a similar result. For example, "'You are forbidden to leave the house!' Dad ordered" or "Was that a car crash I heard?" could be equally effective beginnings.

DIRECTIONS: Write an introductory paragraph with a quote for each of the following topics. (Do not write the complete essay here; just write the opening paragraph.)

Important Inventions of the Twentieth Century

_____

_____

_____

_____

_____

_____

Interesting Facts About My Town

_____

_____

_____

_____

_____

_____

5–13. DEVELOPING THE TOPIC: DESCRIPTION

The paragraphs that follow the introductory paragraph are used to develop the topic of the essay. A short three-paragraph essay will develop the topic with one paragraph between the introductory and concluding paragraphs. Longer essays with more details will need more developmental paragraphs. Regardless of how many there are, the purpose of the **developmental paragraph** or paragraphs is to **explain, describe, or prove the topic** that was stated at the beginning. Some essays lend themselves to development through description, as in this middle paragraph of an essay about a new house.

> The design is modern ranch style—long and low, blending into the surroundings. There is a double-door entry into a square hall with pale green wallpaper and bright Mexican tiles on the floor. The large living room is to the right and a family-sized dining room is on the left. Both have large windows that bring the openness and color of the outdoors into the house. The same is true of the three spacious bedrooms in the rear, each of which has an adjoining tiled bathroom that is reminiscent of ancient Roman baths.

DIRECTIONS: Read the introductory paragraph shown below. Write a developmental paragraph using description to follow it.

Is there one place in the world where you feel happiest and safest? For me, it is my own room.

_____

_____

_____

_____

_____

_____

_____

_____

_____

_____

5–14. DEVELOPING THE TOPIC: EXAMPLES

A good way to develop a topic is to give supporting examples. In a longer essay, a whole paragraph can be used for each example. In a short three-paragraph essay, all the supporting examples will be stated in the middle paragraph, as in this example of a middle paragraph on the value of team sports.

> Team sports promote better school spirit because they involve players, cheerleaders, coaches, teachers, and students in a common goal: to play well and win games. They also help bring a community together, as parents and other residents offer volunteer services and attend games to cheer on their school teams. Most important, they give young people opportunities to grow stronger in body and mind while they learn to work with others in a team effort.

Note how the writer offers three supporting examples—one involving the school, another about the community, and the last concerning individual students—all set out with specific details.

DIRECTIONS: Read the following introductory paragraph for an essay. On the lines below, write a middle paragraph that uses examples to develop the topic stated in the first paragraph.

I'll never forget October 10! It wasn't a holiday or my birthday; it was something even better. On that afternoon, our varsity team, the Vikings, turned what seemed like a sure defeat into victory.

_____

_____

_____

_____

_____

_____

_____

5–15. Developing the Topic: Classification

Some essays lend themselves to development by using supportive details that classify, as in this example, the middle paragraph of an essay called "Neighborhoods of Hillston."

> The oldest section is called Westside. It is a quiet area with big two-story homes on spacious lots. Huge oak trees line the streets, and many of the front yards are graced by colorful gardens. Many business and professional people live there. On the other side of Main Street is a neighborhood called East End. The homes there are newer, smaller, and mostly ranch style. Young families own these homes, so driveways and yards are often littered with bikes and strollers. North of East End, there is a trailer camp that is the town eyesore, with broken-down trailers and not a tree in sight. There is a hopeless feeling in the air of Trailertown. Many of the people who have to live there are unable to find work.

Note how this paragraph develops the topic by classifying the town of Hillston into three neighborhoods (Westside, East End, and Trailertown) and vividly showing the characteristics of each one.

DIRECTIONS: Here is the introductory paragraph of an essay. On the lines below, write a middle paragraph that develops the topic through classification.

Everyone loves a pet! Sometimes it is hard to decide what sort of pet is best for a particular person or family. Pets can be classified into various types. One of these is sure to be right for you.

_____

_____

_____

_____

_____

_____

_____

_____

5–16. DEVELOPING THE TOPIC: CHOOSING THE RIGHT TECHNIQUE

Description, examples, and **classification** are excellent ways to develop a topic. Other techniques that can be equally effective include **definition, sequence,** and **comparison and contrast.** The essay topic will often indicate which technique should be used. For instance, an essay called "Butterflies of the World" will probably work best by using classification. Sequencing might be useful in an essay called "Preparing and Serving a Gourmet Dinner." Description would probably be effective for an essay called "The Best Person I Know." It is the task of the writer to decide on the best way to present the topic.

DIRECTIONS: Write a developmental paragraph to follow each of the introductory paragraphs below. Focus on the topic, and use the technique listed above that seems most appropriate. (Use the back of this sheet if you need more writing space.)

1. "Where shall we eat tonight?" This is a favorite question at my house, since my family enjoys eating out. At least, the rest of my family does. I'm the exception. I like to eat at home. I believe that restaurant food falls short when compared to home-cooked meals.

    _____

    _____

    _____

    _____

    _____

    _____

2. Career Planning Day is coming to our school next month! It should be a great opportunity for students to begin thinking about their futures. The program will include many interesting and important subjects.

    _____

    _____

    _____

    _____

    _____

5–17. Concluding Paragraphs (Part One)

Every story must have an ending, and so must every essay. This ending is called a concluding paragraph. To be effective, the concluding paragraph must do the following:

- Link the end of the essay to the beginning by restating and/or reinforcing the topic presented in the introduction.
- Summarize the points made in the body of the essay.
- Satisfy the reader that no loose ends or unanswered questions remain. The reader should not have to ask, "Then what?" or "What comes next?"

Here is the concluding paragraph of an essay called "The United States: A Beacon of Freedom to the World."

> The United States has proved its commitment to freedom and democracy, first through the American Revolution, then through numerous wars fought to protect the world from fascist and communist dictatorships, and finally through its generous contributions of money, food, and other assistance to struggling young democracies in need. These policies, together with its history as an enduring republic, make the United States an example of freedom.

Note how this concluding paragraph summarizes the points made in the essay and restates the topic in a satisfying way.

DIRECTIONS: On the lines at the bottom of the page, write a concluding paragraph for the following essay.

There are many things that young people can do to protect our Earth and preserve the environment. Just make a few small changes in your daily life, and you will be doing your part to create a better world.

Leg power is a lot cheaper than gasoline and does not pollute the air. Forget the carpool and walk or ride your bike to and from school, shopping centers, the ball field, and so forth. Do you toss empty soda bottles into the garbage? Stop those wasteful ways and put bottles and cans in the recycling bin to be used again. One of our most precious resources is water. Do you waste it by letting it run too long in the sink and shower? Turn off that faucet!

_____

_____

_____

_____

5–18. Concluding Paragraphs (part two)

When writing a concluding paragraph, remember the following principles:

- Link the end of the essay to the beginning by restating and/or reinforcing the topic presented in the introduction.
- Summarize the points made in the body of the essay.
- Satisfy the reader that you have left no loose ends or unanswered questions.

DIRECTIONS: On the lines at the bottom of this page, write a concluding paragraph for the following essay.

How does one become a professional cook? Cooks are usually trained at cooking schools called culinary institutes. You might be surprised at the kinds of courses students take at these special schools.

Classes in cooking and baking are, of course, high on the list of required courses. Many cooking schools also include classes in nutrition, safety, and how to purchase foods. Some even teach their students butchering, business law, and fitness. At the New England Culinary Institute, for example, all students must participate in fitness classes to develop upper-body strength and stamina, so that they can spend up to ten hours a day chopping vegetables, tossing salads, blending sauces, and carving meat. Many culinary institutes operate student-run restaurants where students can not only learn to cook but also learn other aspects of running a successful restaurant.

_____

_____

_____

_____

_____

_____

_____

_____

_____

5–19. ORGANIZING YOUR ESSAY: FOCUS

An architect has to make plans before building a house. First, the concept is explored in his or her mind. Then it is set down on paper. The architect must take into consideration every aspect of the structure—its size, shape, number of rooms, and so on. Every detail is important, from placement of walls and windows to kinds of materials used, even nails and screws. Beyond all of this, the architect has to consider the purpose of the house and the needs of the people who will live in it. All this preliminary work is done before building begins and kept in mind throughout the process.

Writing an essay requires a similar procedure. Before putting a word down on paper, the writer, like the architect, must first know the **purpose** of the task. A house that is built for a large, active family will be different from one that is designed for a more sedentary elderly couple. In the same way, an article describing a park will be different from one that describes the process of building an engine, and both of these will differ from an essay explaining why a particular park or engine is needed in the first place. An essay called "Birds of Florida" will have a different purpose than one called "Pelicans," and both of these will differ from the essay called "My Day at the Bird Sanctuary." The essay writer must focus on the following:

- The purpose of the essay
- Who will read it
- The specific topic

Anything that is not relevant to the topic should be omitted.

DIRECTIONS: In the box below each essay title, list some of the details this essay should focus on. For example, under the title "Pelicans," a list of details might include *size and description, eating habits, mating habits, where they are found, variations in species,* and so on.

A Memorable Class Trip

Types of Cars

5–20. Organizing Your Essay: Order

Before beginning to write, it is helpful to decide what sort of order you plan to use. There are many ways of arranging an essay. The one you choose will be determined by the type of essay you are writing and your perception of it. Here are the most common types of order used in essay writing:

- **Chronological (time) order** arranges items or events in the order in which they occur. This sort of arrangement often uses transitional words and phrases such as *the following day, then, first, next, that summer.* Chronological order works well when narrating a story or experience or when describing a process, such as building a boat.
- **Spatial order** arranges details according to their physical position or relationships. For example, a description of a room might show its contents in order from right to left or back to front, or it might group related items such as bed and night table; desk, chair, and computer; or sofa and coffee table.
- **Order of importance** arranges details from least important to most important, or the other way around. Transitions that are typical in this type of essay are *most important, easiest, most difficult, best, worst,* and so on.
- **Topical order** comes out of the topic itself. For example, a description of a classroom might include size, furnishings, learning devices such as chalkboards and computers, subjects taught there, teacher, students, and so on.

Once you choose an order, keeping the same one throughout the essay will help to avoid confusion on the part of both the reader and the writer.

DIRECTIONS: On the lines below, use one of the types of order listed above to write a paragraph on a topic of your choice. (One paragraph is sufficient here.) Before writing your paragraph, indicate your topic and the type of order you have chosen.

What is your topic?_____

What type of order have you chosen to use? _____

_____

_____

_____

_____

_____

_____

_____

5–21. Writing a Three-Paragraph Essay
(Brainstorming)

DIRECTIONS: Choose one of the following topics for a three-paragraph essay. Place a checkmark next to the topic you have chosen, and then complete the **brainstorming list** below.

❑ *A Famous Person I Admire*
❑ *New Invention Ideas for the Years Ahead*
❑ *The Nature of a Democracy*
❑ *Another topic of your choice (specify):* _____

BRAINSTORMING LIST

1. What is the main topic of this essay? _____

2. What order (circle one) will you use in this essay—**chronological, spatial, importance,** or **topical?**

3. Choose three supporting details for this topic and write them below. Next to each supporting detail, write a list of words and phrases you can use in your description.

Supporting Detail	Words and Phrases
1.	
2.	
3.	

5–22. WRITING A THREE-PARAGRAPH ESSAY (FIRST DRAFT)

DIRECTIONS: Write the first draft of a three-paragraph essay on the topic you have chosen. Use your brainstorming list as a guide. Be sure to stay focused on the topic at all times and to use the type of order you have chosen throughout the essay.

- **The first paragraph** (2 to 3 sentences) should introduce the topic in an interesting way. Be sure that the topic is clearly stated.
- **The second paragraph** (4 to 8 sentences) should develop the topic. Describe the three supporting details that are on your brainstorming list.
- **The concluding paragraph** (2 to 3 sentences) should sum up the topic and bring the essay to a satisfying conclusion.

Write your essay on the lines below. Write the title of the essay on the top line. Indent the first line of each paragraph. Remember that this is a first draft, so you can concentrate on getting your thoughts on paper and not be too concerned with grammar and spelling. (Continue on the back of this sheet if you need more writing space.)

_____

_____

_____

_____

_____

_____

_____

_____

_____

_____

_____

5–23. WRITING A THREE-PARAGRAPH ESSAY
(REVISING AND WRITING A FINAL COPY)

DIRECTIONS: Correct and revise the first draft of your three-paragraph essay. Your teacher will provide you with a list of proofreading symbols to use as you wish. Follow the guidelines below, and check off each item as you complete it.

> ❑ Does your introductory paragraph clearly state the topic?
> ❑ Can you revise the opening sentence to spark the reader's interest?
> ❑ Does the middle paragraph develop the topic? Do you follow the order you have chosen in developing each supporting detail?
> ❑ Do you stay focused on the topic, avoiding irrelevant details?
> ❑ Do you use transitional words where appropriate?
> ❑ Can you add stronger verbs and colorful adjectives to make your writing more vivid?
> ❑ Does the concluding paragraph sum up the topic in a satisfying way?
> ❑ Are your sentences complete? Correct any fragments or run-ons.
> ❑ Do subjects and verbs agree?
> ❑ Check your spelling with a dictionary when in doubt.

DIRECTIONS: Write the final copy of your essay below. Write the title on the top line. Indent at the beginning of each paragraph. (Use the back of this sheet if you need more writing space.)

_____

_____

_____

_____

_____

_____

_____

_____

5–24. WRITING A FIVE-PARAGRAPH ESSAY (OUTLINE)

Most topics can be successfully covered in five paragraphs, as follows:

- **First paragraph:** Introduction and statement of topic
- **Second, third, and fourth paragraphs:** Development of topic in three paragraphs, one for each of three supporting points
- **Fifth paragraph:** Conclusion and summing up of topic

DIRECTIONS: You are going to write a five-paragraph essay called "An Appealing Career" about a career or profession that you find interesting. First, organize your ideas by writing an **outline** on a separate sheet of paper. You can create your own outline, or follow these suggestions.

I. Main topic (for example, *Archaeologist*)

II. First supporting point (for example, *Career Description*)

    A. Detail (for example, *study of ancient civilizations*)

    B. Detail (for example, *learning about artifacts*)

    C. Detail (for example, *fieldwork at digs*)

III. Second supporting point (for example, *Preparation Needed*)

    A. Detail (for example, *college courses*)

    B. Detail (for example, *advanced degrees*)

    C. Detail (for example, *practical experience*)

IV. Third supporting point (for example, *Reasons for Choosing This Career*)

    A. Detail (for example, *interest in history*)

    B. Detail (for example, *love of travel*)

    C. Detail (for example, *curious nature*)

V. Concluding Paragraph

    A. Restate topic

    B. Sum up supporting points

5–25. Writing a Five-Paragraph Essay (first draft)

DIRECTIONS: Write the first draft of a five-paragraph essay called "An Appealing Career." Use your outline as a guide. Be sure to stay focused on the topic at all times.

> - First paragraph (2 to 3 sentences): Introduce the topic in an interesting way. Be sure that the topic is clearly stated.
> - Second paragraph (3 to 6 sentences): Describe the first supporting point.
> - Third paragraph (3 to 6 sentences): Describe the second supporting point.
> - Fourth paragraph (3 to 6 sentences): Describe the third supporting point.
> - Fifth paragraph (2 to 3 sentences): Sum up the topic and conclude the essay.

Begin your essay below, and continue on the back of this sheet if you need more writing space. Write the title on the top line. Indent the beginning of each paragraph. Remember, this is a first draft. Concentrate on getting your thoughts down in an interesting and organized way. Don't be too concerned with grammar or spelling at this point.

5–26. WRITING A FIVE-PARAGRAPH ESSAY
(REVISING AND WRITING A FINAL COPY)

A. DIRECTIONS: Correct and revise the first draft of your five-paragraph essay on an appealing career. Use proofreading symbols if you find them helpful. Follow the guidelines below, and check off each item as you complete it.

❑ Does your introductory paragraph clearly state the topic? Can you revise the opening sentence to spark the reader's interest?

❑ Do each of the three middle paragraphs develop the topic with a supporting point? Do you stay focused on the topic throughout?

❑ Take out any irrelevant details.

❑ Insert transitional words where necessary to make smooth transitions.

❑ Make your writing more vivid by adding strong verbs and colorful adjectives.

❑ Does the concluding paragraph sum up the topic in a satisfying way?

❑ Are your sentences complete? Correct any fragments or run-ons.

❑ Do subjects and verbs agree? Do pronouns agree with their antecedents?

❑ Check your spelling with a dictionary when in doubt.

B. DIRECTIONS: Write the final copy of your essay below. Write the title on the top line, and indent at the beginning of each paragraph. (Use the back of this sheet if you need more writing space.)

_____

_____

_____

_____

_____

_____

_____

_____

_____

_____

TENTH-GRADE LEVEL

ESSAY-WRITING TECHNIQUES PRACTICE TEST

PRACTICE TEST: ESSAY-WRITING TECHNIQUES

Some common sayings have been around for hundreds of years. These sayings are called *adages.* Some well-known adages are listed below.

> ❏ The love of money is the root of all evil.
> ❏ A person is known by the company he keeps.
> ❏ You can lead a horse to water but you can't make him drink.

DIRECTIONS: You are going to write an essay explaining the meaning of one of these adages and discussing whether it is true today. Place a checkmark next to the adage you have chosen, then follow these four steps to write your essay:

- FIRST, on the page labeled "Prewriting," brainstorm essay ideas and examples that support the topic. Include words and phrases you can use.
- SECOND, write the first draft of your essay on a separate sheet of paper. Write your name and date at the top, then the title of the essay. Use your notes from the brainstorming page.
- THIRD, revise and edit your first draft. Use proofreading symbols if you wish. Use the checklist below as a guide, and check off each item when it is revised to your satisfaction.
- FOURTH, write your final copy on a separate sheet of paper with your name and date at the top.

CHECKLIST

❏ Does your introductory paragraph state the topic clearly? Could you say it in a more interesting way by using a surprising statement, a question, or an anecdote?

❏ Does your middle paragraph or paragraphs develop the topic in a clear and logical way?

❏ Do you stay on the subject and use only examples and details that are related to the topic?

❏ Does the concluding paragraph sum up the subject and bring the essay to a satisfying end?

❏ Do all subjects and verbs agree? Do pronouns agree with their antecedents?

❏ Can you add active verbs or sensory words to make your writing more vivid?

❏ Do you use transitional words and phrases to connect ideas smoothly?

❏ Correct any fragments or run-on sentences.

❏ Do you vary sentence length, using short and long sentences?

❏ Check your spelling with a dictionary when in doubt.

PRACTICE TEST: ESSAY-WRITING TECHNIQUES *(continued)*

Prewriting

Use the brainstorming chart below to organize your essay. Arrange the brainstorming chart in any way that will be helpful. Here are some suggestions. At the top, write the adage you are writing about. List at least three supporting points for your topic. Next to each supporting point, write words and phrases you will use for details.

Below the brainstorming chart, write a first sentence for your introductory paragraph that will spark a reader's interest.

Adage: _____

BRAINSTORMING CHART

First sentence of your introductory paragraph: _____

_____

_____

PRACTICE TEST: ESSAY-WRITING TECHNIQUES *(continued)*

Student Samples

DIRECTIONS: Read the sample student essays below. Rate each essay with a score from 1 (lowest) to 6 (highest). Use the information on the scoring guide to help you.

ESSAY A: The Love of Money Is the Root of All Evil

No truer words were ever spoken! The adage, "The love of money is the root of all evil," is as true today as when it was written hundreds of years ago, and continues to cause pain and unhappiness in the world.

This old saying does not mean that money itself is bad. Money is neutral. It is the love of money that brings trouble. Most criminal behaviour results from a desire for money. Bank robbers, burglars, muggers, drug dealers, even murderers have a common goal—money.

Wars usually happen because one country wants something valuable such as gold, oil, or land that the other possesses. This leads to terrible tragedies.

The love of money can also ruin personal relationships. It is good to work hard and be able to live comfortably but when this goal becomes more important than the happiness of family and friends, then love and friendship go down the drain.

Peace and happiness will come about when money is no longer the main goal of people and countries.

Score _____

ESSAY B: The Love of Money Is the Root of All Evil

It is true that money can cause lots of trouble people will do anything to get it and that causes trouble.

My cousin, Josh, got in trouble because he took some money off another kid in his class he took it out of the kids coat pocket hanging on a hook. His father made him give it back he couldve landed in jail.

People like to get expensve presents but it is realy the thought that counts. My mom bakes great cookys and cakes she gives them as presents but people don't appreshiate cause it dont cost money.

Its better when people dont always talk about money and expensve things.

Score _____

Scoring Guide

SCORE	Unsatisfactory—1	Insufficient—2
Content	Attempts to respond to prompt, but provides few details to persuade the reader; may only paraphrase prompt	Presents fragmented information OR may be very repetitive OR may be very undeveloped
Organization	Has no clear organization OR consists of a single statement	Is very disorganized; ideas are weakly connected OR the response is too brief to detect organization
Sentence Structure	Little or no control over sentence boundaries and sentence structure; word choice may be incorrect in much or all of the response	Little control over sentence boundaries and sentence structure; word choice may often be incorrect
Grammar, Usage, and Mechanics	Many errors in grammar or usage (such as tense inconsistency, lack of subject-verb agreement), spelling, and punctuation severely interfere with understanding	Errors in grammar or usage (such as inconsistency, lack of subject-verb agreement), spelling, and punctuation interfere with understanding in much of the response

SCORE	Uneven—3	Sufficient—4
Content	Presents some clear information, but is list-like, undeveloped, or repetitive OR offers no more than a well-written beginning	Develops information with some details; some attempt is made to persuade the reader
Organization	Is unevenly organized; the essay may be disjointed	Is organized with ideas that are generally related but has few or no transitions
Sentence Structure	Exhibits uneven control over sentence boundaries and sentence structure; may have some incorrect word choices	Exhibits control over sentence boundaries and sentence structure, but sentences and word choices may be simple and unvaried
Grammar, Usage, and Mechanics	Errors in grammar or usage (such as tense inconsistency, lack of subject-verb agreement), spelling, and punctuation sometimes interfere with understanding	Errors in grammar or usage (such as tense inconsistency, lack of subject-verb agreement), spelling, and punctuation do not interfere with understanding

SCORE	Skillful—5	Excellent—6
Content	Develops and shapes information with details in parts of the essay	Develops and shapes information with well-chosen details across the essay
Organization	Is clearly organized, but may lack some transitions and/or have lapses in continuity	Is well organized with strong transitions; makes clear persuasive statement
Sentence Structure	Exhibits some variety in sentence structure and some good word choices	Sustains variety in sentence structure and exhibits good word choice
Grammar, Usage, and Mechanics	Errors in grammar, spelling, and punctuation do not interfere with understanding	Errors in grammar, spelling, and punctuation are few and do not interfere with understanding

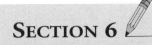

WRITING INFORMATIVE/ EXPOSITORY ESSAYS

Standardized Testing Information

Students in tenth grade taking state or national writing tests will be required to write one or more of the following types of essays: **informative/expository, narrative/imaginative, and persuasive.** This section deals with informative/expository essays.

According to the National Assessment of Educational Progress (NAEP), a sample of informative writing "communicates information to the reader to share knowledge or to convey messages, instructions, and ideas." The topics that students are given in these tests require them "to write on specified subjects in a variety of formats, such as reports, reviews, and letters." The NAEP also recommends that "students should write on a variety of tasks and for many different audiences" and "from a variety of stimulus materials" such as "photographs, cartoons, or poems, . . . newspaper articles, charts." These stimulus materials are called prompts. The NAEP also suggests that "students should generate, draft, revise, and edit ideas and forms of expression in their writing." This suggests mastery of the writing process that is used throughout this resource. The rubric at the end of this section is adapted from NAEP guidelines for scoring informative/expository writing. Information on the NAEP can be found at www.NAGB.org or at www.nces.ed.gov/nationsreportcard.

Most state rubrics are similar to those of the NAEP. The official scoring guide for Florida, for example, offers six levels of achievement from 1 (lowest) to 6 (highest), as in these excerpts:

---

6 Points. The writing is focused, purposeful, and reflects insight into the writing situation. The paper conveys a sense of completeness and wholeness with adherence to the main idea, and its organization pattern provides for a logical progression of ideas. The support is substantial, specific, relevant, concrete, and/or illustrative. The paper demonstrates a commitment to and an involvement with the subject, clarity in presentation of ideas, and use of creative writing strategies appropriate to the purpose of the paper. The writing demonstrates a mature command of language (word choice) with freshness of expression. Sentence structure is varied, and sentences are complete except when fragments are used purposefully. Few, if any, convention errors occur in mechanics, usage, and punctuation.

4 Points. The writing is generally focused on the topic but may include extraneous or loosely related material. An organizational pattern is apparent, although some lapses may occur. The paper exhibits some sense of completeness or wholeness. The support, including word choice, is adequate, although development may be uneven. There is little variation in sentence structure, and most sentences are complete. The paper generally follows the conventions of mechanics, usage, and spelling.

---

2 Points. The writing is related to the topic but includes extraneous or loosely related material. Little evidence of an organizational pattern may be demonstrated, and the paper may lack a sense of completeness or wholeness. Development of support is inadequate or illogical. Word choice is limited, inappropriate, or vague. There is little, if any, variation in sentence structure, and gross errors in sentence structure may occur. Errors in basic conventions of mechanics and usage may occur, and commonly used words may be misspelled.

This is just one example of a state rubric for scoring writing samples. Some are more detailed, but this particular scoring guide gives the teacher or student a clear, concise outline of the basic skills that are being looked at and how they are scored. Whichever rubrics are used, an abundance of guided practice, as in the activities that follow, will thoroughly prepare students for any standardized writing test.

Teacher Preparation and Lessons

The activities in this section are designed to provide a variety of interesting, grade-appropriate experiences in informative/expository writing, with guidelines and supportive instructions that student writers can use to hone their writing skills. Students are encouraged to use the four steps of the writing process as presented in Section 4. Some of the topics, including that used for the PRACTICE TEST on pages 214–217, are adapted from actual prompts from various state and national standardized writing tests.

Each activity has three parts:

- The first part consists of **prewriting activities** such as **brainstorming, clustering,** or **outlining.** This can be done individually, with class participation, or by using some combination of these two procedures.

- The second part is the **writing of a first draft.** Students should be encouraged to write freely at this point, without worrying about grammar, spelling, or punctuation. The aim is to overcome the blocks that so many student writers face by making this part of the process less threatening. Students will also find it helpful to refer to the brainstorming list, cluster, or outline they have already prepared.

- The third part offers directions for **revising and writing a final copy.** The revision and editing process can be done by the individual student alone, in association with the teacher, or with class participation by having students exchange papers and make suggestions for revision. This last method can be valuable for both the writer and the editor, since it is easier for anyone (student or adult) to recognize the flaws in someone else's writing and then transfer this knowledge to his or her own work. Teachers are urged to use this method occasionally in their lessons on revision. Each worksheet on revision contains a checklist of valuable editing suggestions, and students should be instructed to use this checklist. They should also be encouraged to use **proofreading symbols** when revising their work. (See the list of proofreading symbols on page 307 of this resource, and have copies available for students to use.)

The informative/expository writing activities in this section range from simple three-paragraph essays to more detailed and complex essays of five or more paragraphs.

Practice Test: Writing Informative Essays

The sample student essays A and B on page 216 are rated a 5 and a 1, respectively.

Essay A states the topic clearly and develops it in a logical, coherent way. The writer demonstrates an awareness of the audience and presents each supporting point with strong details. Sentence construction and variety are excellent, as are tone and content. Language usage is appropriate, and mechanics of writing, including grammar and spelling, are correct. However, a more mature command of language and freshness of expression would have resulted in a higher score. This essay scored a 5.

Essay B attempts to state a topic, but it is vague and unclear and there seems to be little awareness of the task or audience. Some supporting examples are offered, but their development is limited and weak. There is no apparent organization, and details are scattered and confusing. The language is extremely simplistic. There are frequent errors in spelling, mechanics, and sentence structure. This essay scored a 1.

6–1. A Typical American High School (Prewriting)

DIRECTIONS: Schools are quite different in various parts of the world. You are going to write a short, three-paragraph essay that describes a typical American high school to someone who has just arrived in this country and knows nothing about its educational system. First, prepare a **brainstorming list** that will help you organize your thoughts.

1. In the first column of the chart below, write a list of words and phrases you can use to describe the building (both exterior and interior).

2. In the second column, write a list of words and phrases you can use to describe the courses that are offered.

3. In the third column, write a list of words and phrases you can use to describe the students.

BRAINSTORMING LIST

Building	Courses	Students

On the line below, write an opening sentence for your essay that will spark a reader's interest.

_____

6–2. A TYPICAL AMERICAN HIGH SCHOOL (FIRST DRAFT)

DIRECTIONS: Write the first draft of a three-paragraph essay called "A Typical American High School." Keep your brainstorming list handy and follow this easy guide.

First Paragraph: Use the opening sentence from the brainstorming list and introduce the topic in your introductory paragraph. Write the first paragraph (2 to 4 sentences) here or on another sheet of paper.

_____

_____

_____

_____

Second Paragraph: Develop the topic in your middle paragraph. Use the words and phrases on your brainstorming list to describe the building, courses, and the students. Write the second paragraph (4 to 7 sentences) here or on the other sheet of paper.

_____

_____

_____

_____

_____

_____

Concluding Paragraph: In the third and last paragraph, restate and sum up your topic. It will be satisfying to the reader if you refer to something in the introductory paragraph and bring it to a conclusion. Write your concluding paragraph (at least 2 sentences) here or on the other sheet of paper.

_____

_____

_____

_____

6–3. A TYPICAL AMERICAN HIGH SCHOOL
(REVISING AND WRITING A FINAL COPY)

A. DIRECTIONS: Correct and revise the first draft of "A Typical American High School." Use the list of proofreading symbols your teacher has given you. Follow the guidelines below and check off each one when it has been completed.

❑ Does your first paragraph introduce the topic? Is there any way you can make it more interesting to the reader?

❑ Does the second paragraph develop the topic? Is it organized logically? Have you chosen the most appropriate words and phrases from your brainstorming list?

❑ Does the final paragraph restate and sum up the topic in a satisfying way?

❑ Are your sentences complete? Correct any run-on sentences or fragments.

❑ Do subjects and verbs agree? Do pronouns agree with their antecedents?

❑ Can you add active verbs and sensory language to make your writing more vivid?

❑ Can you add interest to the writing with one simile?

❑ Check spelling with a dictionary when in doubt.

B. DIRECTIONS: Begin the final copy of your essay below, and continue on the back of this sheet. Write the title on the first line, and indent at the beginning of each paragraph.

_____

_____

_____

_____

_____

_____

Name _____ **Date** _____

6–4. An Interesting Period in History (prewriting)

DIRECTIONS: There are many fascinating times in the history of this country and the world. Choose a time in history that you would like to describe. It can be a period and place such as the Renaissance in Europe, ancient Rome, the American Civil War, or Colonial America, or you can write about a particular year and place, such as the world in 1965 or New York City in 1865. Write the title you have chosen on the line below, then follow the directions for preparing a **brainstorming list.**

_____

The organization of your brainstorming list will vary according to the subject you have chosen. For example, for an essay about Colonial America, you might have columns headed "Government and Laws," "Food and Dress," and "Economy." On the other hand, an essay called "The World in 1776" might be organized according to parts of the world, so you could have columns headed "The Americas," "Europe," "Far East," and "Africa." On the brainstorming list below, write headings for each column that are appropriate to your essay. Then, in each column, list words and phrases you will use in your essay about that topic.

BRAINSTORMING LIST

On the line below, write an opening sentence for your essay that will spark a reader's interest.

_____

6–5. An Interesting Period in History (first draft)

DIRECTIONS: Write a five-paragraph essay describing the historical period you have chosen. Use your brainstorming list as a guide, and follow these simple suggestions:

- In the first paragraph (2 to 3 sentences), get the reader's interest with an exciting beginning. You may wish to use the opening sentence from your brainstorming list.
- In the second paragraph (at least 3 sentences), discuss one of your supporting points, using words and phrases from your brainstorming list.
- In the third paragraph (at least 3 sentences), discuss the second point from your brainstorming list.
- In the fourth paragraph (at least 3 sentences), discuss the third heading on your brainstorming list.
- In the fifth paragraph (2 to 3 sentences), restate and sum up the topic.

Begin your essay below, and continue on the back of this sheet. Write the title on the top line, and indent at the beginning of each paragraph. This is a first draft, so just concentrate on getting your thoughts down on paper, and don't be too concerned about spelling or grammar at this point.

_____

_____

_____

_____

_____

_____

_____

_____

_____

_____

6–6. AN INTERESTING PERIOD IN HISTORY
(REVISING AND WRITING A FINAL COPY)

A. DIRECTIONS: Correct and revise your first draft. Use your list of proofreading symbols. Follow and check off the guidelines below.

> ❏ Does the first paragraph introduce the topic? Can you make it more interesting with a question or quotation?
> ❏ Do each of the three middle paragraphs discuss and provide details on one main point?
> ❏ Do you stay on the topic at all times? Delete any irrelevant details.
> ❏ Is your essay organized in a clear and logical way?
> ❏ Does the concluding paragraph restate and sum up the topic in a satisfying manner?
> ❏ Do you use transitional words to connect thoughts and ideas?
> ❏ Can you make your writing more vivid with active verbs and sensory language?
> ❏ Add at least one simile to spark interest.
> ❏ Check spelling with a dictionary when in doubt.

B. DIRECTIONS: Begin the final copy of your essay below, and continue on the back of this sheet. Write the title on the first line, and indent at the beginning of each paragraph.

_____

_____

_____

_____

_____

_____

_____

_____

_____

6–7. GETTING A JOB (PREWRITING)

DIRECTIONS: Many teenagers would like to earn money, either to help out their families or to buy extra things for themselves. Jobs are available for young people, but many teenagers don't know how to go about finding one. You are going to write a five-paragraph essay describing the process of getting a job. First, prepare an **outline.** This preparation will help you focus on the topic and write the essay.

Below is a partial outline for an essay on how to get a job. Fill in the empty spaces with the supporting details you will need. (For example, next to "**A.,**" write the name of one job, such as mowing lawns. Next to "**1.**" and "**2.**" below that, write words or phrases that describe this job.)

OUTLINE

Getting a Job

I. **Jobs Suitable for Teenagers**

   A. (Job #1) _____

      1. (Descriptive detail) _____

      2. (Descriptive detail) _____

   B. (Job #2) _____

      1. (Descriptive detail) _____

      2. (Descriptive detail) _____

   C. (Job #3) _____

      1. (Descriptive detail) _____

      2. (Descriptive detail) _____

II. **Locating a Job**

   A. (Possible source) _____

   B. (Possible source) _____

III. **Applying for a Job**

   A. (Descriptive detail) _____

   B. (Descriptive detail) _____

   C. (Descriptive detail) _____

Name _____ **Date** _____

6–8. Getting a Job (first draft)

DIRECTIONS: Write the first draft of a five-paragraph informative essay explaining to teenagers how to get a job. You have already done an important part of the task by creating an outline. Follow your outline and these simple suggestions:

> - In the first paragraph (2 to 3 sentences), state the topic in a way that will get the reader's interest.
> - In the second paragraph (3 to 6 sentences), refer to "I." on your outline and describe the kinds of jobs that are available.
> - In the third paragraph (3 to 6 sentences), refer to "II." on your outline to discuss the sources available for finding out about these jobs.
> - In the fourth paragraph (3 to 6 sentences), refer to "III." on your outline and describe how to apply for a job.
> - In the fifth paragraph (2 to 3 sentences), restate and sum up the topic.

Begin your essay below, and continue on the back of this sheet. Write a title on the top line, and indent at the beginning of each paragraph. Remember that this is a first draft, so concentrate on getting your thoughts on paper in a clear, organized way, and don't be too concerned about spelling or grammar at this point.

_____

_____

_____

_____

_____

_____

_____

_____

6–9. GETTING A JOB (REVISING AND WRITING A FINAL COPY)

A. DIRECTIONS: Correct and revise your first draft. Use your list of proofreading symbols. Follow the guidelines below and check off each one as you complete it.

> ❑ Does the first paragraph introduce the topic? Can you make the opening more interesting with a startling statement or a question?
>
> ❑ Do the three middle paragraphs each describe and discuss one of the supporting points (jobs available, sources for locating a job, and applying for a job)?
>
> ❑ Do you stay on the topic? Does each paragraph focus on the supporting point it describes? Delete any irrelevant details.
>
> ❑ Is your essay organized in a logical way? Can you change anything to make the topic clearer to the reader?
>
> ❑ Does the concluding paragraph restate and sum up the topic in an interesting way?
>
> ❑ Do your subjects and verbs agree? Do pronouns agree with their antecedents?
>
> ❑ Add some active verbs and sensory language to make your writing vivid.
>
> ❑ Check spelling with a dictionary when in doubt.

B. DIRECTIONS: Begin the final copy of your essay below, and continue on the back of this sheet. Write the title on the first line, and indent at the beginning of each paragraph.

_____

_____

_____

_____

_____

_____

_____

6–10. GAME PLAN (PREWRITING)

DIRECTIONS: Is there a board game or computer game that you like to play? You are going to write an essay describing this game to someone who has never played it before. First, organize your ideas by preparing a **brainstorming list**.

Complete the brainstorming list below for your essay about how to play a board or computer game.

BRAINSTORMING LIST

1. In the box below, write a list of words and phrases you can use to describe the general appearance of the game, such as shapes, colors, objects, and people.

2. In the box below, write a list of words and phrases you can use to describe the goal and rules of the game.

3. In the box below, write a list of words and phrases you can use to describe the process and steps of the game from beginning to end.

4. On the back of this sheet, write a snappy opening, such as "Would you like real excitement in your life? Then rush to the store and get the new board game, 'Rebel.'"

6–11. Game Plan (first draft)

DIRECTIONS: Write the first draft of a five-paragraph essay about a board or computer game. Refer to the work you have already done on your brainstorming list, and follow these simple suggestions:

> • In the first paragraph (2 to 3 sentences), introduce the topic with the snappy opening on your brainstorming list.
> • In the second paragraph (3 to 6 sentences), describe the appearance of the game, using the words and phrases from your brainstorming list.
> • In the third paragraph (3 to 6 sentences), describe the goal and rules of the game, using the words and phrases from your brainstorming list.
> • In the fourth paragraph (3 to 6 sentences), tell how the game is played from beginning to end.
> • In the fifth paragraph (2 to 4 sentences), conclude by referring back to the introductory paragraph and summing up the topic.

Begin your essay below, and continue on the back of this sheet. Write a title on the top line, and indent at the beginning of each paragraph. Remember that this is a first draft. Concentrate on getting your thoughts on paper in a clear and organized manner. Don't be too concerned about spelling or grammar at this point.

_____

_____

_____

_____

_____

_____

_____

_____

6–12. Game Plan (Revising and Writing a Final Copy)

A. DIRECTIONS: Correct and revise your first draft. Use your list of proofreading symbols. Follow the guidelines below and check off each one as you complete it.

> ❑ Does the first paragraph introduce the topic? Can you think of any way to make it even more interesting to the reader?
>
> ❑ Do each of the three middle paragraphs focus on one supporting point (appearance, goals and rules, steps from beginning to end)?
>
> ❑ Are there any irrelevant details? Cut them!
>
> ❑ Is there anything vague or unclear in your description of the game and how it is played? If so, rewrite to clarify.
>
> ❑ Does the concluding paragraph refer back to the introduction and sum up the topic?
>
> ❑ Do subjects and verbs agree? Do pronouns agree with their antecedents?
>
> ❑ Add some active verbs and sensory language to make your writing vivid.
>
> ❑ Add one simile or metaphor.
>
> ❑ Check spelling with a dictionary.

B. DIRECTIONS: Begin the final copy of your essay below, and continue on the back of this sheet. Write the title on the first line, and indent at the beginning of each paragraph.

_____

_____

_____

_____

_____

_____

_____

_____

6–13. Explaining a Poem (Prewriting)

Poets are often able to concentrate a lot of meaning into just a few lines. Here is part of a poem by American poet Edna St. Vincent Millay:

> *My candle burns at both ends;*
> *It will not last the night;*
> *But ah, my foes and oh, my friends—*
> *It gives a lovely light!*

This poem, like many others, can have different meanings for different people. What does it mean to you? You are going to write a simple three-paragraph essay about this poem. First, prepare a **brainstorming list.**

BRAINSTORMING LIST

1. Briefly describe the general meaning of the poem. You don't need complete sentences here, just words and phrases (for example, *burning candles, lighting the darkness, watch out for fires, shortness of life*).

_____

_____

_____

_____

2. What feelings does this poem evoke in you? List words and phrases that describe this feeling (for examples, *sadness, excitement, rebelliousness*).

_____

_____

_____

_____

3. List words and phrases from the poem itself that support your interpretation.

_____

_____

_____

_____

Name _____   Date _____

6–14. EXPLAINING A POEM (FIRST DRAFT)

DIRECTIONS: Write the first draft of a three-paragraph essay, giving your interpretation of the poem by Edna St. Vincent Millay. First, read the poem again and review your brainstorming list. Here are some simple suggestions for organizing your work:

- In the first paragraph (2 to 4 sentences), introduce the topic in an interesting way (for example, "Some words speak to the head; others to the heart. This poem evoked deep feelings within me.").
- In the middle paragraph (4 to 7 sentences), discuss what you believe to be the meaning of this poem and the feelings it brings out. Use quotes from the poem to illustrate your point where possible.
- The concluding paragraph (2 to 4 sentences) should sum up your thoughts and bring the essay to a satisfying conclusion.

Begin your essay below, and continue on the back of this sheet. Write a title on the top line, and indent at the beginning of each paragraph. Remember that this is a first draft. Concentrate on getting your thoughts on paper in a clear and organized manner, and don't be too concerned about spelling or grammar at this point.

6–15. EXPLAINING A POEM
(REVISING AND WRITING A FINAL COPY)

A. DIRECTIONS: Correct and revise the first draft of your essay about Millay's poem. Use proofreading symbols where helpful. Follow the guidelines below, and check off each one as you complete it.

> ❑ Does the first paragraph introduce the topic in an interesting way? Does it state the name of the author and the subject of the poem?
> ❑ Does the middle paragraph clearly express your interpretation of the meaning of this poem? Do you also clearly communicate how it makes you feel?
> ❑ Do you use quotes from the poem to support your conclusions?
> ❑ Does the concluding paragraph restate and sum up the topic?
> ❑ Do subjects and verbs agree? Do pronouns agree with their antecedents?
> ❑ Can you add some active verbs and sensory words to make your writing vivid?
> ❑ Check spelling with a dictionary.

B. DIRECTIONS: Begin the final copy of your essay below, and continue on the back of this sheet. Write the title on the first line and indent at the beginning of each paragraph.

_____

_____

_____

_____

_____

_____

_____

6–16. IMMIGRANTS IN THE UNITED STATES (PREWRITING)

Ever since its founding after the American Revolution, the United States has been a magnet for immigrants from around the world. You are going to write an essay about immigration to the United States and its effect on the nation.

First, organize your ideas by preparing an **outline.** You can write your own outline on a separate sheet of paper, or finish the one that has been started below, adapting it for your essay.

OUTLINE

Immigrants in the United States

I. **Early Immigrants (19th and early 20th centuries)**

    A. (Country or continent of origin) _____

        1. (Reasons for leaving) _____

        2. (Other details) _____

    B. (Another country or continent of origin) _____

        1. (Reasons for leaving) _____

        2. (Other details) _____

II. **More Recent Immigrants (late 20th and early 21st centuries)**

    A. (Country or continent of origin) _____

        1. (Reasons for leaving) _____

        2. (Other details) _____

    B. (Another country or continent of origin) _____

        1. (Reasons for leaving) _____

        2. (Other details) _____

III. **Contributions That Immigrants Have Made**

    A. _____

    B. _____

IV. **Problems Caused by Immigration**

    A. _____

    B. _____

V. **Conclusion (restate the topic and sum up facts)**

6–17. IMMIGRANTS IN THE UNITED STATES (FIRST DRAFT)

DIRECTIONS: Write the first draft of a five- or six-paragraph essay called "Immigrants in the United States." Follow the outline you have prepared. If you used the outline on the Prewriting worksheet, you will have six paragraphs. Here is one suggestion for organizing the essay:

- In the first paragraph (2 to 3 sentences), state the topic in an interesting way (for example, "The United States has always been a haven for immigrants from abroad. Could it be that, in many ways, the immigrants themselves have contributed to the success of the country?").
- In the second paragraph (3 to 6 sentences), describe the immigrants of the 19th and early 20th centuries.
- In the third paragraph (3 to 6 sentences), describe the immigrants of the late 20th and early 21st centuries.
- In the fourth paragraph (3 to 6 sentences), describe contributions that immigrants have made.
- In the fifth paragraph (3 to 6 sentences), describe some problems caused by immigration.
- In the sixth paragraph (2 to 4 sentences), sum up the topic and bring it to a satisfying conclusion.

Begin your essay below, and continue on the back of this sheet. Write a title on the top line, and indent at the beginning of paragraphs. Remember that this is a first draft, so just concentrate on getting your thoughts on paper in a clear, organized way. Don't be too concerned with spelling or grammar at this point.

_____

_____

_____

_____

_____

_____

Name _____   Date _____

6–18. IMMIGRANTS IN THE UNITED STATES
(REVISING AND WRITING A FINAL COPY)

A. DIRECTIONS: Correct and revise the first draft of your essay about immigrants in the United States. Use your list of proofreading symbols if that is helpful, and follow the guidelines below. Check off each one as you complete it.

> ❏ Does the first paragraph introduce the topic? Can you make it more interesting by using a question or a startling statement?
> ❏ Do the three (or four) middle paragraphs develop the topic in a logical, organized way? Does each of these paragraphs state a supporting point and offer details?
> ❏ Do you stay on the topic at all times? Delete any irrelevancies.
> ❏ Does the concluding paragraph sum up the topic and bring it to a satisfying conclusion?
> ❏ Are sentences complete? Correct any fragments or run-ons.
> ❏ Do subjects and verbs agree? Do pronouns agree with their antecedents?
> ❏ Add some active verbs and sensory words to make your writing more vivid.
> ❏ Check spelling with a dictionary.

B. DIRECTIONS: Begin the final copy of your essay below, and continue on the back of this sheet. Write the title on the top line and indent at the beginning of each paragraph.

_____

6–19. KEEPING FIT (PREWRITING)

DIRECTIONS: Athletes are not the only ones who need to stay in shape. All people, regardless of age, will have better physical and mental health if they keep their bodies fit. You are going to write a five-paragraph essay describing ways of staying fit. First, organize your ideas with a **brainstorming list.**

One way of setting up a brainstorming list is to organize your essay paragraph by paragraph. Just follow these directions, and write your brainstorming list below.

Paragraph 1: Briefly state the topic you will introduce in the opening paragraph.

Paragraph 2: State the first supporting point, then list words and phrases you can use to describe it (for example, Types of Exercise—walking, jogging, aerobics, sports, muscle-building, yoga, stretching, fresh air, deep breathing).

Paragraph 3: State the second supporting point, then list words and phrases you can use to describe it (for example, Diet and Nutrition—balanced meals, don't skip breakfast, protein, vegetables and fruit, less fast food).

Paragraph 4: State the third supporting point, then list words and phrases you can use to describe it (for example, Attitude—establish regular routine, challenge yourself, set goals).

Paragraph 5: List words and phrases you can use in your conclusion.

BRAINSTORMING LIST

Paragraph 1: _____

_____

Paragraph 2: _____

_____

_____

Paragraph 3: _____

_____

_____

Paragraph 4: _____

_____

_____

Paragraph 5: _____

_____

Name _____ **Date** _____

6–20. Keeping Fit (first draft)

DIRECTIONS: Use your brainstorming list as your guide to write a five-paragraph essay on keeping fit. Follow the organization you have set up for each paragraph. Here are some suggestions to keep in mind while writing this draft:

- Spark the reader's interest in the opening paragraph with a question, surprising statement, or humorous anecdote.
- Stay on the topic at all times. Avoid irrelevant details. Each paragraph should focus on the supporting point it presents.
- This is just a first draft, so concentrate on getting your thoughts down on paper. Don't be too concerned about spelling or grammar at this point.

Begin the first draft of your essay below, and continue on the back of this sheet. Write a title on the top line, and indent at the beginning of each paragraph.

_____

6–21. Keeping Fit (revising and writing a final copy)

A. DIRECTIONS: Correct and revise the first draft of your essay about keeping fit. Use your list of proofreading symbols if you find it helpful, and follow the guidelines below. Check off each one as you complete it.

> ❏ Is the topic clearly stated in the introductory paragraph? Can you make it more exciting, to spark the reader's interest?
> ❏ Do the three middle paragraphs develop the topic? Does each of these paragraphs explain and detail one supporting point?
> ❏ Do you stay on the topic at all times? Delete any irrelevancies.
> ❏ Does the concluding paragraph restate and sum up the topic?
> ❏ Are all sentences complete? Correct any fragments or run-ons.
> ❏ Do subjects and verbs agree? Do pronouns agree with their antecedents?
> ❏ Do you use transitional words (such as *however, therefore, then, at first,*) to make smooth connections?
> ❏ Add some active verbs and sensory words to make your writing more vivid.
> ❏ Check spelling with a dictionary.

B. DIRECTIONS: Write the final copy of your essay below, and continue on the back of this sheet. Write the title on the top line, and indent at the beginning of each paragraph.

_____

_____

_____

_____

_____

_____

_____

_____

TENTH-GRADE LEVEL

WRITING INFORMATIVE ESSAYS
PRACTICE TEST

PRACTICE TEST: WRITING INFORMATIVE ESSAYS

DIRECTIONS: Often in works of literature there are characters—other than the main character—whose presence in the work is essential. From a work of literature that you have read in or out of school, select a character, other than the main character, who plays a key role. In a well-defined composition, identify the character and explain why this character is important.

Follow these four steps to write your essay:

- FIRST, on the page labeled "Prewriting," brainstorm essay ideas and examples that support the topic. Include words and phrases you can use.

- SECOND, write the first draft of your essay on a separate sheet of paper. Write your name, the date, and the title of the essay at the top. Use your notes from the brainstorming page.

- THIRD, revise and edit your first draft. Refer to your list of proofreading symbols if you wish to make use of them. Use the checklist below as a guide, and check off each item when it is revised to your satisfaction.

- FOURTH, write your final copy on a separate sheet of paper with your name and the date at
the top.

CHECKLIST

- ❏ Does your introductory paragraph state the topic clearly? Can you use a question, a quotation, or a startling statement to make it more interesting?
- ❏ Do your middle paragraphs develop the topic in a clear and logical way? Does each of these paragraphs describe one supporting point or example?
- ❏ Do you stay on the subject at all times?
- ❏ Does the concluding paragraph sum up the topic and bring the essay to a satisfying end?
- ❏ Do subjects and verbs agree? Do pronouns agree with their antecedents?
- ❏ Do you need to add transitional words to make smooth connections?
- ❏ Can you add active verbs or sensory words to make your writing vivid?
- ❏ Correct any fragments or run-ons.
- ❏ Do you vary sentence length, using long and short sentences?
- ❏ Check spelling with a dictionary when in doubt.

PRACTICE TEST: WRITING INFORMATIVE ESSAYS *(continued)*

Prewriting

DIRECTIONS: Use the brainstorming chart below to organize your essay. Arrange the brainstorming chart in any way that will be helpful. Here is one possible arrangement:

Description: words and phrases that describe the character's appearance and character

Relationship: words and phrases describing relationship to main character

Role in story: words and phrases describing the character's actions and how they affect the story and its outcome

BRAINSTORMING CHART

PRACTICE TEST: WRITING INFORMATIVE ESSAYS *(continued)*

Student Samples

DIRECTIONS: Read the sample student essays below. Rate each essay with a score from 1 (lowest) to 6 (highest). Use the information on the scoring guide to help you.

ESSAY A: Minor Characters

In *Les Miserables,* Cosette is the daughter of Fantine and is taken care of by the ex-convict, Jean Valjean. Jean Valjean is the main character we follow through the story. Cosette brings joy and love to his life.

Cosette is important to this story because Jean Valjean's life revolves around her and her well-being. Everything that Jean Valjean does is done, in some part, with Cosette in mind. Every time he does something risky, he is doing it for Cosette and thinking of her needs.

Jean Valjean begins taking care of Cosette because he promised her mother he would when she died. Cosette gives him love and, in return, he would do anything to keep her safe and happy. This causes many of the changes of direction in the story.

Jean Valjean is not the only one affected by Cosette, but also Marius. He, too, constantly thinks of Cosette and they only wish to be together.

Marius' and Cosette's need to be together, and Jean Valjean's need to have her be happy, is what produces the outcome of the story. Cosette is important because most of the other characters' decisions are affected by her. These decisions are what affect the story and its end.

Score _____

ESSAY B: Minor Characters

There are many different ways that the pig played important role.

The first reason why the pig played important role is because the pig was the Kids best friend and the pig was nice. Also the pig helped the boy because there was other pig that was running after boy. So the pig bit the pig that was going after the boy. The next reson why the pig was important in the storie. They killed the pig so that the people could eat. As you can see there are many different reasons why this pig is important in this storie.

Score _____

Scoring Guide

SCORE	Unsatisfactory—1	Insufficient—2
Content	Attempts to respond to prompt, but provides few details; may only paraphrase prompt	Presents fragmented information OR may be very repetitive OR may be very undeveloped
Organization	Has no clear organization OR consists of a single statement	Is very disorganized; ideas are weakly connected OR the response is too brief to detect organization
Sentence Structure	Little or no control over sentence boundaries and sentence structure; word choice may be incorrect in much or all of the response	Little control over sentence boundaries and sentence structure; word choice may often be incorrect
Grammar, Usage, and Mechanics	Many errors in grammar or usage (such as tense inconsistency, lack of subject-verb agreement), spelling, and punctuation severely interfere with understanding	Errors in grammar or usage (such as inconsistency, lack of subject-verb agreement), spelling, and punctuation interfere with understanding in much of the response

SCORE	Uneven—3	Sufficient—4
Content	Presents some clear information, but is list-like, undeveloped, or repetitive OR offers no more than a well-written beginning	Develops information with some details
Organization	Is unevenly organized; the essay may be disjointed	Is organized with ideas that are generally related but has few or no transitions
Sentence Structure	Exhibits uneven control over sentence boundaries and sentence structure; may have some incorrect word choices	Exhibits control over sentence boundaries and sentence structure, but sentences and word choices may be simple and unvaried
Grammar, Usage, and Mechanics	Errors in grammar or usage (such as tense inconsistency, lack of subject-verb agreement), spelling, and punctuation sometimes interfere with understanding	Errors in grammar or usage (such as tense inconsistency, lack of subject-verb agreement), spelling, and punctuation do not interfere with understanding

SCORE	Skillful—5	Excellent—6
Content	Develops and shapes information with details in parts of the essay	Develops and shapes information with well-chosen details across the essay
Organization	Is clearly organized, but may lack some transitions and/or have lapses in continuity	Is well organized with strong transitions; has clear beginning, middle, and end
Sentence Structure	Exhibits some variety in sentence structure and some good word choices	Sustains variety in sentence structure and exhibits good word choice
Grammar, Usage, and Mechanics	Errors in grammar, spelling, and punctuation do not interfere with understanding	Errors in grammar, spelling, and punctuation are few and do not interfere with understanding

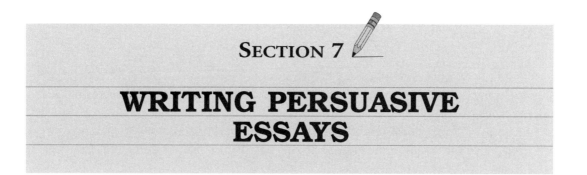
WRITING PERSUASIVE ESSAYS

Standardized Testing Information

Students in tenth grade are often asked to write persuasive essays on state or national assessment tests. Tenth graders usually enjoy this type of writing, since it gives them an opportunity to express their opinions, which are often strongly held. The National Assessment of Educational Progress (NAEP) defines a persuasive essay as one that "seeks to influence the reader to take action or bring about change. It may contain factual information such as reasons, examples, or comparisons; however, its main purpose is to persuade."

The NAEP guidelines go on to say, "In all persuasive writing, authors must choose the approach they will use. They may, for instance, use emotional or logical appeals or an accommodating or demanding tone. Regardless of the situation or approach, persuasive writers must be concerned with having a particular desired effect upon their readers, beyond merely adding to knowledge of the topic."

Most state guidelines for scoring persuasive essays are similar to the NAEP guidelines. The scoring rubric at the end of this section is adapted from the NAEP scoring rubric. Information on the NAEP can be found at www.NAGB.org or at www.nces.ed.gov/nationsreportcard.

A good example of a state rubric is the tenth-grade scoring guide used in Massachusetts. The writing sample is assigned a score from 1 to 6 on topic/idea development and from 1 to 4 on English conventions, as excerpted here:

Topic/Idea Development

- **6 Points**—Rich topic/idea development; careful and/or subtle organization; effective/rich use of language.
- **5 Points**—Full topic/idea development; logical organization; strong details; appropriate use of language.
- **4 Points**—Moderate topic/idea development and organization; adequate, relevant details; some variety in language.
- **3 Points**—Rudimentary topic/idea development; basic supporting details; simplistic language
- **2 Points**—Limited or weak topic/idea development, organization, and/or details.
- **1 Point**—Limited topic/idea development, organization, and/or details; little or no awareness of audience and/or task.

Standard English Conventions

- **4 Points**—Control of sentence structure, grammar and usage, and mechanics (length and complexity of essay provide opportunity for student to show control of standard English conventions)

- **3 Points**—Errors do not interfere with communication and/or few errors relative to length of essay or complexity of sentence structure, grammar and usage, and mechanics
- **2 Points**—Errors interfere somewhat with communication and/or too many errors relative to the length of the essay or complexity of sentence structure, grammar and usage, and mechanics
- **1 Point**—Errors seriously interfere with communication AND little control of sentence structure, grammar and usage, and mechanics

Some states use scoring guides that are more detailed and complex than this example, but it is typical of the specific writing skills and levels of achievement that are rated. The classroom teacher should keep these in mind when leading students through the exercises in this section. The teacher may also find it helpful to occasionally present and discuss selected guidelines from this or other rubrics.

Teacher Preparation and Lessons

The activities in this section are designed to provide a variety of interesting and skill-enhancing experiences in persuasive writing, with guidelines and supportive instructions that will help students reach the level of writing achievement called for both on assessment tests and in life. Each three-part writing assignment guides the student writer through the steps of the writing process, as follows:

- The first part consists of **prewriting activities** such as **brainstorming, outlining,** or **clustering.** These can be done individually, with class participation, or using some combination of these two procedures.
- The second part is the **writing of a first draft.** Students should be encouraged to write freely at this point, without too much concern about grammar, spelling, or punctuation, thus helping to overcome the blocks that many student writers face by making this part of the process less threatening.
- The third part offers directions for **revising and writing a final copy.** The revision and editing process can be done by the individual student alone, in association with the teacher, or with class participation by having students exchange papers with a partner or in small groups and make suggestions for revisions. It will be helpful to review the proofreading symbols on page 307 and encourage their use as part of the revision process.

The persuasive essays in this section range from simple three-paragraph essays to more detailed ones of five or more paragraphs. It is important that students fully understand the nature and purpose of a persuasive essay and what is expected of them. The directions for each activity offer insight into the purpose of persuasive essays and methods of organization, and it is suggested that these be read aloud and discussed.

Practice Test: Writing Persuasive Essays

The sample student essays and their scores are taken from actual examples of student writing on standardized tests. The sample student essays on page 246 are rated 3 and 5, respectively.

Essay A: Giving homeless people a home and a job is the focus of this response. Although the paper lacks a conclusion, an organizational pattern is attempted, as evidenced by the writer's efforts to use transitions ("Because" and "Instead") and cluster information ("crime rate" and "pollution rate"). The supporting ideas relate to the topic but lack sufficient development. Each idea is extended with some specifics, but development remains inadequate (for example, "If the homeless had a home I think the pollution rate would go down . . . because all the bins and dumpsters they set on fire to get warm wouldn't be on fire."). Conventions and word choice are adequate, and there is some sentence variety. To improve this response, the writer needs to develop an effective organizational pattern, elaborate the supporting ideas, and correct punctuation errors. This essay scored a 3.

Essay B: This is a focused response, and there is a logical progression of ideas. Support is ample but not substantial. In the third paragraph, the writer uses the example of the "government shutdown of late 1995 early 1996" to suggest that our "current two-party system does not always work." In this and other sections, elaboration would need to be more specific to earn a higher score. Word choice is often precise ("political hype," "non-offensive manner," and "preyed upon"). Sentence structure is varied, and there are few convention errors. Greater development of support would have improved this response. This essay scored a 5.

7–1. WHEN A DIVORCE IS NECESSARY (PREWRITING)

Divorce is common in today's society. Many children and teens live in homes where a divorce has occurred or have friends who do. Most people would agree that divorce, though not good, is sometimes unavoidable. Under what conditions, if any, do you think a divorce is necessary? Prepare to write an essay expressing your opinion on this subject by preparing a brainstorming list.

BRAINSTORMING LIST

1. On the lines below, write a possible opening sentence or two stating your opinion about this subject (for example, "Call me old-fashioned, but I don't believe that divorce is ever necessary.")

   _____

   _____

2. On the lines below, list three reasons to support your argument. (You don't need complete sentences here; phrases that clearly state your points are enough.) Under each of these supporting points, write words or phrases that you can use to describe this point.

   Supporting point #1: _____

   Words and phrases: _____

   _____

   Supporting point #2: _____

   Words and phrases: _____

   _____

   Supporting point #3: _____

   Words and phrases: _____

   _____

Name _____ **Date** _____

7–2. WHEN A DIVORCE IS NECESSARY (FIRST DRAFT)

DIRECTIONS: Write the first draft of a five-paragraph essay on the topic of when a divorce is necessary. Keep in mind that this is a persuasive essay in which you will be trying to **convince the reader** that your position is the right one. Organize your essay according to your brainstorming list, as follows:

> • In the first paragraph (2 to 4 sentences), introduce the topic and state your opinion. Use the opening from the brainstorming list or improve on it.
>
> • In each of the three middle paragraphs (3 to 6 sentences each), state one supporting point listed on your brainstorming list. Use strong, persuasive details to explain and describe the point fully.
>
> • In the concluding paragraph (2 to 4 sentences), restate and sum up your opinion in a convincing manner.

Begin your essay below, and continue on the back of this sheet. Write a title on the top line, and indent the beginning of each paragraph. This is a first draft, so just concentrate on getting your thoughts down on paper in an organized manner. Don't be too concerned about spelling or grammar at this point.

_____

_____

_____

_____

_____

_____

_____

_____

_____

_____

7–3. When a Divorce Is Necessary
(Revising and writing a final copy)

A. DIRECTIONS: Correct and revise the first draft of your essay. Use your list of proof-reading symbols if this is helpful to you. Keep in mind at all times that you are trying to persuade the reader of the correctness of your opinion. Follow and check off the guidelines below.

❑ Is your opinion clearly stated in the first paragraph? Can you make it more interesting to the reader by using a question or startling statement?

❑ Do each of the three middle paragraphs contain one main point that is supported with details?

❑ Do you stay on the topic? Delete any irrelevant details.

❑ Does the concluding paragraph restate and sum up your opinion? This is your last chance to convince the reader; can you change or add anything to accomplish this?

❑ Are sentences complete? Correct any fragments or run-ons.

❑ Do subjects and verbs agree? Do pronouns agree with their antecedents?

❑ Do you use transitional words to connect thoughts and ideas?

❑ Can you add some active words and sensory language to make your writing more vivid?

❑ Check spelling with a dictionary when in doubt.

B. DIRECTIONS: Begin the final copy of your essay below, and continue on the back of this sheet. Write the title on the first line, and indent the beginning of each paragraph.

_____

_____

_____

_____

_____

_____

_____

_____

_____

7–4. A JOB CHOICE (PREWRITING)

DIRECTIONS: You have two possibilities for summer employment. You can work as a counselor at an athletic camp you have attended for several years, or you can get a job in a local burger chain restaurant. Your parents insist that you take the position of camp counselor. You want to stay home and work at the burger place. You are going to write an essay that will convince your parents to let you take the job of your choice. First, think of convincing arguments you can use and organize them in the brainstorming list below.

- In the first column, list three reasons you can use to support your choice.
- In the second column, write words and phrases you can use to make your argument convincing.

BRAINSTORMING LIST

1.	
2.	
3.	

On the lines below, write an opening sentence that will get your parents' interest in a positive way.

_____

_____

_____

_____

7–5. A JOB CHOICE (FIRST DRAFT)

DIRECTIONS: Write the first draft of a five-paragraph essay about your job choice. Remember, your aim here is to persuade your readers (your parents) that your choice is a good one. Use the notes in your brainstorming list, and organize your essay as follows:

> • In the first paragraph (2 to 4 sentences), state your choice in a way that will get your parents' attention.
>
> • In each of the three middle paragraphs (3 to 5 sentences each), state one reason why this is a good job choice. Use details to strengthen each of these supporting points.
>
> • In the concluding paragraph (2 to 4 sentences), restate and sum up your choice in a convincing manner.

Begin your essay below, and continue on the back of this sheet. Indent the beginning of each paragraph. This is a first draft, so concentrate on getting your thoughts down on paper in an organized, convincing way. Don't be too concerned about spelling and grammar at this point.

_____

_____

_____

_____

_____

_____

_____

_____

_____

7–6. A Job Choice (revising and writing a final copy)

A. DIRECTIONS: Correct and revise the first draft of your essay. Use proofreading symbols if these are helpful to you. Keep in mind that you are trying to persuade your parents to accept your choice of a job. Follow and check off each guideline below.

❑ Is the topic and your choice clearly stated in the first paragraph? Can you make your approach more positive?

❑ Do each of the three middle paragraphs contain one point to support your choice? Can you add more convincing details?

❑ Do you stay on the topic? Delete any irrelevant details.

❑ Does the concluding paragraph restate and sum up your opinion? Can you change or add anything to appear more positive and convincing?

❑ Are sentences complete? Correct any fragments or run-ons.

❑ Do subjects and verbs agree? Do pronouns agree with their antecedents?

❑ Do you use transitional words (for example, *first, then, finally, at last, therefore*) to connect ideas?

❑ Check spelling with a dictionary when in doubt.

B. DIRECTIONS: Begin the final copy of your persuasive essay below, and continue on the back of this sheet. Write the title on the first line, and indent the beginning of each paragraph.

_____

_____

_____

_____

_____

_____

_____

_____

_____

_____

_____

7–7. An Official Language? (Prewriting)

DIRECTIONS: Some people believe that Congress should pass a law establishing English as the official language of the United States. What do you think? Check the box below that states your opinion.

❑ English should be the official language of the United States.
❑ English should not be the official language of the United States.

You are going to write an essay expressing your opinion on this issue and giving facts to support it. First, organize your thoughts by using the **brainstorming list** below.

• In the first column, list three reasons to support your opinion.

• In the second column, next to each supporting point, write words and phrases you can use to strengthen that point.

BRAINSTORMING LIST

Supporting Points/Reasons	Useful Words and Phrases
1.	
2.	
3.	

Name _____ Date _____

7–8. An Official Language? (first draft)

DIRECTIONS: Write the first draft of a five-paragraph essay, stating your opinion about whether Congress should enact a law declaring English to be the official language of the United States. You have already made notes about your position and the reasons for it on your brainstorming list. Consult those notes, and organize your essay as follows:

- In the first paragraph (2 to 4 sentences), introduce the subject in an interesting manner (for example, "French is the official language of France. German is the official language of Germany. The United States should have its own official language, which I believe should be English." or "An official language for the United States? This is a terrible idea! It would have many negative results.")
- In each of the three middle paragraphs (3 to 5 sentences each), state one reason that supports your opinion. Use strong details to strengthen each of these supporting points.
- In the concluding paragraph (2 to 4 sentences), restate the topic (your opinion) in a strong and positive way.

Begin your essay below, and continue on the back of this sheet. Write a title on the first line, and indent the beginning of each paragraph. This is a first draft, so concentrate on organizing your ideas and getting them down on paper as convincingly as possible. Don't be too concerned about spelling and grammar at this point.

7–9. AN OFFICIAL LANGUAGE?
(REVISING AND WRITING A FINAL COPY)

A. DIRECTIONS: Correct and revise the first draft of your essay. Remember that you are trying to persuade your readers that your point of view is correct. Follow and check off each guideline below.

❏ Do you state your opinion clearly in the first paragraph? Can you make the opening more interesting with a question, quote, or exclamation?

❏ Do each of the three middle paragraphs discuss one point that supports your opinion? Can you add more convincing details?

❏ Do you stay on the topic? Delete any irrelevant details.

❏ Does the concluding paragraph restate and sum up your opinion? Can you add anything to make it more convincing to readers?

❏ Do you vary sentence length, using long and short sentences?

❏ Do subjects and verbs agree? Do pronouns agree with their antecedents?

❏ Do you use transitional words to make smooth connections?

❏ Add active verbs and sensory language to make your writing more vivid.

❏ Check spelling with a dictionary when in doubt.

B. DIRECTIONS: Begin the final copy of your persuasive essay below, and continue on the back of this sheet. Write a title on the top line, and indent the beginning of each paragraph.

_____

_____

_____

_____

_____

_____

_____

Name _____   **Date** _____

7–10. COED TEAMS (PREWRITING)

DIRECTIONS: In recent years, there has been pressure on schools to permit girls to play on boys' athletic teams. Do you think this is a good idea? You are going to write an essay to explain what you think about this controversial subject. Check the box next to the statement that expresses your opinion.

> ❏ Girls should be permitted to play on boys' athletic teams.
> ❏ Girls should not be permitted to play on boys' athletic teams.

In this essay, you will use a **compare and contrast** organization. This means that you will compare several supporting points, then come up with a conclusion based on these comparisons. First, prepare a **brainstorming list** to organize your ideas. It will be easy to plan the compare and contrast organization if you follow the format suggested below.

Complete the brainstorming list as follows:

1. Three points to consider are listed in the first column. You can use these, or change them to supporting topics of your own choosing.

2. In the second column, next to each point, list the advantages of that point (words and phrases).

3. In the third column, next to each point, list the disadvantages of that point (words and phrases).

BRAINSTORMING LIST

Points to Consider	Advantages	Disadvantages
1. Effect on girls		
2. Effect on boys		
3. Effect on school and community		

7–11. COED TEAMS (FIRST DRAFT)

DIRECTIONS: Write the first draft of a five-paragraph essay on the topic of whether girls should be permitted to play on boys' athletic teams. Use your brainstorming list as a guide. Here are some suggestions for organizing your essay:

- In the first paragraph (2 to 4 sentences), introduce the topic. State your opinion clearly and in a way that will get the reader's attention (for example, "I know girls with awesome athletic skills! They should not be denied the opportunity to use these skills on the well-financed and more prestigious teams that are now exclusively for males.").
- In each of the three middle paragraphs (3 to 6 sentences each), discuss one consideration. Compare and contrast its advantages and disadvantages as outlined on your brainstorming list.
- In the fifth paragraph (2 to 4 sentences), sum up the topic and conclude in a convincing way.

Begin your essay below, and continue on the back of this sheet. Write a title on the first line, and indent the beginning of each paragraph. This is a first draft, so concentrate on organizing your ideas and getting them down on paper as convincingly as possible. Don't be too concerned about spelling and grammar at this point.

_____

_____

_____

_____

_____

_____

_____

_____

_____

_____

7–12. COED TEAMS (REVISING AND WRITING A FINAL COPY)

A. DIRECTIONS: Correct and revise the first draft of your essay. Keep in mind that you are trying to persuade your readers that your point of view is correct. Follow and check off the guidelines below:

> ❑ Do you state your opinion clearly in the first paragraph? Can you make the opening sentence more exciting with a question, quote, or exclamation?
>
> ❑ Do each of the three middle paragraphs discuss one aspect of this topic, comparing its advantages and disadvantages?
>
> ❑ Do you stay on the topic? Delete any irrelevant details.
>
> ❑ Does the concluding paragraph sum up your opinion? Can you make it stronger and more convincing?
>
> ❑ Do subjects and verbs agree? Do pronouns agree with their antecedents?
>
> ❑ Do you use transitional words to make smooth connections?
>
> ❑ Add active verbs and sensory language to make your writing more vivid.
>
> ❑ Check spelling with a dictionary when in doubt.

B. DIRECTIONS: Begin the final copy of your persuasive essay below, and continue on the back of this sheet. Write a title on the first line, and indent the beginning of each paragraph.

_____

_____

_____

_____

_____

_____

_____

_____

_____

_____

7–13. A SCHOOL DRESS CODE (PREWRITING)

DIRECTIONS: The principal of your school is considering the establishment of a dress code for students, and the editor of the school newspaper has asked you to write an editorial discussing this issue.

An **editorial** is an opinion essay. It follows the same format as any other **persuasive essay.** Newspapers are supposed to be objective in their news reports, but editors have an opportunity to present their opinions in their editorials.

Before writing your editorial, organize your thoughts by using a **brainstorming list,** as follows:

1. On the lines below, write an opening sentence or sentences that express your opinion on the issue of a school dress code.

   _____

   _____

   _____

2. Briefly state two to four reasons for your opinion. For each reason, list words and phrases you can use to support it.

   First point: _____

   Supporting words and phrases: _____

   _____

   Second point: _____

   Supporting words and phrases: _____

   _____

   Third point: _____

   Supporting words and phrases: _____

   _____

   Fourth point: _____

   Supporting words and phrases: _____

   _____

7–14. A School Dress Code (first draft)

DIRECTIONS: Write the first draft of an editorial (opinion article) for your school newspaper about the proposed dress code. Remember that other students will be reading this editorial and they are the ones you want to convince. **The length of this essay is up to you.** You can write a short editorial of three paragraphs, in which all your supporting points are stated in the second paragraph, or you can write a longer essay, using a separate paragraph to discuss each point in greater detail. Consult the notes on your brainstorming list and follow the directions below.

- In the first paragraph (2 to 4 sentences), introduce the topic and state your opinion clearly (for example, "Uniforms are for the armed forces or people in prison. A dress code is a uniform, and young people should not be forced to wear uniforms.")
- In the middle paragraph or paragraphs (3 to 8 sentences each), develop the topic with effective points and details that support your opinion.
- In the concluding paragraph (2 to 4 sentences), sum up and bring the editorial to a close with strong and convincing statements.

Begin your essay below, and continue on the back of this sheet. Write a title (in a newspaper, the title is called a *headline*) on the first line. Indent the beginning of each paragraph. This is a first draft, so concentrate on organizing your thoughts and getting them down on paper. Don't be too concerned about spelling or grammar at this point.

7–15. A SCHOOL DRESS CODE
(REVISING AND WRITING A FINAL COPY)

A. DIRECTIONS: Correct and revise the first draft of your editorial about a school dress code. Follow the guidelines below, and check off each one as you complete it.

> ❏ Do you state your opinion clearly in the first paragraph? Can you make it more exciting with a question or startling statement, so the reader will want to continue?
>
> ❏ Does the middle paragraph or paragraphs clearly present and discuss supporting points for your opinion?
>
> ❏ Do you stay on the topic? Delete any irrelevant details.
>
> ❏ Did you leave out anything important? If so, now is the time to insert it.
>
> ❏ Does the concluding paragraph restate and sum up your opinion?
>
> ❏ Do subjects and verbs agree? Do pronouns agree with their antecedents?
>
> ❏ Add a simile or metaphor to make your writing sparkle.
>
> ❏ Check spelling with a dictionary when in doubt.

B. DIRECTIONS: Begin the final copy of your editorial below, and continue on the back of this sheet. Write a title (headline) on the top line, and indent the beginning of each paragraph.

_____

_____

_____

_____

_____

_____

_____

_____

_____

7–16. ARE PEOPLE BASICALLY GOOD? (PREWRITING)

DIRECTIONS: Most people have read or at least heard of *The Diary of a Young Girl* by Anne Frank, written by a teenage girl about her experiences during World War II. Anne Frank later died in a German concentration camp. In spite of the horror all around her, Anne writes in her diary that she believes people are basically good. Do you agree or disagree with this idea?

Prepare a **brainstorming list** for an essay called "People Are Basically Good" or "People Are Not Basically Good." This type of essay works well with **examples** as supporting points. For instance, if you want to prove that people are basically good, you could describe several examples of events that strengthen your topic statement. If you think that the opposite is true, tell about events that prove your point. Develop your brainstorming list as follows:

1. State your opinion on the line below.

   _____

2. List three examples you can use in your essay to prove that people are or are not basically good. (You don't need to use complete sentences—just phrases.) After each example, write a list of words and phrases that will help you describe that event. For instance, you could cite a recent event in your town in which firefighters went back into a burning building to rescue a family's pet. Or, to prove the opposite, you could describe a time when someone experienced a heart attack and fell down on a city street, only to be ignored by passersby who assumed the person was drunk.

   First example: _____

   Supporting words and phrases: _____

   _____

   Second example: _____

   Supporting words and phrases: _____

   _____

   Third example: _____

   Supporting words and phrases: _____

   _____

7–17. ARE PEOPLE BASICALLY GOOD? (FIRST DRAFT)

DIRECTIONS: Write the first draft of a five-paragraph essay called "People Are Basically Good," or "People Are Not Basically Good." Use the notes from your brainstorming list. Remember that you are trying to persuade your readers to agree with you. Follow these instructions:

> • In the first paragraph (2 to 4 sentences), introduce the topic and state your opinion clearly and in an attention-getting way (for example, "People are basically good? Perhaps an infant might believe that, but not anyone who has seen and read about the terrible things that people do to each other." or "Some people may assume that Anne Frank was innocent or naive. Not me! She had an extraordinary faith in people. If more of us had her outlook, this would be a better world.")
>
> • In each of the three middle paragraphs (3 to 6 sentences each), write about one example that supports your opinion.
>
> • In the concluding paragraph (2 to 4 sentences), conclude your essay by summing up the topic in a strong, convincing way.

Begin your essay below, and continue on the back of this sheet. Write the title on the top line, and indent the beginning of each paragraph. This is a first draft, so concentrate on organizing your thoughts and getting them down on paper. Don't be too concerned about spelling or grammar at this point.

Name _____ Date _____

7–18. ARE PEOPLE BASICALLY GOOD?
(REVISING AND WRITING A FINAL COPY)

A. DIRECTIONS: Correct and revise the first draft of your essay. Use proofreading symbols if they are helpful to you. Follow the guidelines below, and check off each one as you complete it.

> ❑ Do you state your opinion clearly in the first paragraph? Can you use a question, quote, or startling statement to grab the reader's interest?
> ❑ Does each of the three middle paragraphs develop the topic by offering one example that supports your opinion?
> ❑ Can you make these events more interesting with strong details, active verbs, and sensory language?
> ❑ Do you stay on the topic at all times?
> ❑ Does the concluding paragraph restate and sum up your opinion? Can you make it stronger and more convincing?
> ❑ Are sentences complete? Correct any fragments or run-ons.
> ❑ Do subjects and verbs agree? Do pronouns agree with their antecedents?
> ❑ Can you add transitional words (for example, *then, therefore, however, in addition*) to make smoother connections?
> ❑ Check spelling with a dictionary when in doubt.

B. DIRECTIONS: Begin the final copy of your essay below, and continue on the back of this sheet. Write the title on the top line, and indent the beginning of each paragraph.

_____

_____

_____

_____

_____

_____

_____

_____

_____

7–19. CUTTING PROGRAMS (PREWRITING)

What are they going to cut? In classrooms, halls, and campuses, wherever groups of students gather, this is the main topic of conversation. The school district is in a budget crunch. There must be cutbacks! Among other cost-saving measures, it has been decided that one course will be eliminated from the school curriculum. Which one will it be? Some possibilities that have been mentioned are art, music, one of the athletic teams, and advanced physics.

The editor of your school newspaper has asked you to write an editorial on this topic. This editorial (opinion article) will be read by students, faculty, administrators, and parents. Your words will have the power to influence opinion on this issue, so before you begin the article, give some thought to what your recommendation will be. Then organize your ideas on the **brainstorming list** below.

BRAINSTORMING LIST

1. On the lines below, write an opening sentence (or sentences) recommending which program should be cut.

   _____

   _____

   _____

2. List three supporting points for your opinion. (You don't need to write sentences—just phrases.) Under each supporting point, list words and phrases that provide more details.

   First point:_____

   _____

   Words and phrases:_____

   _____

   Second point: _____

   _____

   Words and phrases:_____

   _____

   Third point:_____

   _____

   Words and phrases:_____

   _____

7–20. CUTTING PROGRAMS (FIRST DRAFT)

DIRECTIONS: Write the first draft of an editorial (opinion article) for your school newspaper on the subject of cutting one course from the school curriculum. You want your article to be strong and convincing so that it will influence the students, teachers, parents, and administrators who read it. Consult the notes you have made on your brainstorming list, and follow the suggestions below.

> - In the first paragraph (2 to 4 sentences), introduce the topic and your opinion in a way that will attract the attention of your readers (for example, "What a terrible choice! Losing even one program from the excellent curriculum our school offers will be a tragedy. If it must be done, however, let us eliminate advanced physics.").
> - In each of the three middle paragraphs (3 to 6 sentences each), discuss one of the supporting points on your brainstorming list.
> - In the concluding paragraph (2 to 4 sentences), sum up and restate your opinion in a strong, convincing way.

Begin your essay below, and continue on the back of this sheet. Write a title on the top line. (In a newspaper, the title is called a *headline.*) Indent the beginning of each paragraph. This is a first draft, so don't be too concerned about spelling or grammar at this point. Concentrate on organizing your thoughts and getting them down on paper.

7–21. CUTTING PROGRAMS
(REVISING AND WRITING A FINAL COPY)

A. DIRECTIONS: Correct and revise the first draft of your editorial about cutting a program from the curriculum. Follow the guidelines below, and check off each one as you complete it.

> ❑ Is your opinion clearly expressed in the introductory paragraph? Can you begin with a question or startling statement that will grab the reader's interest?
>
> ❑ Do each of the three middle paragraphs develop the topic by presenting one supporting point? Can you enhance any of these arguments with stronger details?
>
> ❑ Do you stay on the topic? Delete any irrelevant details.
>
> ❑ Have you left out anything important that would strengthen your argument? If so, insert it now.
>
> ❑ Does the concluding paragraph sum up and restate your position convincingly?
>
> ❑ Do subjects and verbs agree? Do pronouns agree with their antecedents?
>
> ❑ Do you need to add transitional words to make smoother connections?
>
> ❑ Add active verbs and sensory language to make your writing vivid.
>
> ❑ Check spelling with a dictionary when in doubt.

B. DIRECTIONS: Begin the final copy of your editorial below, and continue on the back of this sheet. Write a title (headline) on the top line, and indent the beginning of each paragraph.

_____

_____

_____

_____

_____

_____

_____

Tenth-Grade Level

Writing Persuasive Essays
Practice Test

PRACTICE TEST: WRITING PERSUASIVE ESSAYS

DIRECTIONS: Can the United States be a better place in which to live than it is now? What changes do you think the government can make to achieve this goal?

Follow these four steps to write your essay:

- FIRST, on the page labeled "Prewriting," brainstorm essay ideas and examples that support the topic and will be convincing to your reader. Include words and phrases you can use to flesh out your ideas.
- SECOND, write the first draft of your essay on a separate sheet of paper. Write your name, the date, and the title of your essay at the top of the page. Consult your notes from the brainstorming page.
- THIRD, revise and edit your first draft. Refer to your list of proofreading symbols if you wish. Use the checklist below as a guide, and check off each item when it has been revised to your satisfaction.
- FOURTH, write your final copy on a separate sheet of paper with your name and date at the top.

CHECKLIST
- ❏ Does your introductory paragraph state the topic clearly? Can you use a question, quotation, or startling statement to grab the reader's attention?
- ❏ Do your middle paragraphs develop the topic in a logical, convincing way? Does each of these paragraphs describe one supporting point or example that strengthens your point of view?
- ❏ Do you stay on the subject at all times?
- ❏ Does the concluding paragraph sum up the topic in a convincing way and bring the essay to a satisfying close?
- ❏ Do subjects and verbs agree? Do pronouns agree with their antecedents?
- ❏ Do you need to add transitional words to make smooth connections?
- ❏ Correct any fragments or run-ons.
- ❏ Do you vary sentence length, using long and short sentences?
- ❏ Check spelling with a dictionary when in doubt.

PRACTICE TEST: WRITING PERSUASIVE ESSAYS *(continued)*

Prewriting

Think about three main points you will use in your opinion essay suggesting changes that should be made by the United States government. List these three points in the box below. You can arrange them as an outline, a brainstorming list, or a cluster. For each point, add words and phrases that will give supporting details.

PRACTICE TEST: WRITING PERSUASIVE ESSAYS *(continued)*

Student Samples

DIRECTIONS: Read the sample student essays below. Rate each essay with a score from 1 (lowest) to 6 (highest). Use the information on the scoring guide to help you.

ESSAY A

I think one change that would make this country a better place to live is to give all the homeless people a home and a job. This one change would make the United States a better place to live because if we had no homeless people I think that a lot of the crime rate would go down. People wouldn't have to rob stores and jump people for their money and gold to get food for themselves and their families if they had a job. If the homeless had a home I think the pollution rate would go down. The pollution rate would go down because all the bins and dumpsters they set on fire to get warm wouldn't be on fire. Instead the homeless would be in their homes with heat and blankets to keep themselves warm.

Score _____

ESSAY B

The United States may be an excellent place to live, but, like anything, there is always room for improvement. On thing that could make our country a better place to live is a government that works under the basic idea of peace and unity. It would help our people understand who is right and wrong while giving us a sense of belonging.

Today, innocent people are being preyed upon by those whose ways are selfish. What we need is to get the government to show our citizens how to improve our own status without hurting others. This could be done by speaking to us without the usual political hype. It is up to the government to show us how things should be done. After all, they make the decisions for our nation.

Another way the United States could be improved would be to have the government work together respectfully. The government shutdown of late 1995 early 1996 shows how our current two-party system does not always work. In order to give the nation a sense of equality and belonging we must first see it in the government. This would mean no political parties, just people working under the principals of peace and unity.

Last of all, if our government were to preach harmony in a non-offensive manner, maybe the people could see how violence is a beast that must be slain. Once again, people's selfish ideas lead to violent acts upon those who oppose them. People should be able to better themselves without imposing on others. The government could teach these things by setting up more programs to help children understand how to treat each other equally. We must start out young because children are our future.

In closing, what our nation needs is a government that will focus on equality and unity of the people and will lead us to harmony. If everyone lived with these ideas, the Earth could be an Eden after all.

Score _____

Scoring Guide

SCORE	Unsatisfactory—1	Insufficient—2
Content	Attempts to respond to prompt, but provides few details to persuade the reader; may only paraphrase prompt	Presents fragmented information OR may be very repetitive OR may be very undeveloped
Organization	Has no clear organization OR consists of a single statement	Is very disorganized; ideas are weakly connected OR the response is too brief to detect organization
Sentence Structure	Little or no control over sentence boundaries and sentence structure; word choice may be incorrect in much or all of the response	Little control over sentence boundaries and sentence structure; word choice may often be incorrect
Grammar, Usage, and Mechanics	Many errors in grammar or usage (such as tense inconsistency, lack of subject-verb agreement), spelling, and punctuation severely interfere with understanding	Errors in grammar or usage (such as inconsistency, lack of subject-verb agreement), spelling, and punctuation interfere with understanding in much of the response

SCORE	Uneven—3	Sufficient—4
Content	Presents some clear information, but is list-like, undeveloped, or repetitive OR offers no more than a well-written beginning	Develops information with some details
Organization	Is unevenly organized; the essay may be disjointed	Is organized with ideas that are generally related but has few or no transitions
Sentence Structure	Exhibits uneven control over sentence boundaries and sentence structure; may have some incorrect word choices	Exhibits control over sentence boundaries and sentence structure, but sentences and word choices may be simple and unvaried
Grammar, Usage, and Mechanics	Errors in grammar or usage (such as tense inconsistency, lack of subject-verb agreement), spelling, and punctuation sometimes interfere with understanding	Errors in grammar or usage (such as tense inconsistency, lack of subject-verb agreement), spelling, and punctuation do not interfere with understanding

SCORE	Skillful—5	Excellent—6
Content	Develops and shapes information with details in parts of the essay	Develops and shapes information with well-chosen details across the essay
Organization	Is clearly organized, but may lack some transitions and/or have lapses in continuity	Is well organized with strong transitions
Sentence Structure	Exhibits some variety in sentence structure and some good word choices	Sustains variety in sentence structure and exhibits good word choice
Grammar, Usage, and Mechanics	Errors in grammar, spelling, and punctuation do not interfere with understanding	Errors in grammar, spelling, and punctuation are few and do not interfere with understanding

NARRATIVE WRITING

Standardized Testing Information

Students generally find narrative writing the easiest type to do and the most fun, because this type of writing allows for flexibility in structure and content as well as the use of imagination and personal experience. Many assessment tests use narrative prompts. These include personal narratives (true stories about something that has happened to or been observed by the writer) and stories (fictional narratives where the details arise from the imagination of the writer.) Both personal narratives and imaginative stories use similar narrative techniques and are grouped together in this section.

The National Assessment of Educational Progress (NAEP) defines narrative writing as "the production of stories or personal essays." The NAEP guidelines go on to say that narrative writing "encourages writers to use their creativity and powers of observation to develop stories that can capture a reader's imagination." Information on the NAEP can be found at www.NAGB.org or at www.nces.ed.gov/nationsreportcard.

Narrative writing, therefore, is of two types:

1. The **personal narrative, or narrative essay,** is usually written from the writer's point of view. Generally, the subject is something that has actually happened, and events are related in chronological order. The people and places are real, as is any dialogue that is used.

2. An **imaginative narrative** is also usually narrated in chronological order, but is fictional, with fictional characters and fictional dialogue.

Following are two examples of prompts that have been used in tenth-grade assessment tests. The first prompt is clearly for a personal narrative. The second is a story prompt.

Example 1: Many times in life we avoid experiences because we are afraid to do them, or we dread the thoughts of a negative experience. Other times we have no choice and must do what we dread most. In some instances, our worst fears are realized, but more often we learn that our fears were unjustified. Write about an experience you dreaded but discovered was not nearly so bad as you had expected.

Example 2: You are shipwrecked on an island for a month with only your backpack. Tell how you survive with the items in your backpack.

Guidelines for narrative writing vary slightly from state to state, but the following set of scoring rubrics from Pennsylvania is similar to most.

The "Pennsylvania Writing Assessment Domain Scoring Guide" is divided into five categories: focus, content, organization, style, and conventions. These earn scores from 1 (lowest) to 4 (highest), as excerpted on the next page.

4. **Focus:** Sharp, distinct controlling point made about a single topic with evident awareness of task (mode). **Content:** Substantial, specific and/or illustrative content demonstrating strong development and sophisticated ideas. **Organization:** Sophisticated arrangement of content with evident and/or subtle transitions. **Style:** Precise, illustrative use of a variety of words and sentence structures to create consistent writer's voice and tone, appropriate to audience. **Conventions:** Evident control of grammar, mechanics, spelling, usage, and sentence formation.

3. **Focus:** Apparent point made about a single topic with sufficient awareness of task (mode). **Content:** Sufficiently developed content with adequate elaboration or explanation. **Organization:** Functional arrangement of content that sustains a logical order with some evidence of transitions. **Style:** Generic use of a variety of words and sentence structures that may or may not create writer's voice and tone appropriate to audience. **Conventions:** Sufficient control of grammar, mechanics, spelling, usage, and sentence formation.

2. **Focus:** No apparent point but evidence of a specific topic. **Content:** Limited content with inadequate elaboration or explanation. **Organization:** Confused or inconsistent arrangement of content with or without attempts at transition. **Style:** Limited word choice and control of sentence structures that inhibit voice and tone. **Conventions:** Limited control of grammar, mechanics, spelling, usage, and sentence formation.

1. **Focus:** Minimal evidence of a topic. **Content:** Superficial and/or minimal content. **Organization:** Minimal control of content arrangement. **Style:** Minimal variety in word choice and minimal control of sentence structures. **Conventions:** Minimal control of grammar, mechanics, spelling, usage, and sentence formation.

These guidelines and rubrics are typical. The classroom teacher should keep them in mind when leading students through the exercises in this section. The teacher may also find it helpful to occasionally present and discuss with the students selected guidelines from this or other state rubrics.

Teacher Preparation and Lessons

The activities in this section are designed to provide a variety of interesting experiences in narrative writing, with guidelines and supportive instructions that will lead the students through the writing process and enhance their skills while also stimulating interest in this kind of writing.

Each activity has three parts:

- The first part consists of **prewriting** activities such as **brainstorming, clustering,** or **outlining.** These can be done individually, in small groups, with whole-class participation, or using some combination of these three procedures. In addition to jotting down ideas and making lists of words and phrases to be used in the essay, students should also be advised and guided to use this step of the writing process to provide an organizational framework for their writing.

- The second part is the **writing of a first draft.** Students should be encouraged to write freely at this point, without too much concern about grammar, spelling, and punctuation, thus helping to overcome the blocks that many student writers face by making this part of the process less threatening. This is especially important in narrative writing, which calls for a free flow of imagination and creativity.

- The third part offers directions for **revising and writing a final copy.** The revision and editing process can be done by the individual student alone, in association with the teacher, or with class participation by having students exchange papers and make suggestions for revision. Each revision activity includes a checklist for students to refer to during the editing process. When necessary, this would be a good point at which to review basic elements of essay writing, such as the purpose and nature of a good introductory paragraph, developing the topic, staying on the subject, and using transitional words. It will be helpful to review the proofreading symbols on page 307. Students should have copies of these on hand and should be encouraged to use them as part of the revision process.

This unit on narrative writing should be introduced in a positive, upbeat, exciting manner that makes it clear that this is the sort of activity that students will truly enjoy. The teacher can say something like, "How many 'compositions' do you put together every day? Probably at least one personal narrative—a true story about something that has happened to you or to someone you know. You usually tell these stories orally to your friends, family, and teachers. With a little practice, you can easily acquire the skill to write down these personal narratives in a way that will be interesting to other people."

It is important to point out to the students that narrative writing differs in at least one significant way from informative and persuasive essays, which usually begin with a topic statement, then develop the topic with supporting facts or details. In a five-paragraph informative or persuasive essay, each of the three middle paragraphs may present one of these supporting facts. **Narrative writing** also begins with a statement of the subject, but then usually develops it **chronologically, telling the story in sequences of events or scenes.**

Before beginning activities that involve writing imaginative stories, it can be helpful for the teacher or students to read aloud one or more exciting passages from a work of fiction, to prepare the students for their own flights of imagination.

Note that tenth-grade assessment tests include personal narrative prompts more frequently than they include imaginative narratives. Therefore, most of the activities in this section will concentrate on personal narratives.

The directions for each activity will help students understand the purposes and methods of narrative writing. It is suggested that the directions be read aloud and discussed.

Practice Test: Narrative Writing

The sample student essays and their scores are taken from actual examples of student writing on standardized tests. The sample student essays on page 276 are rated 6 and 1, respectively.

Essay A has a strong, clearly written controlling point about conquering a fear of job hunting. This fear controls the content throughout the narrative development of the essay. The essay is well organized, with good transitions. A variety of words and sentence structures create a consistent writer's voice, and there is evident control of grammar, mechanics, spelling, usage, and sentence formation. This essay received a score of 6.

Essay B has minimal evidence of a topic. The narrative is disorganized and confusing. Who asked the guy out—the writer, another girl, or another guy? The content and details are superficial and confusing. Lack of control in the conventions of grammar, mechanics, spelling, usage, and sentence formation prevent any style or coherence from emerging. This essay received a score of 1.

8–1. LEARNING FROM EXPERIENCE (PREWRITING)

It is easy and fun to write about things that have happened to you or that you have observed. This kind of essay is called a **personal narrative.** Personal narratives differ from informative and persuasive essays in the way they are developed. In an informative or persuasive essay, the main subject is developed with supporting points or subtopics. Narrative writing, however, is often organized **chronologically** (by time) in sequences of events or scenes. Keep this in mind whenever you write a narrative.

Life is full of experiences that teach us lessons. Write about an experience that taught you an important lesson. First, prepare a **brainstorming list,** following the directions below.

BRAINSTORMING LIST

1. On the line below, describe briefly where this experience occurred. Then list words and phrases you can use in your description of the place.

   Where: _____

   Descriptive words and phrases: _____

2. On the line below, tell when this experience occurred (for example, what month or year, your age at the time). Then list words and phrases you can use in describing the time.

   When: _____

   Descriptive words and phrases: _____

3. On the line below, tell who else was present. Then list words and phrases you can use to describe the person or persons.

   Who: _____

   Descriptive words and phrases: _____

4. Organize the development of your narrative by dividing it into several segments of time, and describe each one briefly below. (For example, the first segment could introduce the time and place. The second segment could tell how the incident began, the third segment could tell what happened next, and the last segment could tell how the incident ended.) Think of each segment as part of a scene in a story or movie.

   First segment: _____

   Second segment: _____

   Third segment: _____

5. Describe briefly what this experience taught you.

   _____

8–2. LEARNING FROM EXPERIENCE (FIRST DRAFT)

DIRECTIONS: Write the first draft of a narrative telling about an experience that taught you a lesson. Use your **brainstorming list** as a guide, and follow these suggestions:

- In the first paragraph (2 to 4 sentences), introduce the topic in a way that will grab the reader's interest (for example, "Do you continue to make the same mistakes over and over? If so, you are like most people, including me. Once, however, I had an experience that taught me an important lesson.")
- In each of the middle paragraphs (3 to 7 sentences each), develop your narrative by describing what happened. Begin by telling where and when the experience occurred and who was there. Then narrate the events in chronological order, as a series of scenes. Use as many paragraphs as you need for the development. Complete this section by telling how the experience ended.
- In your concluding paragraph, sum up the experience and explain what you learned from it.

Begin your narrative on the lines below, and continue on the back of this sheet. Write a title on the top line, and indent the beginning of each paragraph. This is just a first draft, so concentrate on getting your thoughts on paper without too much concern for spelling and grammar.

8–3. LEARNING FROM EXPERIENCE
(REVISING AND WRITING A FINAL COPY)

A. DIRECTIONS: Revise and correct the first draft of your narrative about a learning experience. Use proofreading symbols if they are helpful to you. Follow the guidelines below, and check off each one as you complete it.

❑ Does the first paragraph introduce the subject in an interesting way? Can you use a question, quotation, or startling statement to grab the reader's attention?

❑ Do the middle paragraphs develop the narrative by telling what happened chronologically in a clear and organized way?

❑ Do you begin by telling where and when the experience occurred?

❑ Do you introduce and describe the people involved?

❑ Do you describe clearly when and how the incident came to an end?

❑ Does the concluding paragraph sum up the experience and state clearly what lesson you learned?

❑ Can you add active verbs and colorful adjectives to make your writing vivid?

❑ Are sentences complete? Correct any fragments or run-ons.

❑ Do subjects and verbs agree? Do pronouns agree with their antecedents?

❑ Do you use transitional words (such as *then, therefore, however, at first*) to make smooth connections?

❑ Check spelling with a dictionary when in doubt.

B. DIRECTIONS: Begin the final copy of your narrative below, and continue on the back of this sheet. Write a title on the top line, and indent the beginning of each paragraph.

_____

_____

_____

_____

_____

_____

8–4. MAKING A DECISION (PREWRITING)

When we are young children, our parents make most of our decisions for us. Growing up requires us to make our own decisions. Think about a time when you had to make an important decision and what resulted from that decision. You are going to write an essay about that experience. First, organize your thoughts by preparing a **cluster.** Follow the directions below.

DIRECTIONS: On a separate sheet of paper, prepare a cluster for this essay, as follows:

1. Draw a large circle on a sheet of paper. Write the subject in the middle of the circle in big letters.

2. Divide your decision-making experience into scenes from beginning to end. Give each scene a title, and write each title in somewhat smaller print in different parts of the circle around the subject (for example, "where and when," "people present," "problem to be solved," "factors to be considered," "final decision").

3. Near each title, use even smaller lettering to write words and phrases that describe it.

Here is an example of how your cluster might look:

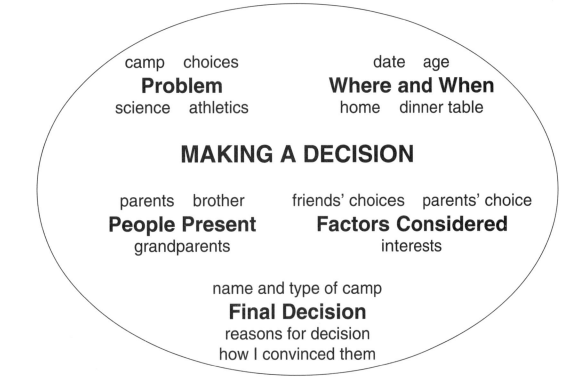

8–5. MAKING A DECISION (FIRST DRAFT)

DIRECTIONS: Write the first draft of an essay describing a time when you had to make an important decision. Use your cluster as a guide, and follow these suggestions.

- In the first paragraph (2 to 4 sentences), introduce the topic in a way that will spark a reader's interest (for example, "'It's your choice, kid.' I couldn't believe my father's words! I was only eight; how could I make such an important decision?").

- Describe this experience, from beginning to end, in the middle paragraphs (3 to 7 sentences each). Describe the problem and how it came about. Then tell what happened, in chronological order. Say who was there and how they influenced your decision, if at all. What other factors were involved? The number of middle paragraphs will vary, but don't include more than one or two points (or steps) in each paragraph. End this middle part of the essay with your decision.

- In the concluding paragraph (2 to 4 sentences), restate the subject and describe what resulted from the decision you made and how you felt about it.

Begin your narrative on the lines below, and continue on the back of this sheet. Write a title on the top line, and indent the beginning of each paragraph. This is just a first draft, so concentrate on getting your thoughts on paper without too much concern for spelling and grammar at this point.

_____

_____

_____

_____

_____

_____

_____

_____

8–6. MAKING A DECISION
(REVISING AND WRITING A FINAL COPY)

A. DIRECTIONS: Revise and correct the first draft of your essay about making a decision. Use proofreading symbols if you find them helpful. Follow the guidelines below, and check off each one as you complete it.

❑ Does the first paragraph introduce the subject in an interesting way? Can you use a question, quotation, or startling statement to spark the reader's interest?

❑ Do the middle paragraphs develop the narrative by explaining what happened in a clear and logical way?

❑ Do you describe the problem and tell where and when it happened?

❑ Do you introduce and describe the people who were involved?

❑ Do you clearly describe your decision and the factors involved in making it? Did you omit any important details? If so, add them now.

❑ Does the concluding paragraph sum up the experience and describe the result?

❑ Are sentences complete? Correct any run-ons or fragments.

❑ Can you add active verbs and colorful adjectives to make the writing vivid?

❑ Do subjects and verbs agree? Do pronouns agree with their antecedents?

❑ Do you use transitional words (such as *then, at first, however, later*) to make smooth connections?

❑ Check spelling with a dictionary.

B. DIRECTIONS: Begin the final copy of your essay below, and continue on the back of this sheet. Write a title on the top line, and indent the beginning of each paragraph.

_____

_____

_____

_____

_____

_____

8–7. FEELING NERVOUS (PREWRITING)

DIRECTIONS: Think about a time when you were nervous. It might have been before a big test or a recital. It might have been the first time you were up to bat, your first plane ride, playing an important role in the drama club production, a blind date, or the first time you had to give a speech in front of a class.

You are going to write a narrative essay about one time that you were nervous. Describe what happened and how you reacted. First, prepare the **brainstorming list** below.

BRAINSTORMING LIST

1. On the line below, state briefly what the occasion was. (See the examples at the top of the page for ideas.)

   _____

2. On the line below, state when and where this experience happened.

   _____

3. On the line below, say who else was there.

   _____

4. On the lines below, briefly summarize what happened (for example, "When I finally got up the courage to tell my parents, instead of being angry, they said they would try to help me turn things around by hiring a tutor.")

   _____

   _____

5. On the line below, write a list of words and phrases you can use when describing this event.

   _____

6. On the line below, write a list of words and phrases you can use to describe your feelings about this experience.

   _____

8–8. FEELING NERVOUS (FIRST DRAFT)

DIRECTIONS: Write the first draft of a narrative essay describing a time when you felt nervous about something you had to do or something that was going to happen. Use your brainstorming list as a guide, and follow these suggestions:

- In the first paragraph (2 to 4 sentences), introduce the topic in an interesting way (for example, "My hour of doom! My heart pounded and my knees quaked as I thought about the dreaded moment I would soon be facing.").
- In the middle paragraphs (3 to 7 sentences each), describe this experience in chronological order from beginning to end. Begin by telling where and when it occurred. Then describe it step by step. Begin a new paragraph each time a new step occurs. Keep your reader in suspense about the outcome until the end.
- In the concluding paragraph (2 to 4 sentences), restate the theme and describe the effect the experience had on you.

Begin your essay below and continue on the back of this sheet. Write a title on the top line, and indent the beginning of each paragraph. This is just a first draft, so don't be too concerned about spelling and grammar at this point. Concentrate on getting your thoughts on paper.

8–9. FEELING NERVOUS
(REVISING AND WRITING A FINAL COPY)

A. DIRECTIONS: Revise and correct the first draft of your essay about a time you felt nervous. Use proofreading symbols if you find them helpful. Follow the guidelines below, and check off each one as you complete it.

> ❏ Does the first paragraph introduce the subject? Can you make it more interesting with a startling statement or question?
>
> ❏ Do the middle paragraphs describe the experience chronologically in a clear and logical progression? Did you leave out anything important? If so, insert it now.
>
> ❏ Do you tell where and when this happened and who was present?
>
> ❏ Do you vividly describe your feelings?
>
> ❏ Do you describe the outcome and how it affected you?
>
> ❏ Does the concluding paragraph sum up the experience and its effect on you?
>
> ❏ Can you add active verbs and sensory language to make your writing stronger?
>
> ❏ Add at least one simile or metaphor.
>
> ❏ Do subjects and verbs agree? Do pronouns agree with their antecedents?
>
> ❏ Do you use transitional words and phrases (such as *at first, finally, at last, then, however*) for smooth connections?
>
> ❏ Check spelling with a dictionary.

B. DIRECTIONS: Begin the final copy of your essay below, and continue on the back of this sheet. Write the title on the top line, and indent the beginning of each paragraph.

_____

_____

_____

_____

_____

_____

_____

Name _____ Date _____

8–10. PERSONAL PERSPECTIVE (PREWRITING)

It has been noted that three onlookers describing a traffic accident will give three different descriptions of what happened. Think of a recent incident you observed in your school or classroom that caused a lot of comment and discussion. You are going to write a description of that incident. When you have finished, it will be fun to compare your description with those of others who have written about the same or similar events, to see the similarities and differences.

First, prepare a **brainstorming list,** as follows:

- In the first column below, write a list of words and phrases you can use to describe where and when this incident occurred.

- In the second column, write a list of words and phrases you can use to describe who and what (people and objects) were present.

- In the third column, write a list of words and phrases that describe the details of the incident and its outcome.

BRAINSTORMING LIST

Where and When	People and Objects	Details

Write an opening sentence that will spark reader interest (for example, "The science lesson was suddenly interrupted by an ear-splitting crash.")

_____

_____

Name _____ **Date** _____

8–11. PERSONAL PERSPECTIVE (FIRST DRAFT)

DIRECTIONS: Write the first draft of a narrative essay describing a recent exciting or unexpected incident that you saw in your classroom or school. Use your brainstorming list as a guide, and follow these suggestions:

> • In the first paragraph (2 to 4 sentences), introduce the topic in an interesting way. Use the opening sentence from your brainstorming list.
>
> • In the middle paragraphs (3 to 6 sentences each), recount exactly what occurred, as you observed it. Describe the people and things involved and precise details of the incident, including the result. Use as many paragraphs as you need for this development.
>
> • In the concluding paragraph (2 to 4 sentences), sum up the incident and its effect on you and others.

Begin your essay below, and continue on the back of this sheet. Write a title on the first line (for example, "A Fight That Got Out of Hand"). Indent the beginning of each paragraph. This is a first draft, so just concentrate on getting your thoughts on paper, and do not be too concerned about spelling and grammar at this point.

8–12. PERSONAL PERSPECTIVE
(REVISING AND WRITING A FINAL COPY)

A. DIRECTIONS: Revise and correct the first draft of your essay about a recent incident you witnessed in your classroom or elsewhere at school. Use proofreading symbols if you find them helpful. Follow the guidelines below. Check off each one as you complete it.

❑ Does the first paragraph introduce the subject? Can you make it more interesting with a question or a startling statement?

❑ Do the middle paragraphs describe the incident with clear details from beginning to end? Did you leave out anything important? If so, insert it now.

❑ Do you tell exactly where and when this event occurred and who was involved?

❑ Do you describe the outcome and its effect on you and others?

❑ Does the concluding paragraph sum up the incident and its importance?

❑ Add active verbs and sensory language to make your description more vivid.

❑ Add at least one simile or metaphor.

❑ Do subjects and verbs agree? Do pronouns agree with their antecedents?

❑ Do you use transitional words (such as *at first, then, next, finally, therefore*) to make smooth connections?

❑ Do you vary sentence length, using some short and some long sentences?

❑ Check spelling with a dictionary.

B. DIRECTIONS: Begin the final copy of your essay below, and continue on the back of this sheet. Write the title on the top line, and indent at the beginning of each paragraph. If you can, share your final essay with others who wrote about the same incident. Compare similarities and differences.

_____

_____

_____

_____

_____

_____

_____

8–13. A Celebrity and You (Prewriting)

Everyone has a favorite celebrity—a film or TV star, a politician, an athlete, an author, or someone from the world of business or education. You have been given the opportunity to spend a day with your favorite celebrity. Write a narrative about how you will spend that day and why it is a meaningful experience for you.

First, organize your thoughts by completing this **brainstorming list:**

BRAINSTORMING LIST

1. Write the name of your celebrity and state the field in which he or she is well known.

   _____

2. Write a list of words and phrases that describe this person.

   _____

3. State where and when your day with your celebrity will begin.

   _____

4. Explain briefly the first thing you will do.

   _____

5. Briefly tell what will happen next.

   _____

6. Write one thing you might say to this person. (Use quotation marks.)

   _____

7. Write one thing this person might say to you. (Use quotation marks.)

   _____

8. How will this day end?

   _____

Name _____ Date _____

8–14. A Celebrity and You (first draft)

DIRECTIONS: Write the first draft of a narrative about a day you might spend with your favorite celebrity. Use your brainstorming list as a guide. Here is one way you might organize this essay:

- In the first paragraph (2 to 4 sentences), introduce the subject in an interesting way (for example, "I must be the luckiest teenager in the world. Imagine being able to spend an entire day with . . . .").
- In the second paragraph (3 to 6 sentences), describe your celebrity and tell why you admire this person.
- In the third paragraph (3 to 6 sentences), narrate the first half of your day with your celebrity. Include one thing you might say to him or her.
- In the fourth paragraph (3 to 6 sentences), narrate the second half of your day together. Include one thing he or she might say to you.
- In the concluding paragraph (2 to 4 sentences), sum up your day with this special person and describe why it is important to you.

Begin your narrative below, and continue on the back of this sheet. Write a title on the top line (for example, "My Incredible Day with a Legend"). This is a first draft, so concentrate on getting your thoughts on paper. Don't be too concerned about spelling and grammar at this point.

_____

_____

_____

_____

_____

_____

_____

_____

_____

_____

8–15. A CELEBRITY AND YOU
(REVISING AND WRITING A FINAL COPY)

A. DIRECTIONS: Revise and correct the first draft of your essay about spending a day with your favorite celebrity. Use proofreading symbols if you find them helpful. Follow the guidelines below. Read each one carefully before you check it off.

> ❑ Does the first paragraph introduce the subject? Can you use a question or a startling statement to spark the reader's interest?
>
> ❑ Do the middle paragraphs relate the events of the day in the order in which they occur? Do you describe the celebrity fully? Can you add anything about his or her appearance, attitude, personality, or character? Do you include your own feelings and reactions to this person?
>
> ❑ Have you put quotation marks around any dialogue that is used?
>
> ❑ Does the concluding paragraph sum up the experience and tell why it is important to you?
>
> ❑ Do you use strong active verbs and sensory language?
>
> ❑ Add at least one simile or metaphor.
>
> ❑ Do subjects and verbs agree? Do pronouns agree with their antecedents?
>
> ❑ Do you use transitional words (such as *therefore, next, at last)* to make smooth connections?
>
> ❑ Check spelling with a dictionary.

B. DIRECTIONS: Begin the final copy of your narrative below, and continue on the back of this sheet. Write the title on the first line, and indent at the beginning of each paragraph.

_____

_____

_____

_____

_____

_____

_____

8–16. SURVIVING A SHIPWRECK (PREWRITING)

DIRECTIONS: You are shipwrecked on a deserted island for a month with only your backpack. Write a narrative telling how you survive, using only the items in your backpack. First, organize your narrative by preparing a **brainstorming list.**

1. In the first column below, list the items in the backpack.

2. In the second column, next to each item, list words and phrases to describe it.

3. In the third column, list words and phrases to describe how each item could be used to survive.

BRAINSTORMING LIST

Item	Description	Uses

4. Write an attention-getting opening sentence or sentences for this narrative (for example, "The first thing I saw when I opened my eyes was my backpack on the sand beside me. What had happened? Where was I?")

_____

_____

8–17. SURVIVING A SHIPWRECK (FIRST DRAFT)

DIRECTIONS: Write the first draft of your narrative about being shipwrecked on an island and surviving for a month by using the items in your backpack. Use your brainstorming list as a guide, and organize your essay as follows:

> • In the first paragraph (2 to 4 sentences), use the opening sentences from your brainstorming list to introduce the subject in an interesting way.
>
> • In the middle paragraphs (3 to 6 sentences each), develop the narrative in one of two ways:
>
>   (1) Tell the story chronologically from the time of the shipwreck until you are rescued, with several key incidents in each paragraph, or
>
>   (2) Feature each item from the backpack in a separate paragraph and relate how it helped you survive.
>
> • In the concluding paragraph (2 to 4 sentences), sum up the story and bring it to a satisfying conclusion.

Begin your narrative below, and continue on the back of this sheet. Write a title on the top line, and indent the beginning of each paragraph. This is a first draft, so don't be too concerned about spelling and grammar at this point. Concentrate on getting your thoughts down on paper.

_____

_____

_____

_____

_____

_____

_____

_____

Copyright © 2004 by John Wiley & Sons, Inc.

8–18. SURVIVING A SHIPWRECK
(REVISING AND WRITING A FINAL COPY)

A. DIRECTIONS: Revise and correct the first draft of your essay about surviving a shipwreck, using only the items in your backpack. Use proofreading symbols if you find them helpful. Follow the guidelines below. Read each one carefully before you check it off.

> ❑ Does the first paragraph introduce the subject of the narrative? Can you think of a better beginning that will spark the reader's interest?
> ❑ Do the middle paragraphs relate the story in a clear and organized way, either chronologically or by featuring each item and how it helped you survive?
> ❑ Does the concluding paragraph sum up the story and bring it to a satisfying end?
> ❑ Do you hold the reader's interest with exciting active verbs and sensory language?
> ❑ Add at least one simile or metaphor.
> ❑ Are sentences complete? Correct any fragments or run-ons.
> ❑ Do subjects and verbs agree? Do pronouns agree with their antecedents?
> ❑ Can you add some transitional words or phrases to make smooth connections?
> ❑ Check spelling with a dictionary when in doubt.

B. DIRECTIONS: Begin the final copy of your narrative below, and continue on the back of this sheet. Write the title on the top line, and indent at the beginning of each paragraph.

_____

_____

_____

_____

_____

_____

_____

_____

8–19. An Important Object (Prewriting)

> *There was a child who went forth every day,*
> *And the first object he look'd upon, that object he became,*
> *And that object became part of him for*
>   *The day or a certain part of the day,*
> *Or for many years or stretching cycles of years.*
>   —Walt Whitman

DIRECTIONS: This excerpt from a poem by Walt Whitman suggests that certain objects become important to us and remain important to us even if we no longer have them.

Write a story in which you tell about an object that remains important to the main character over a period of years. The main character could be you, someone you know, or a fictional character. In your story, describe the following:

- The main character's first encounter with the object
- Why the object is important to the character
- How, over the years, the object remains a part of the character's life

Before you begin your story, complete the **brainstorming list** below.

BRAINSTORMING LIST

1. What is this object? _____

2. Write a list of words and phrases describing the object. _____
_____

3. What is the name of the main character? _____

4. Write a list of words and phrases describing the main character. _____
_____

5. How old was the main character when he or she first encountered the object?
_____

6. Write a list of words and phrases that describe the setting in which this occurred.
_____

7. Write a list of words and phrases that describe events that occur involving this object. _____

8. State briefly why this object is so important to the character. _____
_____

9. State briefly how this object remains part of the character's life. _____
_____

Name _____ Date _____

8–20. AN IMPORTANT OBJECT (FIRST DRAFT)

> *There was a child who went forth every day,*
> *And the first object he look'd upon, that object he became,*
> *And that object became part of him for*
> *The day or a certain part of the day,*
> *Or for many years or stretching cycles of years.*
> —Walt Whitman

DIRECTIONS: Write the first draft of your story about an object and the person to whom it remains important over a period of years. Use your brainstorming list as a guide. Here are some helpful hints:

- Open the story with a sentence or sentences that will catch the reader's interest (for example, "Matt's friends teased him. His father laughed. No one could understand why he kept the strange object he had found on the beach on that long-ago day during the summer he turned twelve.").
- Describe the main character and the object early in the narrative.
- Describe, in chronological order, events that occurred through the years involving the main character and the object. Make them exciting and suspenseful.
- Describe other characters and places in the story with vivid, colorful language.
- Show how the main character feels about the object and tell how long it remains part of his or her life.
- Use dialogue to show the characters speaking to one another. When writing dialogue, begin a new paragraph each time someone begins to speak. Place quotation marks around each quote.
- Bring the story to an end that will satisfy the reader.

Write your story on a separate sheet of paper. Put your name and date at the top of the page. Decide on a title and write it at the beginning. Indent at the beginning of each paragraph or whenever a character begins to speak. This is a first draft, so concentrate on getting your thoughts down on paper. Don't be too concerned about spelling or grammar at this point.

Name _____   Date _____

8–21. AN IMPORTANT OBJECT
(REVISING AND WRITING A FINAL COPY)

A. DIRECTIONS: Revise and correct the first draft of your story about an object and the importance it has in the life of the main character. Use proofreading symbols if you find them helpful. Follow the guidelines below, and check off each one as you complete it.

❑ Does the story begin in an interesting way that will spark the reader's interest? Can you make it more suspenseful and exciting?

❑ Do you introduce the main character and the object early in the story?

❑ Do you describe the setting in which the story begins, as well as other background settings that occur later?

❑ Do you describe other characters and their importance to the story? Are there any characters who are not important and should be taken out?

❑ Do you show clearly why the object is important to the main character?

❑ Do you describe chronological events that show the object's importance?

❑ Can you make these events more exciting with strong, active verbs and sensory language?

❑ Add at least one simile or metaphor.

❑ Do you begin a new paragraph when someone speaks and put quotation marks around what they say?

❑ Can you add transitional words (such as *then, at first, later, therefore*) to make smoother connections?

❑ Does your conclusion end the story in a satisfying way?

❑ Check spelling with a dictionary.

B. DIRECTIONS: Begin the final copy of your story below, and continue on the back of this sheet. Write the title on the top line, and indent at the beginning of each paragraph.

_____

_____

_____

_____

_____

_____

_____

TENTH-GRADE LEVEL

NARRATIVE WRITING PRACTICE TEST

PRACTICE TEST: NARRATIVE WRITING

DIRECTIONS: You are going to write an essay based on the prompt below. Read the prompt carefully, and be sure you understand the topic before beginning.

Many times in life we avoid experiences because we are afraid of them, or we dread having a negative experience. Other times we have no choice and must do what we dread the most. In some instances, our worst fears are realized, but more often we learn that our fears were unjustified. Write about an experience you dreaded but discovered was not nearly so bad as you had expected.

Follow these four steps to write your essay:

- FIRST, on the page labeled "Prewriting," brainstorm ideas, facts, and examples that support the topic. Include a variety of words and phrases you can use to develop the narrative.

- SECOND, write the first draft of your essay on a separate sheet of paper. Write your name and the date at the top of the page, followed by the title of your essay. Consult your notes from the brainstorming page.

- THIRD, revise and edit your first draft. Refer to your list of proofreading symbols if you wish. Use the checklist below as a guide, and check off each item when it has been revised to your satisfaction.

- FOURTH, write your final copy on a separate sheet of paper with your name and date at the top.

CHECKLIST

❑ Does your introductory paragraph state the topic clearly? Can you use a question, quotation, or startling statement to grab the reader's interest?

❑ Do your middle paragraphs develop the topic in a logical, convincing way, showing that this experience was not so bad as you had expected?

❑ Do you present specific reasons, details, facts, and examples to develop your narrative?

❑ Do you stay on the subject at all times? Delete any irrelevant material.

❑ Does the concluding paragraph sum up the topic in a convincing way and bring the narrative to a satisfying conclusion?

❑ Do you use a variety of well-constructed, complete sentences? Correct any fragments or run-ons.

❑ Do subjects and verbs agree? Do pronouns agree with their antecedents?

❑ Do you need to add transitional words to make smoother connections?

❑ Correct any errors in spelling, punctuation, capitalization, and usage. Use a dictionary when in doubt.

PRACTICE TEST: NARRATIVE WRITING *(continued)*

Prewriting

Re-read the prompt to be sure you are writing about the correct topic. Think about the experience you have chosen to illustrate the point that an experience one dreads often turns out to be not nearly so bad as expected. Organize your ideas by making notes on this page with a brainstorming list, a cluster, or an outline. Be sure to list a variety of words and phrases you can use to develop your narrative.

PRACTICE TEST: NARRATIVE WRITING *(continued)*

Student Samples

DIRECTIONS: Read the sample student essays below. Rate each essay with a score from 1 (lowest) to 6 (highest). Use the information on the scoring guide to help you.

ESSAY A

Sweet sixteen. Ahhh . . . driver's license, car, new found freedom and independence. These were the words which came to my mind on my sixteenth birthday. My parents paused my jubilation though when they uttered the words they associated with sixteen years old: get a job. The thought of going out and talking with strangers about my future employment status was terrifying. Rejection? Let's not even go there!

My mom helped me compile a resume of my experience (5 years of babysitting) and my activities and various awards. She had me get dressed up, dropped me off at a mall, told me to fill out some applications, and she'd be back in an hour. It was the longest hour of my life.

The first place I went into was a card shop. I smiled at the woman who gently informed me that they weren't hiring. Okay, I thought, move along. I thanked her and went on to the video store. Yes, they were looking for applicants. I filled out an application (talk about tedious) and left my resume. I had gotten four more applications done by the time my mom came around again.

Three days went by without any word, when out of the blue came a call from a family-owned bread company. They wanted to interview me. My stomach was in knots as questions were fired at me from a lanky guy partially hidden behind a starched white apron. He seemed about as friendly as I was nervous—extremely. He told me he would call the next day.

It turned out I was exactly what they were looking for and I started training immediately. Finding a job wasn't nearly as traumatic as I thought it would be. Everyone experiences rejection at some point in life. I learned many things about the job-application process as well as that it's not always a bad thing to tackle your fears and go for it.

Score _____

ESSAY B

I was afraid about ask a gye out. He was not bad looking. It was abarrisment to ask him out. She did ask him. It was not that bad it was cool. He ask her out that same day. It feelt good that he ask me out.

Score _____

SCORE	Unsatisfactory—1	Insufficient—2
Content	Attempts to respond to prompt, but provides few details; may only paraphrase prompt	Presents fragmented information OR may be very repetitive OR may be very undeveloped
Organization	Has no clear organization OR consists of a single statement	Is very disorganized; ideas are weakly connected OR the response is too brief to detect organization
Sentence Structure	Little or no control over sentence boundaries and sentence structure; word choice may be incorrect in much or all of the response	Little control over sentence boundaries and sentence structure; word choice may often be incorrect
Grammar, Usage, and Mechanics	Many errors in grammar or usage (such as tense inconsistency, lack of subject-verb agreement), spelling, and punctuation severely interfere with understanding	Errors in grammar or usage (such as inconsistency, lack of subject-verb agreement), spelling, and punctuation interfere with understanding in much of the response

SCORE	Uneven—3	Sufficient—4
Content	Presents some clear information, but is list-like, undeveloped, or repetitive OR offers no more than a well-written beginning	Develops information with some details
Organization	Is unevenly organized; the narrative may be disjointed	Is organized with ideas that are generally related but has few or no transitions
Sentence Structure	Exhibits uneven control over sentence boundaries and sentence structure; may have some incorrect word choices	Exhibits control over sentence boundaries and sentence structure, but sentences and word choices may be simple and unvaried
Grammar, Usage, and Mechanics	Errors in grammar or usage (such as tense inconsistency, lack of subject-verb agreement), spelling, and punctuation sometimes interfere with understanding	Errors in grammar or usage (such as tense inconsistency, lack of subject-verb agreement), spelling, and punctuation do not interfere with understanding

SCORE	Skillful—5	Excellent—6
Content	Develops and shapes information with details in parts of the narrative	Develops and shapes information with well-chosen details across the narrative
Organization	Is clearly organized, but may lack some transitions and/or have lapses in continuity	Is well organized with strong transitions
Sentence Structure	Exhibits some variety in sentence structure and some good word choices	Sustains variety in sentence structure and exhibits good word choice
Grammar, Usage, and Mechanics	Errors in grammar, spelling, and punctuation do not interfere with understanding	Errors in grammar, spelling, and punctuation are few and do not interfere with understanding

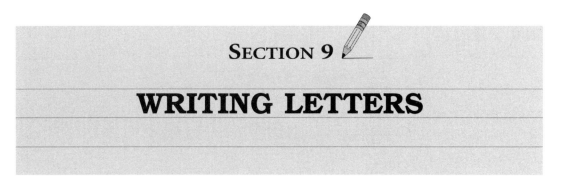
WRITING LETTERS

Standardized Testing Information

It is not unusual for the prompt in a writing assessment test to require a response in letter format. Informative/expository, persuasive, or narrative responses may be requested.

Letter responses in these assessments do not require formal personal or business letter format, except in the greeting and closing.

National and state rubrics do not differentiate between letter and essay form responses. The state of Oregon, for example, rates writing samples on a scale of 6 (highest) to 1 (lowest) in each of the following categories: ideas/content, organization, voice, and word choice. Here are some excerpts from the Oregon official scoring guide:

Ideas/Content

6. The writing is exceptionally clear, focused, and interesting. It holds the reader's attention throughout. Main ideas stand out and are developed by strong support and rich details suitable to audience and purpose.

3. The reader can understand the main ideas, although they may be overly broad or simplistic, and the results may not be effective. Supporting detail is often limited, insubstantial, overly general, or occasionally slightly off-topic.

1. The writing lacks a central idea or purpose.

Organization

6. The organization enhances the central idea(s) and its development. The order and structure are compelling and move the reader through the text easily. The writing is characterized by
   - Effective, perhaps creative, sequencing; the organizational structure fits the topic, and the writing is easy to follow.
   - A strong, inviting beginning that draws the reader in and a strong, satisfying sense of resolution or closure.
   - Smooth, effective transitions among all elements.
   - Details that fit where placed.

3. An attempt has been made to organize the writing; however, the overall structure is inconsistent or skeletal. The writing is characterized by
   - Attempts at sequencing, but the order or relationship among ideas may occasionally be unclear.
   - A beginning and an ending which, although present, are either undeveloped or too obvious.

- Transitions that sometimes work.
- Placement of details may not always be effective.
1. The writing lacks coherence; organization seems haphazard and disjointed. Even after rereading, the reader remains confused.

Voice

6. The writer has chosen a voice appropriate for the topic, purpose, and audience. The writer seems deeply committed to the topic, and there is an exceptional sense of "writing to be read." The writing is expressive, engaging, or sincere.
3. The writer's commitment to the topic seems inconsistent. A sense of the writer may emerge at times; however, the voice is either inappropriately personal or inappropriately impersonal.
1. The writing seems to lack a sense of involvement or commitment.

Word Choice

6. Words convey the intended message in an exceptionally interesting, precise, and natural way appropriate to audience and purpose. The writer employs a rich, broad range of words which have been carefully chosen and thoughtfully placed for impact.
3. Language is quite ordinary, lacking interest, precision and variety, or may be inappropriate to audience and purpose in places. The writer does not employ a variety of words, producing a sort of "generic" paper filled with familiar words and phrases.
1. The writing shows an extremely limited vocabulary or is so filled with misuses of words that the meaning is obscured. Only the most general kind of message is communicated because of vague or imprecise language.

The classroom teacher should keep these and other state rubrics in mind when leading students through the letter-writing exercises in Section 9.

Teacher Preparation and Lessons

There are six letter-writing activities in this section, two each of informative, persuasive, and narrative. Although state and national assessments do not require knowledge of correct letter form, samples of business and personal letter models are offered on page 282 to acquaint students with the useful skill of writing a standard letter. The teacher may choose to use these formats for one or more of the activities in this section with the clear understanding that assessment tests call only for the use of a greeting and closing in the response to a letter-writing prompt.

Like the other essay-writing activities in this resource, each activity in this section has three parts:

- The first part consists of **prewriting** activities such as **brainstorming, clustering,** or **outlining** to be done individually, in small groups, or with whole-class participation, at the teacher's discretion. Students should be advised to use this step of the writing process to provide an organizational framework for their writing. Personal and business letter models will also be introduced in some of these prewriting activities.

- The second part is the writing of a **first draft.** Students should be encouraged to write freely at this point, without too much concern about grammar, spelling, and punctuation, in an effort to overcome blocks that are all too common when students face a writing assignment.
- The third part offers directions for **revising and writing a final copy.** The revision and editing process can be done by the individual student writer alone, in association with the teacher, or with class participation (exchange of papers). Each revision activity includes a checklist for students to refer to during the editing process. It may be helpful to review the proofreading symbols on page 307.

These letter-writing activities offer an opportunity for a discussion of the concept of readership. Even more than other essay-writing assignments, a letter is usually intended for the eyes of one particular recipient. A class discussion of this subject will help students learn to focus on the reader, not only when writing letters, but in other writing activities as well. At the beginning of the first letter-writing activity, therefore, the teacher could ask the following questions:

1. Who is meant to read this letter?
2. What can the writer do to focus the message for that particular reader?

The discussion can then be expanded to include previously completed essay-writing assignments and their intended readership. Elicit from students the ways in which letters are similar to essays in having the following elements:

- A beginning that identifies the topic
- A middle (one or more paragraphs) that develops the topic
- An ending

Elicit from the students the aspects of letter-writing that differ from essay composition, and write these on the board:

- An essay is addressed to a general group of readers, while a letter is addressed to one individual.
- The tone of a letter is more personal, resembling one part of a dialogue between two individuals.
- The structure of a letter, while having a beginning, middle, and end, is somewhat looser and more flexible than that in an essay.

Practice Test: Writing Letters

The student letter samples on page 304 are rated 5 and 2, respectively.

Letter A uses pertinent details to make a point, as "This doesn't mean your work must be humorous or adventurous. It simply means you have to keep the reader's attention." Though the paragraphs do not flow smoothly one to the other, the logical order of this response overall makes it cohesive. The student provides sentence variety and makes accurate word choices and few errors. This letter scored a 5.

Letter B makes at attempt at organization, but the response is fairly repetitive, as in this excerpt: "Advice that has been given to me is to think of a topic and make an outline. For your outline think ideas about your topic topic, and then organize your ideas." The student's writing is unclear in parts. The response also shows some lack of control over sentence structure and contains awkward constructions. This letter scored a 2.

Sample Letter Forms

1. BUSINESS LETTER

Your Street Address
Your City, State, and ZIP Code
Today's Date

Name of Recipient
Street Address of Recipient
City, State, and ZIP Code of Recipient

Greeting*

MESSAGE

Closing**
Your signature

*The greeting is followed by a colon or comma (for example, "Dear Mr. Jones:" or "Dear Mr. Jones,").

**The closing is followed by a comma (for example, "Yours truly,").

2. PERSONAL LETTER

(Address optional)
Today's Date

Greeting*

MESSAGE

Closing**
Your signature

*The greeting is followed by a comma (for example, "Dear Aunt Jennifer,").

**The closing is followed by a comma (for example, "Love,").

Name _____   **Date** _____

9–1. A Typical Day (prewriting)

You have been asked to write to a foreign exchange student about a typical day at your school. This person will spend next year at your school and needs to know what to expect. When writing your letter, keep in mind why your description of the events of a typical day will be meaningful to the exchange student.

First, organize your thoughts by completing the **brainstorming list** below.

BRAINSTORMING LIST

1. Your letter will be written to one of the following exchange students. Check the one you have chosen.

   ❑ Patrick, a sixteen-year-old boy in Belfast, Ireland
   ❑ Michiko, a sixteen-year-old girl in Osaka, Japan
   ❑ Elena, a sixteen-year-old girl in Bogota, Colombia
   ❑ Sven, a sixteen-year-old boy in Stockholm, Sweden

2. Divide your chronological description of a typical day at your school into two parts: morning and afternoon. In the first column of the box labeled "Morning Activities," list three morning **activities.** In the second column, list words and phrases you will use to describe the **places** where each activity occurs. In the third column, list words and phrases that describe **people and things** involved in each of these activities.

3. Follow the same procedure for the box labeled "Afternoon Activities."

Morning Activities

Afternoon Activities

9–2. A TYPICAL DAY (FIRST DRAFT)

DIRECTIONS: Write the first draft of your letter to a foreign exchange student about a typical day at your school. Keep in mind the purpose of this letter and what your reader needs to know. Use your brainstorming list as a guide, and organize your letter as follows:

> - **Begin with a greeting followed by a comma (for example, "Dear Patrick,").**
>
> - In the first paragraph of the letter (2 to 4 sentences), introduce yourself and tell why you are writing (for example, "Are you nervous about going to school in a country so far from your own? Don't be scared! My name is Alison Bernini and I'm going to tell you exactly what to expect here.")
>
> - In the second paragraph (4 to 8 sentences), describe, chronologically, activities that take place in the morning.
>
> - In the third paragraph (4 to 8 sentences), describe, chronologically, activities that take place in the afternoon.
>
> - In the concluding paragraph, sum up a typical day at your school in a friendly, welcoming way.
>
> - Write a closing, followed by a comma (for example, "Your new friend,"). *Note:* Only the first word of the closing is capitalized.

Begin your letter below, and continue on the back of this sheet. This is a first draft, so concentrate on getting your thoughts down on paper, and don't be too concerned about spelling or grammar. Don't forget to include the greeting and closing (followed by commas) and to indent the beginning of each paragraph.

_____

_____

_____

_____

_____

_____

9–3. A TYPICAL DAY (REVISING AND WRITING A FINAL COPY)

A. DIRECTIONS: Revise and correct the first draft of your letter to a foreign exchange student about a typical day at your school. Use proofreading symbols if you find them helpful. Follow the guidelines below, and check off each one as you complete it.

❑ Do you begin the letter with a greeting followed by a comma?

❑ Do you introduce yourself and the topic of the letter in the first paragraph? Can you make it more interesting or exciting with a question or exclamation?

❑ Do the middle paragraphs describe a typical day at your school in chronological order? Did you leave out anything important? If so, add it now.

❑ In your narration, do you consider the point of view of the exchange student and what he or she needs to know? Take out anything that is irrelevant or superfluous.

❑ Do you include descriptions of the people and places in the school that will satisfy the curiosity of the exchange student? Add at least one more description of a person or a school location.

❑ Would any of your comments be unclear to someone who has never been to this country? If so, revise them in a way that will be understood by a foreign student.

❑ Does the concluding paragraph sum up the day in an interesting way? Can you add anything to make the new student feel at ease when he or she arrives?

❑ Did you place a comma after the closing?

❑ Do subjects and verbs agree? Do pronouns agree with their antecedents?

❑ Add some transitional words (such as *at first, then, afterward, finally*) to make smoother connections.

❑ Check spelling with a dictionary.

B. DIRECTIONS: Begin the final copy of your letter below, and continue on the back of this sheet. Don't forget the greeting and closing. Indent the beginning of each paragraph.

_____

_____

_____

_____

_____

_____

9–4. MAGIC CARPET (PREWRITING)

There are many wonderful places to visit in your state, your country, and the world. Think about one spot that you've always wanted to see. Pretend that you have been whisked aboard a magic carpet and taken there. You are going to write a letter home describing this place and what happens to you there.

First, organize your thoughts by preparing a **brainstorming list.**

BRAINSTORMING LIST

1. What is the name of the place you are visiting? _____

2. State one reason why you want to go there. _____

3. To whom will you write this letter (parents, friend, or someone else)? _____

4. In the first column of the box below, make a list of words and phrases you can use to describe what this place *looks like.* In the second column, write words and phrases describing *people and animals* you will see there. In the third column, write words and phrases to describe *buildings and other objects* you will see there.

Appearance	People and Animals	Objects

5. List four things that will happen to you in this place (for example, riding on the back of an elephant).

_____

_____

_____

_____

9–5. Magic Carpet (first draft)

DIRECTIONS: Write the first draft of your letter to someone at home describing your visit to a place you have always wanted to see. Use your brainstorming list as a guide. There are various ways you could organize this narrative. Here is one way that is easy to follow:

- Begin with a greeting followed by a comma (for example, "Dear Rose,").
- In the first paragraph, state the topic of the letter in an interesting way that will grab the reader's attention (for example, "You'll never believe where I am writing this! I am sitting on a platform high in a tree in the Amazon forest of South America. This has been the greatest adventure of my life, and I am going to share it with you.")
- In the second paragraph, tell how you got there and what it looks like.
- In the third paragraph, describe the people and/or wildlife you have seen.
- In the fourth paragraph, relate the things you have done and what has happened to you since your arrival.
- In the concluding paragraph, sum up the topic and bring your narrative to a satisfying ending.
- Write a closing, followed by a comma (for example, "Your sister,").
- Sign your name under the closing.

Begin your letter below, and continue on the back of this sheet. Don't forget to include the greeting and the closing (followed by commas). Indent the beginning of each paragraph. This is a first draft, so concentrate on getting your thoughts down on paper. Don't be too concerned about spelling or grammar at this point.

_____

_____

_____

_____

_____

_____

Name _____ **Date** _____

9–6. MAGIC CARPET (REVISING AND WRITING A FINAL COPY)

A. DIRECTIONS: Revise and correct the first draft of your letter describing your visit to a place you have always wanted to see. Use proofreading symbols if they are helpful to you. Follow the guidelines below, and check off each one as you complete it.

> ❑ Do you begin the letter with a greeting followed by a comma?
> ❑ Do you introduce the topic in the first paragraph? Can you make it more exciting with a question or a startling statement?
> ❑ Do the middle paragraphs clearly describe the place you are visiting and what happens to you there?
> ❑ Do you stay on the topic? Take out any irrelevancies.
> ❑ Add some transitional words to make smooth connections between sentences.
> ❑ Add strong, active verbs and colorful adjectives to make your writing more vivid.
> ❑ Add at least one simile or metaphor.
> ❑ Do subjects and verbs agree? Do pronouns agree with their antecedents?
> ❑ Does the last paragraph bring the narrative to a satisfying conclusion?
> ❑ Did you place a comma after the closing?
> ❑ Don't forget to sign your name under the closing.
> ❑ Check spelling with a dictionary.

B. DIRECTIONS: Begin the final copy of your letter below, and continue on the back of this sheet. Don't forget the greeting, the closing, and your signature. Indent the beginning of each paragraph.

9–7. LETTER TO THE EDITOR (PREWRITING)

The editor of your school newspaper has written several editorials on subjects of interest to students. There is a newspaper page called "Letters to the Editor." You are going to write a letter to the editor telling whether you agree or disagree with her position and giving your reasons for this opinion. Respond to one of the following editorial subjects:

> ❏ The school cafeteria franchise should be turned over to a fast-food supplier such as McDonald's or Burger King. The editor is in favor of this change.
> ❏ Student lockers should be searched for drugs on a regular basis. The editor opposes this proposal.
> ❏ The school sponsors a senior prom and a junior prom. The editor thinks there should be a sophomore prom as well.

1. Place a checkmark next to one of the editorial subjects. Indicate here whether you agree or disagree with the editor. _____

2. Organize your ideas for this letter by preparing a cluster, as follows:
   • Write the main topic in the center of the circle below, using large letters.
   • Write three or four supporting points around the topic, using smaller letters.
   • Write detail words and phrases around each supporting point, using tiny letters.
   Note: You can use different colors instead of different letter sizes.

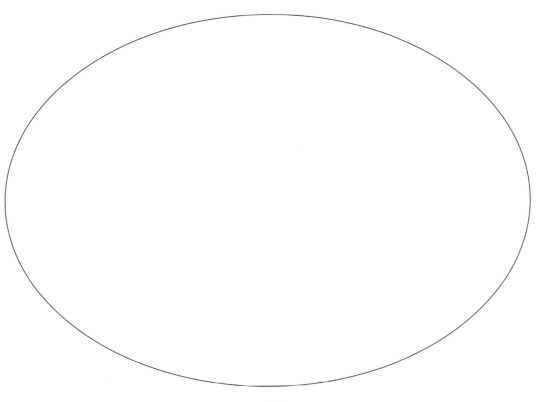

9–8. LETTER TO THE EDITOR (FIRST DRAFT)

DIRECTIONS: Write the first draft of a letter to the editor of your school newspaper agreeing or disagreeing with an editorial. Use your cluster as a guide, and follow these suggestions for organizing your letter:

- Begin with a greeting followed by a comma (for example, "Dear Editor,").
- In the first paragraph (2 to 4 sentences), state the topic and indicate whether or not you agree with the view of the editor (for example, "Hot dogs, hamburgers, and fries sound like hog heaven to teenagers, but is it really in our best interest to have this diet thrust on us day after day? Most of us would have to agree, reluctantly, that it is not.")
- In the second paragraph (3 to 6 sentences), discuss in persuasive detail one point that supports your opinion.
- In the third paragraph (3 to 6 sentences), discuss another supporting point.
- In the fourth paragraph (3 to 6 sentences), discuss one more supporting point.
- In the concluding paragraph (2 to 4 sentences), sum up the topic and bring your letter to a satisfying end.
- Write a closing followed by a comma (for example, "A concerned student,").
- Sign your name under the closing.

Begin your letter below, and continue on the back of this sheet. Don't forget to include the greeting and the closing (both followed by commas). Indent the beginning of each paragraph. This is a first draft, so concentrate on getting your thoughts down on paper. Don't be too concerned at this point about spelling or grammar.

_____

_____

_____

_____

_____

_____

Name _____ Date _____

9–9. LETTER TO THE EDITOR
(REVISING AND WRITING A FINAL COPY)

A. DIRECTIONS: Correct and revise the first draft of your letter to the editor of the school newspaper. Use proofreading symbols if you find them useful. Follow the guidelines below, and check off each one after you complete it.

> ❏ Do you begin the letter with a greeting followed by a comma?
> ❏ Do you introduce the topic in the first paragraph? Is your position on the topic clear to the reader? Can you spark the reader's interest by beginning with a question or a startling statement?
> ❏ Does each of the middle paragraphs discuss one supporting point? Do you use details that will convince the reader? Can you add other important facts?
> ❏ Do you stay on the topic? Take out any irrelevant details.
> ❏ Does the concluding paragraph sum up your opinion in a satisfying way? Can you make it stronger?
> ❏ Add strong, active verbs and sensory language to make your writing vivid.
> ❏ Add at least one simile or metaphor.
> ❏ Add transitional words, where necessary, to make smoother connections between sentences or paragraphs.
> ❏ Are sentences complete? Correct any fragments or run-ons.
> ❏ Do subjects and verbs agree? Do pronouns agree with their antecedents?
> ❏ Did you place a comma after the closing, and sign your name below?
> ❏ Check spelling with a dictionary.

B. DIRECTIONS: Begin the final copy of your letter below, and continue on the back of this sheet. Don't forget the greeting, the closing, and your signature. Indent the beginning of each paragraph.

_____

_____

_____

_____

_____

Name _____ Date _____

9–10. APPLYING FOR A JOB (PREWRITING)

Many prospective employers prefer to see a job candidate's qualifications in writing before granting an interview. A well-written **letter of application** can determine whether that candidate will even reach the interview process.

DIRECTIONS: You are going to write a letter of application for a summer job. The following positions have been advertised. Check the one for which you would like to apply.

> ❑ Warren Galen, the owner of Galen's Garage, wants an assistant to clean the premises, run errands, and learn automobile mechanics.
> ❑ The Pelican Beach Club is hiring lifeguards for their pool and beach. The manager's name is Frank Tuscan.
> ❑ Marcia Kahn, owner of the Eagle Travel Agency, is offering a summer position to someone who would like to learn about the travel industry. Good computer skills are required.
> ❑ A local radio station, WQQA, has a position available for a trainee. The station manager is Jennifer Sanchez.
> ❑ The school district has an opening for a teacher's aide trainee in its preschool summer program. The program director is Luke Bookman.

In your letter of application, you want to persuade the person to whom you are writing to hire you. First, organize your thoughts by completing the **brainstorming list** below. In the first column, list words and phrases describing the skills you can bring to the job. In the second column, list words and phrases to describe any job experience you have had. In the third column, list words and phrases describing the personal qualities that make you perfect for this job.

BRAINSTORMING LIST

Skills	Experience	Personal Qualities

9–11. Applying for a Job (first draft)

DIRECTIONS: Write the first draft of a letter applying for a summer job. Your teacher will give you a handout that shows the correct form for this type of business letter. Use this handout and your brainstorming list as a guide, and follow these suggestions:

- Write your address and the date on three lines at the right, as illustrated on the handout.
- Write the name and address of the person to whom you are writing at the left margin, as illustrated on the handout.
- Write the greeting, followed by a colon or comma (for example, "Dear Ms. Sanchez,").
- In the first paragraph (2 to 4 sentences), introduce yourself and explain the purpose of the letter (for example, "The position of trainee that you advertised is made to order for me. For years, I have dreamed of working in radio. I am sixteen years old and finishing my sophomore year at Leland High School.").
- In the second paragraph (3 to 6 sentences), describe any skills you have that will be useful in this job.
- In the third paragraph (3 to 6 sentences), describe any experience you have had that will be useful for this job.
- In the fourth paragraph (3 to 6 sentences), describe how your personal qualities make you ideal for this job.
- In the concluding paragraph (2 to 4 sentences), restate and sum up your qualifications in a positive way.
- Write the closing, followed by a comma, and sign your name below.

Begin the first draft of your letter below, and continue on the back of this sheet. This is a first draft, so just concentrate on getting your thoughts on paper. Use correct business letter form as illustrated on the handout.

_____

_____

_____

_____

_____

_____

9–12. APPLYING FOR A JOB
(REVISING AND WRITING A FINAL COPY)

A. DIRECTIONS: Correct and revise the first draft of your letter applying for a job. Use proofreading symbols if you find them useful. Follow the guidelines below, and check off each one after you complete it.

❑ Did you write your street address, city, state, and ZIP Code and today's date at the upper right?

❑ Did you write the name, street address, city, state, and ZIP Code of the person to whom you are writing at the left margin?

❑ Did you use a greeting followed by a comma?

❑ Do you introduce yourself and explain the purpose of the letter in the first paragraph? Can you make this opening more interesting with a question or strong statement?

❑ Does each of the middle paragraphs give strong details about one aspect of your qualifications for the job?

❑ Does your letter stay focused on the topic? Take out any irrelevancies.

❑ Are sentences complete? Do subjects and verbs agree?

❑ Does the concluding paragraph sum up your qualifications in a convincing way?

❑ Did you write the closing at the bottom right, followed by a comma?

❑ Did you sign your name beneath the closing?

❑ Check spelling with a dictionary.

B. DIRECTIONS: Begin the final copy of your letter of application below, and continue on the back of this sheet. Follow correct business letter form, and indent the beginning of each paragraph.

_____

_____

_____

_____

_____

_____

Name _____ **Date** _____

9–13. PARTY PLANNING (PREWRITING)

You are planning a party for your parents' twenty-fifth wedding anniversary. Your mom's sister, your Aunt Linda, will be helping with the preparations. You don't want your parents to find out about the party, so instead of talking to Aunt Linda on the phone, where you might be overheard, you have decided to write her a letter with all the details.

First, prepare the **brainstorming list** below.

BRAINSTORMING LIST

1. Write the date, time, and place for the party below.

_____

2. In the box below, write a list of words and phrases you can use to describe the guests, invitations, and decorations.

3. In the box below, write a list of words and phrases you can use to describe the preparation and service of food and refreshments for the party.

4. In the box below, write a list of words and phrases you can use to describe additional preparations for the party.

5. In the first column below, write words and phrases to describe your preparations. In the second column, write words and phrases to describe the plans for which your aunt will be responsible.

9–14. PARTY PLANNING (FIRST DRAFT)

DIRECTIONS: Write the first draft of a letter to your Aunt Linda (you can use the name of a real relative or family friend if you prefer) about the party for your parents' twenty-fifth wedding anniversary. Use your brainstorming list as a guide. Here is one way to organize your letter:

> - Write the greeting followed by a comma (for example, "Dear Aunt Linda,").
> - In the first paragraph, state the subject of the letter and why you are writing it (for example, "I'm determined that this party will be a surprise, but the walls in this house have ears! I'm afraid of being overheard on the phone, so I'm writing this letter reviewing our plans for my parents' twenty-fifth anniversary celebration.").
> - In the second paragraph, state the date, time, and place of the party, and discuss guests, invitations, and decorations.
> - In the third paragraph, discuss the food and any additional arrangements.
> - In the fourth paragraph, discuss how the party preparations will be divided between Aunt Linda and you.
> - In the concluding paragraph, sum up and bring your letter to an end.
> - Write a closing, followed by a comma (for example, "Your excited nephew,").

Begin the first draft of your letter below, and continue on the back of this sheet. This is a first draft, so just concentrate on getting your thoughts down on paper. Don't forget to include a greeting and closing (followed by commas). Indent the beginning of each paragraph.

_____

_____

_____

_____

_____

_____

_____

_____

9–15. PARTY PLANNING
(REVISING AND WRITING A FINAL COPY)

A. DIRECTIONS: Revise and correct the first draft of your letter to your aunt (or other relative) about plans for a twenty-fifth anniversary party for your parents. Use proofreading symbols if you find them helpful. Follow the guidelines below, and check off each one as you complete it.

❏ Do you use a greeting followed by a comma?

❏ Do you clearly state the purpose of the letter in the first paragraph?

❏ Do the middle paragraphs develop the topic in a logical way? Do you completely cover one aspect of the planning before going on to another?

❏ Does your letter clearly indicate which tasks will be done by you and which will be taken care of by your aunt?

❏ Does the concluding paragraph sum up the topic and end the letter on a positive note?

❏ Are sentences complete? Correct any fragments or run-ons.

❏ Do subjects and verbs agree? Do pronouns agree with their antecedents?

❏ Is there a comma after the closing?

❏ Check spelling with a dictionary when in doubt.

B. DIRECTIONS: Begin the final copy of your letter below, and continue on the back of this sheet. Don't forget to include a greeting and closing (followed by commas) and to indent the beginning of each paragraph.

_____

_____

_____

_____

_____

_____

_____

_____

_____

9–16. GETTING RESEARCH INFORMATION (PREWRITING)

Sometimes it is necessary to write a letter to get information. Jason Brentano's class was working on a unit about important inventions. Jason had to write a report about the typewriter. He looked it up in the encyclopedia and in library books. One of the books said that more information could be obtained from the Milwaukee Public Museum. Jason copied the address and wrote the following letter:

> 54 Basking Road
> Rochester, NY 14618
> April 3, 2004
>
> Milwaukee Public Museum
> 800 West Wells Street
> Milwaukee, WI 53233
>
> Dear Sirs:
>
> I am doing a school report on the invention and history of typewriters. My research indicates that your museum has a large collection of artifacts and original documents on this subject.
> I would appreciate any information you could send me about this invention. I am particularly interested in descriptions of early writing machines.
> Thank you.
>
> Yours truly,
>
> Jason Brentano

This letter did the job! The Milwaukee Museum sent Jason several pamphlets with many interesting facts. He was able to write a detailed report that received a high grade.

You are going to write a letter requesting information for a report you have been assigned on one of the following topics:

- ❏ *Animals of the Southwestern United States*
- ❏ *How Wildfires Affect Our Forests*
- ❏ *The Alligators of Florida*

Put a checkmark next to the box you have chosen. (You don't have to write the report, just a letter as part of your research.)

You can get information on any of these subjects from the National Museum of Natural History. Here is the address for your letter: National Museum of Natural History, Washington, DC 29560.

Write a possible first sentence for your letter on the back of this sheet.

9–17. GETTING RESEARCH INFORMATION (FIRST DRAFT)

DIRECTIONS: Write the first draft of a letter to the National Museum of Natural History asking for information about the subject you selected on your prewriting sheet. Use the sample letter as a model, and follow these guidelines:

- Use the correct form for a business letter. Write your street address; your city, state, and ZIP Code; and today's date on the first three lines at the right.
- Write the name and address of the museum (2 lines) at the left margin. Write a greeting below, followed by either a comma or a colon. (A colon is preferred in a business letter.)
- In the first paragraph, state your reason for writing the letter. Use the opening sentence from your prewriting sheet.
- In the middle paragraph or paragraphs (one will probably be sufficient), explain in detail the information you need.
- In the concluding paragraph, express your appreciation for the museum staff's assistance.
- Write the closing at the right, followed by a comma.
- Sign your name beneath the closing.

Begin your letter below, and continue on the back of this sheet. This is just a first draft, so don't be too concerned about spelling or grammar. Concentrate on getting your thoughts down on paper. Be sure to follow the correct form for a business letter, and indent the beginning of each paragraph.

_____

_____

_____

_____

_____

_____

_____

_____

9–18. Getting Research Information
(Revising and Writing a Final Copy)

A. DIRECTIONS: Revise and correct the first draft of your letter to the National Museum of Natural History requesting information for your report. Use proofreading symbols if they are helpful to you. Follow the guidelines below, and check off each one as you complete it.

> ❑ Is the form of your letter correct? Check it against the letter on the prewriting sheet.
> ❑ Do your street address, city, state, and ZIP Code, and today's date appear at the right on the top three lines?
> ❑ Did you write a greeting at the left margin? Is it followed by a colon or a comma?
> ❑ Do you introduce yourself and explain the purpose of the letter in the first paragraph?
> ❑ In the middle paragraph(s), do you clearly outline the information you would like to receive, including specific details?
> ❑ Do you end the letter politely in the last paragraph?
> ❑ Do you stay on the topic? Remove any irrelevancies.
> ❑ Are your sentences complete? Correct any fragments or run-ons.
> ❑ Do subjects and verbs agree?
> ❑ Add transitional words where needed to make smooth connections between sentences or paragraphs.
> ❑ Did you write a closing at the bottom right, followed by a comma?
> ❑ Did you sign your name beneath the closing?
> ❑ Check spelling with a dictionary when in doubt.

B. DIRECTIONS: Begin the final copy of your letter below, and continue on the back of this sheet. Use correct business letter form.

_____

_____

_____

_____

_____

_____

TENTH-GRADE LEVEL

WRITING LETTERS
PRACTICE TEST

PRACTICE TEST: WRITING LETTERS

DIRECTIONS: You are going to write a letter based on the prompt below. Read the prompt carefully and be sure you understand the topic before beginning.

Your school has a program in which a tenth grader acts as a mentor to a junior high school student at the end of each year. The mentor's job is to help the younger student have a successful experience when he or she enters your school. Your student is worried about being able to write well enough for high school classes.

Write a letter to your junior high student explaining what kind of writing is expected in high school classes and what the student can do to be a successful writer in high school. As you plan your responses, think about your own writing experiences. How would you describe "good" writing? What advice about writing has been helpful to you? What writing techniques do you use?

Follow these four steps to write your letter:

- FIRST, on the page labeled "Prewriting," brainstorm ideas and examples that support and develop the topic. Include a variety of words and phrases you can use.

- SECOND, write the first draft of your letter on a separate sheet of paper. Write your name and the date at the top. Consult your notes from the brainstorming list.

- THIRD, revise and edit your first draft. Refer to your list of proofreading symbols if you wish. Use the checklist below as a guide, and check off each item when it has been revised to your satisfaction.

- FOURTH, write your final copy on a separate sheet of paper with your name and the date at the top.

CHECKLIST

❑ Do you begin with a greeting followed by a comma?

❑ Does your introductory paragraph tell why you are writing this letter and state the topic?

❑ Do your middle paragraphs develop the topic in a logical way?

❑ Do you clearly present your definition of good writing, with examples for each point?

❑ Do you stay on the subject? Delete any irrelevant details.

❑ Does the concluding paragraph sum up the topic in an encouraging way?

❑ Is there a comma after the closing? Did you sign your name beneath it?

❑ Do you use a variety of well-constructed, complete sentences? Do subjects and verbs agree? Correct any fragments or run-ons.

❑ Correct any errors in punctuation, capitalization, or usage.

❑ Check spelling with a dictionary when in doubt.

PRACTICE TEST: WRITING LETTERS (continued)

Prewriting

Re-read the prompt to be sure you are writing about the correct topic. Think about the writing skills you have learned that will be helpful to an incoming student. What is good writing? What advice has been helpful to you? What writing techniques do you use? Organize your ideas by making notes on this page with a brainstorming list, a cluster, or an outline. Be sure to list a variety of words and phrases you can use to develop your suggestions.

Practice Test: Writing Letters *(continued)*

Student Samples

DIRECTIONS: Read the sample student essays below. Rate each essay with a score from 1 (lowest) to 6 (highest). Use the information on the scoring guide to help you.

LETTER A

Dear Junior High School student,

I understand that you are concerned with becoming a successful writer in high school. High school teachers expect their students to have good writing skills and to effectively use them. There are many things that I would advice you to do.

First of all, in order to have an effective piece of writing, you must keep the audience interested. This doesn't mean your work must be humorous or adventurous. It simply means you have to keep the reader's attention. One way to keep the attention of the audience is to use description just enough to make it interesting, but not too much to bore the reader. Another bit of advice is to reveal to the reader how you feel about the subject and make them feel a certain way.

I was once given some advice concerning keeping the reader's attention. The suggestion was to start with a very interesting and eye-catching introduction. That way, the audience is interested from the very beginning.

One technique that is useful in becoming a successful writer is to include more than one strategy in your writing, for example, you could include an anecdote in a compare and contrast essay or you could combine division and classification techniques in your essay. Just be sure that what you are saying is always relevant to the subject.

If you follow these suggestions and present your topic and supporting details clearly, you should have no trouble with high school writing assignments.

Your mentor,

Score _____

LETTER B

Dear Junior High student,

I am here to help you with your problems in writing. When you take high school classes, you will be doing a lot of writing. There are different types of writing in different classes. Advice that has been given to me is to think of a topic and make an outline. For your outline think ideas about your topic topic, and then organize your ideas.

A good writing technique to think about the five punctuation patterns your English teacher will give you. When you are writing a paper these patterns will help you a lot.

Your mentor,

Score _____

SCORE	Unsatisfactory—1	Insufficient—2
Content	Attempts to respond to prompt, but provides few details; may only paraphrase prompt	Presents fragmented information OR may be very repetitive OR may be very undeveloped
Organization	Has no clear organization OR consists of a single statement	Is very disorganized; ideas are weakly connected OR the response is too brief to detect organization
Sentence Structure	Little or no control over sentence boundaries and sentence structure; word choice may be incorrect in much or all of the response	Little control over sentence boundaries and sentence structure; word choice may often be incorrect
Grammar, Usage, and Mechanics	Many errors in grammar or usage (such as tense inconsistency, lack of subject-verb agreement), spelling, and punctuation severely interfere with understanding	Errors in grammar or usage (such as inconsistency, lack of subject-verb agreement), spelling, and punctuation interfere with understanding in much of the response

SCORE	Uneven—3	Sufficient—4
Content	Presents some clear information, but is list-like, undeveloped, or repetitive OR offers no more than a well-written beginning	Develops information with some details
Organization	Is unevenly organized; the letter may be disjointed; has greeting/and or closing	Is organized with ideas that are generally related but has few or no transitions
Sentence Structure	Exhibits uneven control over sentence boundaries and sentence structure; may have some incorrect word choices	Exhibits control over sentence boundaries and sentence structure, but sentences and word choices may be simple and unvaried
Grammar, Usage, and Mechanics	Errors in grammar or usage (such as tense inconsistency, lack of subject-verb agreement), spelling, and punctuation sometimes interfere with understanding	Errors in grammar or usage (such as tense inconsistency, lack of subject-verb agreement), spelling, and punctuation do not interfere with understanding

SCORE	Skillful—5	Excellent—6
Content	Develops and shapes information with details in parts of the letter	Develops and shapes information with well-chosen details across the letter
Organization	Is clearly organized, but may lack some transitions and/or have lapses in continuity	Is well organized with strong transitions; follows letter format
Sentence Structure	Exhibits some variety in sentence structure and some good word choices	Sustains variety in sentence structure and exhibits good word choice
Grammar, Usage, and Mechanics	Errors in grammar, spelling, and punctuation do not interfere with understanding	Errors in grammar, spelling, and punctuation are few and do not interfere with understanding

Proofreading Symbols

⁊	indent first line of paragraph
≡	capitalize
∧ or ∨	add
℘	remove
⊙	add a period
/	make lowercase
ↄ	move
∼	transpose
∼∼	boldface
—	italicize
…	stet or restore crossed-out words

PREPARING YOUR STUDENTS FOR STANDARDIZED PROFICIENCY TESTS

Even as the debate over the value and fairness of standardized tests continues, standardized tests are an annual event for millions of students. In most school districts the results of the tests are vitally important. Scores may be used to determine if students are meeting district or state guidelines, they may be used as a means of comparing the scores of the district's students to local or national norms, or they may be used to decide a student's placement in advanced or remedial classes. No matter how individual scores are used in your school, students deserve the chance to do well. They deserve to be prepared.

By providing students with practice in answering the kinds of questions they will face on a standardized test, an effective program of preparation can familiarize students with testing formats, refresh skills, build confidence, and reduce anxiety, all critical factors that can affect scores as much as basic knowledge. Just like the members of an orchestra rehearse to get ready for a concert, the dancer trains for the big show, and the pianist practices for weeks before the grand recital, preparing students for standardized tests is essential.

To be most effective a test-preparation program should be comprehensive, based on skills your students need to know, and enlist the support of parents. Because students often assume the attitudes of their parents regarding tests—for example, nervous parents frequently make their children anxious—you should seek as much parental involvement in your test preparations as possible. Students who are encouraged by their parents and prepared for tests by their teachers invariably do better than those who come to the testing session with little preparation and support.

What Parents Need to Know About Standardized Tests

While most parents will agree it is important for their children to do well on standardized tests, many feel there is little they can do to help the outcome. Consequently, aside from encouraging their children to "try your best," they feel there is nothing more for them to do. Much of this feeling arises from parents not fully understanding the testing process.

To provide the parents of your students with information about testing, consider sending home copies of the following reproducibles:

- ✏ The Uses of Standardized Tests
- ✏ Test Terms
- ✏ Common Types of Standardized Tests
- ✏ Preparing Your Child for Standardized Tests

You may wish to send these home in a packet with a cover letter (a sample of which is included) announcing the upcoming standardized tests.

The Uses of Standardized Tests

Schools administer standardized tests for a variety of purposes. It is likely that your child's school utilizes the scores of standardized tests in at least some of the following ways.

- Identify strengths and weaknesses in academic skills.

- Identify areas of high interest, ability, or aptitude. Likewise identify areas of average or low ability or aptitude.

- Compare the scores of students within the district to each other as well as to students of other districts. This can be done class to class, school to school, or district to district. Such comparisons help school systems to evaluate their curriculums and plan instruction and programs.

- Provide a basis for comparison of report card grades to national standards.

- Identify students who might benefit from advanced or remedial classes.

- Certify student achievement, for example, in regard to receiving awards.

- Provide reports on student progress.

Test Terms

Although standardized tests come in different forms and may be designed to measure different skills, most share many common terms. Understanding these "test terms" is the first step to understanding the tests.

- ✏ *Achievement tests* measure how much students have learned in a particular subject area. They concentrate on knowledge of subject matter.

- ✏ *Aptitude tests* are designed to predict how well students will do in learning new subject matter in the future. They generally measure a broad range of skills associated with success. Note that the line between aptitude and achievement tests is often indistinct.

- ✏ *Battery* refers to a group of tests that are administered during the same testing session. For example, separate tests for vocabulary, language, reading, spelling, and mathematics that comprise an achievement test are known as the *test battery.*

- ✏ *Correlation coefficient* is a measure of the strength and direction of the relationship between two items. It can be a positive or negative number.

- ✏ *Diagnostic tests* are designed to identify the strengths and weaknesses of students in specific subject areas. They are usually given only to students who show exceptional ability or serious weakness in an area.

- ✏ *Grade equivalent scores* are a translation of the score attained on the test to an approximate grade level. Thus, a student whose score translates to a grade level of 4.5 is working at roughly the midyear point of fourth grade. One whose score equals a grade level of 8.0 is able to successfully complete work typically given at the beginning of eighth grade.

- ✏ *Individual student profiles* (also referred to as *reports*) display detailed test results for a particular student. Some of these can be so precise that the answer to every question is shown.

- ✏ *Item* is a specific question on a test.

- ✏ *Mean* is the average of a group of scores.

- ✏ *Median* is the middle score in a group of scores.

- ✏ *Mode* is the score achieved most by a specific group of test takers.

- ✏ *Normal distribution* is a distribution of test scores in which the scores are distributed around the mean and where the mean, median, and mode are the same. A normal distribution, when displayed, appears bell-shaped.

- ✏ *Norming population* is the group of students (usually quite large) to whom the test was given and on whose results performance standards for various age or grade levels are based. *Local norms* refer to distributions based on a particular school or school district. *National norms* refer to distributions based on students from around the country.

- ✏ *Norm-referenced tests* are tests in which the results of the test may be compared with other norming populations.

Test Terms *(continued)*

✏ *Percentile rank* is a comparison of a student's raw score with the raw scores of others who took the test. The comparison is most often made with members of the norming population. Percentile rank enables a test taker to see where his or her scores rank among others who take the same test. A percentile rank of 90, for example, means that the test taker scored better than 90% of those who took the test. A percentile rank of 60 means the test taker scored better than 60% of those who took the test. A percentile rank of 30 means he or she scored better than only 30% of those who took the test, and that 70% of the test takers had higher scores.

✏ *Raw score* is the score of a test based on the number correct. On some tests the raw score may include a correction for guessing.

✏ *Reliability* is a measure of the degree to which a test measures what it is designed to measure. A test's reliability may be expressed as a reliability coefficient that typically ranges from 0 to 1. Highly reliable tests have reliability coefficients of 0.90 or higher. Reliability coefficients may take several forms. For example, parallel-form reliability correlates the performance on two different forms of a test; split-half reliability correlates two halves of the same test; and test-retest reliability correlates test scores of the same test given at two different times. The producers of standardized tests strive to make them as reliable as possible. Although there are always cases of bright students not doing well on a standardized test and some students who do surprisingly well, most tests are quite reliable and provide accurate results.

✏ *Score* is the number of correct answers displayed in some form. Sometimes the score is expressed as a *scaled score*, which means that the score provided by the test is derived from the number of correct answers.

✏ *Standard deviation* is a measure of the variability of test scores. If most scores are near the mean score, the standard deviation will be small; if scores vary widely from the mean, the standard deviation will be large.

✏ *Standard error of measurement* is an estimate of the amount of possible measurement error in a test. It provides an estimate of how much a student's true test score may vary from the actual score he or she obtained on the test. Tests that have a large standard error of measurement may not accurately reflect a student's true ability. The standard error of measurement is usually small for well-designed tests.

✏ *Standardized tests* are tests that have been given to students under the same conditions. They are designed to measure the same skills and abilities for everyone who takes them.

✏ *Stanine scores* are scores expressed between the numbers 1 and 9 with 9 being high.

✏ *Validity* is the degree to which a test measures what it is supposed to measure. There are different kinds of validity. One, *content validity,* for example, refers to the degree to which the content of the test is valid for the purpose of the test. Another, *predictive validity,* refers to the extent to which predictions based on the test are later proven accurate by other evidence.

Common Types of Standardized Tests

Most standardized tests are broken down into major sections that focus on specific subjects. Together these sections are referred to as a *battery*. The materials and skills tested are based on grade level. The following tests are common throughout the country; however, not all schools administer every test.

- *Analogy tests* measure a student's ability to understand relationships between words (ideas). Here is an example: Boy is to man as girl is to woman. The relationship, of course, is that a boy becomes a man and a girl becomes a woman. Not only does an analogy test the ability to recognize relationships, it tests vocabulary as well.

- *Vocabulary tests* determine whether students understand the meaning of certain words. They are most often based on the student's projected grade-level reading, comprehension, and spelling skills.

- *Reading comprehension tests* show how well students can understand reading passages. These tests appear in many different formats. In most, students are required to read a passage and then answer questions designed to measure reading ability.

- *Spelling tests* show spelling competence, based on grade-level appropriate words. The tests may require students to select a correctly spelled word from among misspelled words, or may require students to find the misspelled word among correctly spelled words.

- *Language mechanics tests* concentrate on capitalization and punctuation. Students may be required to find examples of incorrect capitalization and punctuation as well as examples of correct capitalization and punctuation in sentences and short paragraphs.

- *Language expression tests* focus on the ability of students to use words correctly according to the standards of conventional English. In many "expression" tests, effective structuring of ideas is also tested.

- *Writing tests* determine how effectively students write and can express their ideas. Usually a topic is given and students must express their ideas on the topic.

- *Mathematics problem-solving tests* are based on concepts and applications, and assess the ability of students to solve math problems. These tests often include sections on number theory, interpretation of data and graphs, and logical analysis.

- *Mathematics computation tests* measure how well students can add, subtract, multiply, and divide. While the difficulty of the material depends on grade level, these tests generally cover whole numbers, fractions, decimals, percents, and geometry.

- *Science tests* measure students' understanding of basic science facts and the methodology used by scientists in the development of theoretical models that explain natural phenomena.

- *Social studies tests* measure students' understanding of basic facts in social studies.

Preparing Your Child for
Standardized Tests

As a parent, there is much you can do to help your son or daughter get ready for taking a standardized test.

During the weeks leading up to the test . . .

- ✏ Attend parent–teacher conferences and find out how you can help your child succeed in school.

- ✏ Assume an active role in school. Seeing your commitment to his or her school enhances the image of school in your child's eyes.

- ✏ Find out when standardized tests are given and plan accordingly. For example, avoid scheduling doctor or dentist appointments for your child during the testing dates. Students who take standardized tests with their class usually do better than students who make up tests because of absences.

- ✏ Monitor your child's progress in school. Make sure your child completes his or her homework and projects. Support good study habits and encourage your child to always do his or her best.

- ✏ Encourage your child's creativity and interests. Provide plenty of books, magazines, and educational opportunities.

- ✏ Whenever you speak of standardized tests, speak of them in a positive manner. Emphasize that while these tests are important, it is not the final score that counts, but that your child tries his or her best.

During the days immediately preceding the test . . .

- ✏ Once the test has been announced, discuss the test with your child to relieve apprehension. Encourage your son or daughter to take the test seriously, but avoid being overly anxious. (Sometimes parents are more nervous about their children's tests than the kids are.)

- ✏ Help your child with any materials his or her teacher sends home in preparation for the test.

- ✏ Make sure your child gets a good night's sleep each night before a testing day.

- ✏ On the morning of the test, make sure your child wakes up on time, eats a solid breakfast, and arrives at school on time.

- ✏ Remind your child to listen to the directions of the teacher carefully and to read directions carefully.

- ✏ Encourage your child to do his or her best.

Cover Letter to Parents
Announcing Standardized Tests

Use the following letter to inform the parents of your students about upcoming standardized tests in your school. Feel free to adjust the letter according to your needs.

Dear Parents/Guardians,

On _____(dates)_____ , our class will be taking the _____(name of test)_____. During the next few weeks students will work on various practice tests to help prepare for the actual test.

You can help, too. Please read the attached materials and discuss the importance of the tests with your child. By supporting your child's efforts in preparation, you can help him or her attain the best possible scores.

Thank you.

Sincerely,

(Name)

What Students Need to Know
About Standardized Tests

The mere thought of taking a standardized test frightens many students, causing a wide range of symptoms from mild apprehension to upset stomachs and panic attacks. Since even low levels of anxiety can distract students and undermine their achievement, you should attempt to lessen their concerns.

Apprehension, anxiety, and fear are common responses to situations that we perceive as being out of our control. When students are faced with a test on which they don't know what to expect, they may worry excessively that they won't do well. Such emotions, especially when intense, almost guarantee that they will make careless mistakes. When students are prepared properly for a test, they are more likely to know "what to expect." This reduces negative emotions and students are able to enter the testing situation with confidence, which almost always results in better scores.

The first step to preparing your students for standardized tests is to mention the upcoming tests well in advance—at least a few weeks ahead of time—and explain that in the days leading up to the test, the class will be preparing. Explain that while they will not be working with the actual test, the work they will be doing is designed to help them get ready. You may wish to use the analogy of a sports team practicing during the pre-season. Practices help players sharpen their skills, anticipate game situations, and build confidence. Practicing during the pre-season helps athletes perform better during the regular season.

You might find it useful to distribute copies of the following reproducibles:

✏ Test-taking Tips for Students

✏ Test Words You Should Know

Hand these out a few days before the testing session. Go over them with your students and suggest that they take them home and ask their parents to review the sheets with them on the night before the test.

TEST-TAKING TIPS FOR STUDENTS

1. Try your best.

2. Be confident and think positively. People who believe they will do well usually do better than those who are not confident.

3. Fill out the answer sheet correctly. Be careful that you darken all "circles." Be sure to use a number 2 pencil unless your teacher tells you otherwise.

4. Listen carefully to all directions and follow them exactly. If you don't understand something, ask your teacher.

5. Read all questions and their possible answers carefully. Sometimes an answer may at first seem right, but it isn't. Always read all answers before picking one.

6. Try to answer the questions in order, but don't waste too much time on hard questions. Go on to easier ones and then go back to the hard ones.

7. Don't be discouraged by hard questions. On most tests for every hard question there are many easy ones.

8. Try not to make careless mistakes.

9. Budget your time and work quickly.

10. Be sure to fill in the correct answer spaces on your answer sheet. Use a finger of your non-writing hand to keep your place on the answer space.

11. Look for clues and key words when answering questions.

12. If you become "stuck" on a question, eliminate any answers you know are wrong and then make your best guess of the remaining answers. (Do this only if there is no penalty for guessing. Check with your teacher about this.)

13. Don't leave any blanks. Guess if you are running out of time. (Only do this if unanswered questions are counted wrong. Check with your teacher.)

14. Double-check your work if time permits.

15. Erase completely any unnecessary marks on your answer sheet.

Test Words You Should Know

The words below are used in standardized tests. Understanding what each one means will help you when you take your test.

all	double-check	opposite
always	end	order
answer sheet	error	oval
best	example	part
blank	fill in	passage
booklet	finish	pick
bubble	following	punctuation
capitalization	go on	question
check	item	read
choose	language expression	reread
circle	language mechanics	right
column	mark	row
complete	match	same as
comprehension	missing	sample
continue	mistake	section
correct	name	select
definition	never	stop
details	none	topic
directions	not true	true
does not belong	number 2 pencil	vocabulary

Creating a Positive
Test-taking Environment

Little things really do matter when students take standardized tests. Students who are consistently encouraged to do their best throughout the year in the regular classroom generally achieve higher scores on standardized tests than students who maintain a careless attitude regarding their studies. Of course, motivating students to do their best is an easy thing to suggest, but not such an easy goal to accomplish.

There are, fortunately, some steps you can take to foster positive attitudes on the part of your students in regard to standardized tests. Start by discussing the test students will take, and explain how the results of standardized tests are used. When students understand the purpose of testing, they are more likely to take the tests seriously. Never speak of tests in a negative manner, for example, saying that students must work hard or they will do poorly. Instead, speak in positive terms: by working hard and trying their best they will achieve the best results.

To reduce students' concerns, assure them that the use of practice tests will improve their scores. Set up a thorough test-preparation schedule well in advance of the tests, based upon the needs and abilities of your students. Avoid cramming preparation into the last few days before the test. Cramming only burdens students with an increased workload and leads to anxiety and worry. A regular, methodical approach to preparation is best, because this enables you to check for weaknesses in skills and offer remediation.

The value of preparation for standardized tests cannot be understated. When your students feel that they are prepared for the tests, and that you have confidence in them, they will feel more confident and approach the tests with a positive frame of mind. Along with effective instruction throughout the year, a focused program of test preparation will help ensure that your students will have the chance to achieve their best scores on standardized tests.